Bauwelt Fundamente 176

T0364990

Edited by

Elisabeth Blum
Jesko Fezer
Günther Fischer
Angelika Schnell

Frida Grahn (Ed.)

**Denise Scott Brown
In Other Eyes
Portraits of an Architect**

Bauverlag

Gütersloh · Berlin

Birkhäuser

Basel

The Bauwelt Fundamente series was founded in 1963 by Ulrich Conrads; it was edited from the early 1980s to 2015 jointly with Peter Neitzke.

Supervising editor of this volume: Elisabeth Blum

Front cover: The portrait of Denise Scott Brown was taken in 1978 by Lynn Gilbert during her work on the pioneering publication *Particular Passions: Talks with Women Who Have Shaped Our Times* (1981, with Gaylen Moore) © Lynn Gilbert.

Back cover: Robert Venturi and Denise Scott Brown with an interior model of the Children's Museum of Houston. Photograph by Matt Wargo, c. 1987. Courtesy of VSBA.

Frontispiece: A Philadelphia street scene reminiscent of the Smithsons' London street studies. Mothers could keep an eye on children playing in the street, while their workplace was within walking distance of home. Photograph by Denise Scott Brown, 1961.

Library of Congress Control Number: 2022942164

Bibliographic information published by the German National Library
The German National Library lists this publication in the Deutsche Nationalbibliografie; detailed bibliographic data are available on the Internet at http://dnb.dnb.de.

This publication is also available as an e-book (ISBN PDF 978-3-0356-2625-4)

Distribution via bookstores is exclusively through Birkhäuser Verlag.
© 2022 Birkhäuser Verlag GmbH, Basel
P.O. Box 44, 4009 Basel, Switzerland
Part of Walter de Gruyter GmbH, Berlin/Boston and Bauverlag BV GmbH, Gütersloh, Berlin

Printed on acid-free paper produced from chlorine-free pulp. TCF ∞
Printed in Germany

ISBN 978-3-0356-2624-7

MIX
Papier aus verantwortungsvollen Quellen
FSC® C089473
www.fsc.org

98765432
www.birkhauser.com

With the kind support of:
Peter Fischer Cooke, Jr., Philadelphia

Istituto di storia e teoria dell'arte e dell'architettura

Contents

Part II
1960s: Teaching 107

Part III
1970s –2020s: Designing 197

Denise Scott Brown, 1970s.

Preface

Mary McLeod

> The task set ... is certainly an impossible one. As such, it should be approached with a true sense of adventure and with the courage and gaiety of despair.[1]
> —Denise Scott Brown, *Form, Forces and Function in Santa Monica*

Like the studio program that Denise Scott Brown set for her students at UCLA, any attempt to describe her long and multifaceted life and career as an architect, planner, urban designer, writer, teacher, and mentor is a nearly impossible task. However, *Denise Scott Brown In Other Eyes: Portraits of an Architect*, edited by Frida Grahn, begins to do just that, providing a wonderful introduction to Scott Brown's many accomplishments and contributions to architecture. This rich and diverse collection of twenty-three essays and recollections also reveals her conviction in facing adversity with courage, gaiety, and a sense of adventure.

As an outsider—a woman, Jewish, and a foreigner—she surmounted formidable odds and forged a remarkable career spanning more than sixty years, one that helped change American architecture and studio teaching in fundamental ways. Although she remained a functionalist to the core and sought, as Le Corbusier had before her, to make other eyes "see" (if in a very different world of freeways, neon signs, strip malls, and mobile homes), she brought a concern for social factors, an appreciation of everyday life, and an attention to popular taste and mass culture that countered many of the prevailing norms in architecture. She also helped transform architectural education in radical ways, and by 1964 had created a new kind of design studio that emphasized urban research and documentation while proposing minimal design interventions; just as important, she introduced more collaborative, participatory, pluralist, and interdisciplinary modes of working, challenging the long-standing ethos of competition and the idea of the individual creative genius. Knowledge was something to be collectively gained—not from a master but from one another, from local residents, and from close observation of the surrounding environment.

What has been less recognized but emerges as an underlying thread in several of the essays is Scott Brown's feminism—both her personal struggle to obtain status and recognition in a white, male, star-studded profession and her strong commitment to helping other women do the same. As she declared in 1981, she became a feminist mainly because of "experiences in my professional life"; and throughout her career, in her writings, practice, and teaching, she has actively campaigned to change that profession. Her own life was a "quarry," and she was not afraid to draw from her own struggles with discrimination, petty slights, and lack of recognition to write about what must be done to make architecture a more egalitarian, humane, and diverse profession. Sometimes this meant tackling the failure of architects to address the needs—even the smallest, most mundane ones—of women in their daily lives, as she did in her marvelous 1967 essay "Planning the Powder Room." (What woman, even today, has not experienced some of the frustrations she so wittily described?) In other instances, it meant confronting head-on the culture of the profession itself, as she did in a talk in 1973 at the Alliance of Women in Architecture and then again in her 1975 essay "Sexism and the Star System," a somewhat shorter version of which was published in the feminist anthology *Architecture: A Place for Women* in 1989. She attacked the blatant sexism in the profession—the notion of the sole "designer on top," the cult of personality, the boys' club atmosphere, the exclusion of women at professional gatherings, the press's lack of coverage of women architects, and the glass ceiling that prohibited women's advancement. Moreover, in contrast to many women architects of her generation, she did not take pride in being "an exceptional one"; indeed, she delighted in the rise of women in the field in the mid-1970s and in how the "talent and enthusiasm of these young women has burst creativity into the profession." But she was also a hard-core realist about their prospects, recognizing that they too would face discrimination, and she urged them to have a "feminist awareness" as they confronted professional obstacles.

Of her practice with Robert Venturi, Scott Brown wrote in 2007: "using heart, mind, and artistry, we still hope naively, like Arthur Korn, to do good and achieve beauty." This book is a testament to that hope and how architecture has been enriched by it.

Notes

1   The epigraph is from Denise Scott Brown studio
program *Form, Forces and Function in Santa Monica,* 41, UCLA 401, Fall 1966, Venturi Scott Brown
Collection, by the gift of Robert Venturi and Denise
Scott Brown, the Architectural Archives at the University of Pennsylvania, Philadelphia. Subsequent
quotations by Denise Scott Brown are from her interview with Lynn Gilbert, appearing in Gilbert and
Moore, *Particular Passions,* 315 and her essays
"Room at the Top?," in *Having Words,* 87–88; and
"Towards an Active Socioplastics," also appearing
in *Having Words,* 51.

Denise Scott Brown in the Las Vegas desert, off the Strip.
Photo by Robert Venturi, Las Vegas, 1966.

Introduction: Portraits of an Architect

Frida Grahn

> Today, when I look at this image and myself then, confidently stand-
> ing there, hands on hips, I see someone who is happy with her profes-
> sional life and happier still with her personal life. I also see someone who
> is feeling triumphant and daring anyone to say otherwise.
> —Denise Scott Brown, *From Soane to the Strip: Soane Medal Lecture 2018*

This collection of essays, published on the fiftieth anniversary of *Learning from Las Vegas*, celebrates the life and career of Denise Scott Brown. Although the seminal Las Vegas treatise, coauthored with Robert Venturi and Steven Izenour, was heavily indebted to Scott Brown's work and ideas, she has so far only sparingly been subject to scholarly attention.

In my conversations with Scott Brown, conducted as a part of my Ph.D. research, she has often struck me with amazement: doors kept opening to unexpected fields, and I realized how little is commonly known about her. Notwithstanding her great skill as a writer and communicator, keys for entering her intellectual universe have been missing, and few commentators have gone beyond the instant allure of the well-known catchphrases. So I was thrilled when Elisabeth Blum spoke to me about her idea of publishing an anthology on Scott Brown in the Bauwelt Fundamente series, and I immediately started work on planning the book and sending out invitations to write essays for it. Many contemporary scholars and architects clearly felt a desire to reflect further on Scott Brown's life and work, and their positive responses soon began filling my inbox.

Scott Brown is known for celebrating the vitality of the contemporary city, its richness, layers, and contrasts. Her genius lies in her ability to channel transdisciplinary knowledge into new syntheses, combining innovative thinking with an infectious passion and enthusiasm for countless subjects that has enriched architecture's set of techniques. She is a mediator among professions, cultures, and continents, making a mark on cultural discourse as few others have done, going beyond the fields of architecture and urbanism. But her contributions have long remained unrecognized or wrongly attributed, as described in her essay "Room at the Top? Sexism and the Star System in Architecture" (1989). She was one of the first to speak out against sexism and misogyny in architecture, and the photo of her in front of the Las Vegas Strip in 1966—radiating joy, strength, and confidence—has become a symbol for empowerment and an inspiration for women who share her struggle.

This anthology is more than an homage—it aims to open up new perspectives on Scott Brown and her thinking in ways that reflect her holistic approach and the broad range of her professional identities, which encompass architect, planner, urbanist, theorist, writer, and educator. The term "architect" in the subtitle "Portraits of an Architect" is meant to imply all dimensions and scales of design, from regional planning to architectural detailing. The plural form "portraits" indicates a multitude of views. Similarly, the phrase "In Other Eyes" conveys the authors' various approaches to the different phases of Scott Brown's biography. As an initial attempt to portray Scott Brown, this volume is also an invitation to further research and debate.

The book consists of twenty-three chapters, including new essays by international scholars interspersed with more personal reflections by architects who are friends and colleagues of Scott Brown, which together bridge the divisions among history, theory, and practice. The longer essays are based on extensive studies of unpublished archival material, primarily in the Venturi Scott Brown Collection at the Architectural Archives, University of Pennsylvania. They build on and critically assess Scott Brown's rich production of writings over six decades, in books such as *Urban Concepts* (1990) and *Having Words* (2009), as well as (with Venturi) *A View from the Campidoglio* (1984) and *Architecture as Signs and Systems: For a Mannerist Time* (2004). The contributors and I have also had the honor of receiving Scott Brown's invaluable help and guidance while disentangling archival findings and reconstructing the details of certain historical events. Editing this book, compiling these stories, and looking at Scott Brown through the eyes of others has been a privilege and a delight.

The chapters of this book are grouped into three main sections, in a loose and overlapping chronology. They cover her intellectual formation in the 1950s, how she developed her ideas through teaching in the 1960s, and her design practice from the 1970s onward.

The introductory chapter by Craig Lee examines how Scott Brown's youth in Johannesburg would influence her view of the American everyday environment. The chapter by one of Scott Brown's oldest friends, Robin Middleton, provides unique insight into their joint work on the exhibition "Man Made Johannesburg" (1951) and the intellectual milieu at the University of the Witwatersrand, where Scott Brown started her architectural education in 1949. She continued her education at the Architectural Association School of Architecture (AA) in London in 1952, where she encountered the British reception of mannerism. This overlooked episode in contemporary historiography is explored in the essay by Andrew Leach. Alongside mannerism, functionalism occupies a central position in Scott Brown's thinking; Denise Costanzo sheds light on her decade-long preoccupation with that concept. Other early influences, such as contact with the New Brutalists and growing social concerns in architecture, continued to resonate in her work during her time in Rome, as described in Carolina Vaccaro's chapter. In 1958, Denise Scott Brown and her first husband, Robert Scott Brown, moved to Philadelphia to continue their studies at the University of Pennsylvania (Penn). The influence of the sociologist Herbert Gans at Penn is the focus of Marianna Charitonidou's essay, ending the first section.

The book's second section highlights the 1960s as a creative period centered on Scott Brown's teaching commitments at a number of American universities, where she developed methods and theoretical concepts. She began teaching after receiving a master's degree in city planning in 1960. Lee Ann Custer examines the way in which Scott Brown's teaching at Penn served as a testing ground for ideas such as the communicative power of urban form, which would serve as the basis of later studies of Las Vegas. At Penn, Paul Davidoff became an important influence on Scott Brown, as described in a contribution by James Yellin, one of her first planning students and later US Ambassador to Burundi. Scott Brown started teaching at the School of Architecture and Urban Planning at UCLA in 1966. Sylvia Lavin's chapter outlines how she created a curriculum that would explain urban life with "the widest possible angle of vision." Also in 1966, Scott Brown invited Venturi, whom she had met in 1960 while teaching at Penn, to Las Vegas; they married in 1967 in Santa Monica and returned to Philadelphia, where she joined Venturi's architectural office. One of her first projects there involved working as an advocacy planner for the impoverished South Street area in central Philadelphia, described in the chapter by Sarah Moses. Her commitment to the everyday urban landscape, to the conventional and ordinary, was expressed in her (and Venturi's) defense of Co-op City in New York, a little-known intervention in architectural debate, described in Joan Ockman's essay. Scott Brown and Venturi's legendary *Learning from Las Vegas* research studio at Yale School of Architecture in 1968 and the aforementioned book with that title have been the subject of many excellent studies, among them *Eyes That Saw: Architecture After Las Vegas* (2020), edited by Stanislaus von Moos and Martino Stierli. Valéry Didelon provides a new reading, drawing parallels with Susan Sontag's concept of "camp." After the Las Vegas studio, they offered one on Levittown, which resulted in the exhibition *Signs of Life: Symbols in the American City* at the Renwick Gallery, Smithsonian Institution, Washington, DC (1976). Katherine Smith's chapter sheds light on the connection between pop art and the studios at Yale and its place in Scott Brown's thinking in general.

The third section, "1970–2020s: Designing," explores her shift from studio teaching to design, and is presented as a collage on methods and influences, personal reflections, and biographical episodes. Inès Lamunière shows how Scott Brown and Venturi's work has informed her architectural practice in Geneva. My own chapter reconnects to Geneva, a city that was to become something of a European second home for Scott Brown after her parents moved there in the 1960s. Outside the city, at the castle of La Sarraz, Scott Brown and Venturi both gave lectures on the occasion of CIAM's fiftieth anniversary in 1978, an ambivalent celebration given the postmodern critique of functionalist urban planning. Christopher Long revisits Scott Brown's critique of modernism by looking at her intellectual kinship with the Austrian architect Josef Frank. In her view, postmodernism, often mistaken for frivolity, is rooted in the darkest moments of twentieth-century history. Her response to the Holocaust and other atrocities, such as the Vietnam War, was to advocate for humanism and cultural pluralism, as well as to repudiate universal solutions and aesthetic totalitarianism.

Her political awareness often leads her to consider social and architectural questions together. This is evident in her reconsideration of the everyday, an important current in architectural discourse during the 1970s. The topic reappears in my conversation with Jacques Herzog, in which he gives his perspective on Scott Brown, whose thinking he sees as having parallels with that of Lucius Burckhardt. Stanislaus von Moos, in turn, sees similarities between her work as an urbanist and that of Herzog de Meuron, with an emphasis on the city as a floating, ever-changing system. A related idea, namely of the city as a nervous system, is at the heart of Hilary Sample's essay on Scott Brown's studio on health at Harvard Graduate School of Design in 1989; her ambitious syllabus in that course has a new relevance in the light of the current pandemic and its social consequences. Aron Vinegar explores the relationship between evidence and speculation in Scott Brown's writings—in particular, the abundance of evidence immanent in her notion of "learning from everything." An example of an architecture without "paralipomena"—things that are left out—is given by Françoise Blanc in her recollections on the Provincial Capitol Building in Toulouse (1999).

The penultimate piece in the volume is a new text by Scott Brown herself, written in the form of a letter to Biljana Arandelovic, but also by implication to the many scholars and architects who are inspired by her work today. In the letter, she gives us her view of what has happened since the Las Vegas studio, focusing on her work on university campuses and returning to the Provincial Capitol in Toulouse. That project illustrates the way in which Scott Brown's analysis of activity patterns can be used as a design tool—seen most clearly in the diagonal configuration of the site, inspired by Alison and Peter Smithson's paths across orthogonal squares, which connects the medieval city with a nearby shopping center. The shortcut is a recurring element in her designs. In the letter, Scott Brown also highlights the intertwining of ideas in her collaboration with Venturi, and how "one plus one" can become more than two. The anthology's final piece is a joint contribution by Scott Brown and her long-time collaborator and friend Jeremy Eric Tenenbaum. It explores Scott

Brown's acclaimed photography, giving us an insight into how she uses photos to develop and relay her ideas about architecture, urbanism, art, and communication.

This book has taken shape during my doctoral research at the USI Accademia di architettura, Mendrisio, Switzerland, where Scott Brown was awarded an honorary doctorate in 2021. I would like to thank my Ph.D. supervisor, Prof. Sonja Hildebrand, for supporting this endeavor, as well as Prof. Daniela Mondini and Prof. Christoph Frank of the Istituto di storia e teoria dell'arte e dell'architettura (ISA) for financial help with the publishing subsidy. I would also like to thank my co-supervisor at Columbia University, Prof. Mary McLeod, for the preface and for her invaluable support, inspiration and advice. I am grateful to Elisabeth Blum, as instigator and coeditor of the Bauwelt Fundamente series, for a joyful, tireless collaboration, for editorial guidance, and for her faith in me. Thanks also go to René Furer, who taught extensively on Scott Brown and Venturi at ETH Zurich in the 1970s, and whose idea of connecting Blum and myself made the project possible in the first place.

Deserving special acknowledgment are the contributors to this volume for their insights, their dedication, enthusiasm, commitment, and friendly cooperation. My thanks to Lynn Gilbert for giving us permission to use as the image on the book's cover her portrait of Scott Brown, taken in 1978 during Gilbert's work on the pioneering publication *Particular Passions: Talks with Women Who Have Shaped Our Times* (1981). I am indebted to William Whitaker, curator and collections manager at the Architectural Archives of the University of Pennsylvania, and to two archivists there, Heather Isbell Schumacher and Allison Rose Olsen, for providing additional images and for their support for the authors. I would also like to acknowledge Emma Brown for her helpfulness in organizing photographs from the archive of Scott Brown and VSBA Architects & Planners. My appreciation goes to Michael Robertson for carefully copy-editing the manuscript and to Katharina Kulke for coordinating the project at Birkhäuser. As always, my warm thanks to Carl and my family for their support. Finally, I would like to express my heartfelt gratitude to Denise Scott Brown, who has generously shared her time during work on the anthology. Thank you, Denise—I hope you will like the result.

"I grew up surrounded by my mother's Africa of the mind. Stories of her beloved wilderness imbued me with my own love for the veld, and a preference for occupying the outskirts, the edge of things."

—Denise Scott Brown, *From Soane to the Strip: Soane Medal Lecture 2018*

Part I
1950s: Learning

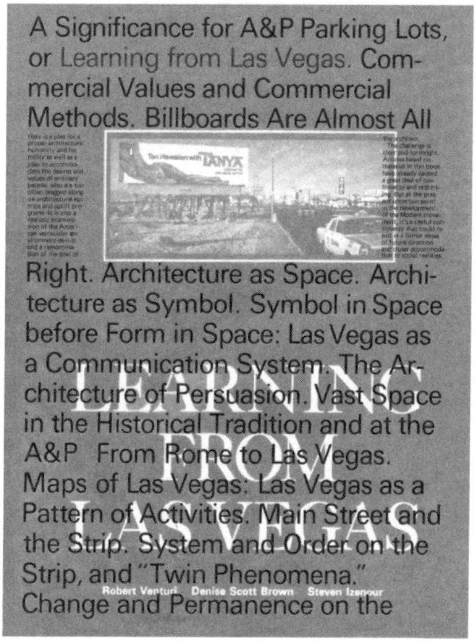

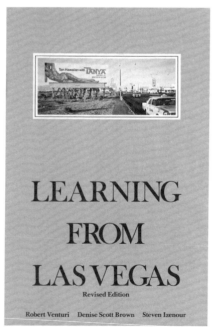

A Significance for A&P Parking Lots, or Learning from Las Vegas. Commercial Values and Commercial Methods. Billboards Are Almost All
Tan Hawaiian with TANYA
Right. Architecture as Space. Architecture as Symbol. Symbol in Space before Form in Space: Las Vegas as a Communication System. The Architecture of Persuasion. Vast Space in the Historical Tradition and at the A&P From Rome to Las Vegas. Maps of Las Vegas: Las Vegas as a Pattern of Activities. Main Street and the Strip. System and Order on the Strip, and "Twin Phenomena." Change and Permanence on the
LEARNING FROM LAS VEGAS
Robert Venturi Denise Scott Brown Steven Izenour

Figure 1: ***Learning from Las Vegas,*** **cover with glassine dust jacket, 1972.**

Tan Hawaiian with TANYA
LEARNING
FROM
LAS VEGAS
Revised Edition
Robert Venturi Denise Scott Brown Steven Izenour

Figure 2: ***Learning from Las Vegas,*** **revised edition, cover, 1977.**

On the Outside Looking Around:
"Mine is an African View of Las Vegas"

Craig Lee

Twelve years after the 1972 publication of *Learning from Las Vegas*, written by Robert Venturi, Denise Scott Brown, and Steven Izenour, Scott Brown emphasized her perspective on the project: "Mine is an African view of Las Vegas."[1] In her statement, a point of view reiterated in subsequent writings and interviews, she was calling attention to her individual biography.[2] This "African view"—a term explored in this essay—reflected her upbringing in Johannesburg as well as her transnational experience as a South African national, student in London and Philadelphia, and American immigrant and then American citizen.[3] It also embodied a position, continually on the margin, that had a formative role in her work and thinking about the everyday cultural landscape. Considering Scott Brown's place-based biography uncouples her from her coauthors in *Learning from Las Vegas* to detail a way of looking at the American built environment and her leading contribution to this influential study.

Learning from Las Vegas—the 1968 Yale architecture studio, the 1972 first edition, the 1977 revised edition, and the 2017 facsimile edition—was a career-defining project and a landmark in architectural discourse (fig. 1 and fig. 2).[4] In it, the authors studied the signs and symbols on the Las Vegas Strip to understand the iconography of the city's "commercial vernacular." Their close and serious attention to the mainstream reality of Main Street—in the overblown form of the Strip—stressed the need to look at the full scope of the built environment with all-embracing tastes. In particular, it was the condition of the commonplace that held important lessons for architecture and urbanism. "Learning from the existing landscape," they argued in the opening line, "is a way of being revolutionary for architects."[5]

If the call was for revolution, then it was Scott Brown who led the charge. She designed the studio programs and work topics.[6] Izenour later attested to the primacy of her role: "The Las Vegas [project] was totally dependent on Denise for the intellectual rigor of it."[7] So much so that some early manuscripts placed her name first, though the publication led with Venturi, for various reasons, owing to him writing "the larger portion of the first draft" and to his seniority and name recognition with his acclaimed book *Complexity and Contradiction in Architecture*, published in 1966.[8] The intent of this essay is not to claim Scott Brown as the sole or "true" author of *Learning from Las Vegas*, but rather to tease out her individual perspective and focus on her contribution in the Las Vegas studio, study, publication, and its reception.[9] It is an effort to discern the notion of "joint creativity" that Scott Brown has called for in recognition of her work and practice, and also in partnership with Venturi.[10]

Learning in and from Johannesburg

Scott Brown's commitment to popular architecture and the cultural landscape stemmed from her experiences at a young age. Through her family, Scott Brown (née Lakofski), the eldest of four, with two sisters and a brother, was attuned to architecture and an awareness of its larger surroundings from early on.[11] Born on October 3, 1931 in Nkana, Northern Rhodesia (now Kitwe, Zambia), an area with extensive copper mines, the Lakofski family moved from the rural wilderness to the urban and suburban environs of Johannesburg when she was two years old (fig. 3). At age six, she began at Kingsmead College, a private girls' primary and secondary school in Melrose, a northern suburb of Johannesburg, and graduated in 1947.[12] Her father, Shim Lakofski, a "quintessential entrepreneur," owned several little stores in Northern Rhodesia, including the Nkana Trading Store.[13] In Johannesburg he began a stockbroking firm with his cousin, before becoming a movie distributor with several movie houses. Later, he became a successful real estate developer with, as Scott Brown recalls, "a brilliant but unusual mind" and "a sort of intuitive sense about where areas will develop," leading him to construct lucrative office buildings in an emerging financial district.[14] From this work, she

Figure 3: Denise as a baby with her parents Phyllis (née Hepker) and Shim Lakofski, Nkana, Northern Rhodesia (now a suburb of Kitwe, Zambia), fall 1931.

remembers, "I watched my father, a developer, walk Johannesburg, looking and learning," with an eye on the city.[15]

This roving attention to the city in various forms was an important part of Scott Brown's childhood. Her mother Phyllis Lakofski (née Hepker) was vital in instilling an approach and appreciation to see what is close at hand. Scott Brown later recalled, "During my childhood she looked out on the African landscape with a sense of elation and celebration and she taught me to look around me ... My mother, my sister and I would drive around Johannesburg sightseeing, looking mainly at houses."[16] Furthermore, Scott Brown remembered art classes with Rosa van Gelderen, a Dutch-Jewish refugee, whose instruction to "paint what's around you" had a lasting impact: "[It] made me notice where I was [in Africa] and awoke my interest in popular culture."[17] In the street, she found "an intriguing folk/pop culture in their irrepressible adaptations and interpretations of western commercial and industrial artefacts—bead-covered Coca Cola bottles or sandals made from old car tyres—and in their hybrid African-American music."[18] For Scott Brown, consideration of architecture and popular culture was instilled at a young age.

Phyllis Lakofski had studied architecture for two years at the University of Witwatersrand (Wits) during an exciting period when the ideas of the modern movement and Le Corbusier influenced the curriculum.[19] Her father's failing health, however, caused her to withdraw from school so that she could work to help her parents in Northern Rhodesia. Her time as an architecture student had later importance: It set a precedent for her daughters to view architecture as "women's work," prompting Scott Brown, upon entering her first year architecture program at Wits with only five other women and seeing all the men in the classroom, to think, "What are they doing here?"[20] Lakofski's dedication to modern architecture prompted the Lakofski family, in 1934, to commission, for their home in suburban Dunkeld, one of the earliest modernist houses in South Africa, designed by her friend and former classmate, Norman Hanson, and his practice at the time, Hanson, Tomkin, and Finkelstein (fig. 4).[21]

The Lakofski house was completed in 1935 when Scott Brown was four years old. She remembers "really *blue* prints" and the imaginative possibilities of growing up in an International Style house: "I don't have the sentimental

Figure 4: Denise Scott Brown's childhood home with her parents, Shim and Phyllis Lakofski, in Johannesburg, South Africa, by Hanson, Tomkin, and Finkelstein. Designed in 1934 and built in 1935, it has now been demolished. Photographed 1936.

memories of the attic and the steps up to the attic, and the oak paneling. What I have is strip windows, which have walls that don't quite come up to the window, and there's a little piece between that you can peep through and listen through."[22] She further reminisced, "I climbed its steel columns and played ships on its spiral stair and deck. You can have mythic allusions in houses with flat roofs, and you can also play on the roof."[23] In this way, her exposure to modernist ideas of the period was personal and experiential, framing her identity to this day. Though often labeled a postmodernist, she has declared, "I am an old-fashioned modernist in a 1930s mold. I still believe that function is one of the glories of architecture—for aesthetic as well as moral reasons."[24] Among the moral reasons are her warm memories of the house accommodating various members of her large, extended family, along with lodgers too, which left a positive impression of the practical value of modern architecture to contribute to family life.[25] In other words, her self-avowed alignment with the 1930s modernists first began when she was a child at home.

By the time Scott Brown enrolled at Wits in 1948, the architecture program was no longer the model of progressive modernist thinking that it had been nearly twenty years earlier when her mother was there.[26] To augment the instruction, and during the difficult period when the legislation for apartheid was being introduced, Scott Brown joined various student societies and surrounded herself with a group of like-minded peers who would likewise become architectural emigrants in America: Robert Scott Brown (1931–1959), who would become Denise Scott Brown's first husband; Diana Evenary (b. 1932), later a key advocate in the fight to save Pennsylvania Station in New York who married Marc Goldstein, a partner at Skidmore, Owings and Merrill in San Francisco; and Robin Middleton (b. 1931), later a professor of architectural history at Columbia University.[27] More than just a group for discussion and debate, together they planned an exhibition titled "Man Made Johannesburg."[28] For their role, Denise and Robert Scott Brown explored the city by motorbike, seeing buildings, visiting architects, and gathering photographs for the exhibition, which consumed much of their energies to the detriment of their schoolwork.[29] Such activities engaged skills learned in childhood, namely to look openly and critically at the surrounding built environment. The exhibition, with its survey of buildings in Johannesburg from the 1910s to 1940s, is a key example of Denise Scott Brown's frame of viewing and method of photographic documentation that would carry on to Las Vegas.[30]

In contrast to the urbanism of Johannesburg, Scott Brown learned important lessons from camping and fossil-hunting trips in the vast rural veld expanses in the Makapan Valley, outside Potgietersrus (now Mokopane), a three-hour drive to the north (fig. 5).[31] "Alone in the veld in the sun," she recalled, "if you kept still enough, you could hear a thousand insects buzzing and small animals would come up close. The veld has given me empty spaces in my head that have been important in my life."[32] Paradoxically, but profoundly, Scott Brown was able to see the shared relationships between rural and urban spaces: "Eventually I came to compare our wilderness landscapes with the city, feeling that both established complex laws with or without our intervention."[33] The landscape, climate, and geography fostered a design approach that was mindful of environmental conditions.

But the veld also became a touchstone for questioning cultural and colonial identity. From an early age, Scott Brown noted the disjuncture between her physical reality and a perceived colonial ideal:

Figure 5: Photograph by Denise Scott Brown of veld landscape in South Africa, taken after her return from Europe, 1957.

As a child, I too saw almost exclusively English places in the books I read. I lived in a harsher, drier landscape and, although I found the high veld incredibly beautiful, English people around me seemed to like it only to the extent that it reminded them of "home." Why, I wondered, must my landscape look like Surrey to be beautiful? And I became an African xenophobe.[34]

This disjuncture, this "African xenophobia" that suggested an aversion to the African landscape, even though she found it beautiful, was radicalizing: "I became a patriot for the African bush veld and scorned expats who preferred Surrey."[35] It became an early experience of "is" and "ought," a kind of binary framework which, as she would later learn from social scientists at the University of Pennsylvania (Penn), could be used to explain these conflicting cultural value systems—in this case, the "is" of the colony and the "ought" of the mother country.[36] Simply put, she asked herself, "Where did we fit, culturally and artistically? With Africa or with England?"[37]

This dichotomy and self-awareness placed her in an interstitial position: in one sense peripheral to the colonial metropole, and in another still very privileged in its local context, as a white, upper-middle-class citizen. Scott Brown recognized her position, later recalling she "felt guilty, even as a child, that I had privilege beyond what I deserved in South Africa."[38] And yet, growing up Jewish—a reason she was bullied at school—amidst the specter of Nazism in Europe and as a white person in apartheid South Africa, it also made her question the simple strictures of dogma and ideology: "They made me consider the complexity that ideologists ignore, and the conflicts of values that individuals face within themselves. For example, Afrikaners, proud of their heritage, were among the leaders of the anti-apartheid movement in South Africa."[39] The complex social, racial, and personal conditions that were Scott Brown's life in Johannesburg proved to be critical to her outlook. In response to a question about being conscious of humanistic issues in her work, Scott Brown was unequivocal: "Very much so. Because you can't be South African and not be conscious of it."[40] Her status as an outsider, in these various ways, left her not so much on the outside looking in, but rather on the outside looking around.

An "African View"

Throughout her career, Scott Brown has used the phrase an "African view" to describe an important part of herself that informed her understanding of and approach to architecture and urbanism in the United States as she studied, lived, taught, practiced, and wrote about it. In the 1986 essay "Invention and Tradition," about the nature of American architecture and drawing parallels with her own history, she concluded:

> In this thesis on colonies and mother cultures I have tried to suggest that the colonial paradoxes are as much opportunities as problems and that they add intensity and uniqueness to American architecture. Two "colonial" heritages, one American and the other African, both set in a European mould, have helped define my argument. Its edge probably derives from the marginal nature of my relation to dominant cultures.[41]

Her position on various cultural and colonial edges informed her perspective, especially on Las Vegas, as she explained: "It was relatively easy to transfer my African xenophobia to America, and to suggest that American architects, for the sake of cultural relevance and artistic vitality, look at the landscape around them and learn."[42] That is, growing up as a South African in a former colony still dominated by English culture, Scott Brown perceived and resisted what she saw as colonial ideologies dismissive of South African surroundings and experiences. Her "African xenophobia" was a term that described a British "expat xenophobia" in South Africa that became a powerful cautionary tale for her against dismissing American surroundings and experiences, instead encouraging her to find their value.[43] When this 1986 essay was republished in 2009, Scott Brown added a sentence, reinforcing her point of view: "In that sense, mine is an African view of Las Vegas."[44]

However, her first published use of the phrase appears two years earlier, in the February 1984 issue of *Architectural Record*.[45] In recounting her "worm's eye view of recent architectural history" to counter dominant narratives and misconceptions, Scott Brown underlined the importance of "learning from the cultural landscape" in her life and work, especially from growing up in South Africa. From seeing at a young age—especially through her art classes—the reuse and appropriation of commercial objects and industrial culture in the painting and sculpture of African folk artists, she absorbed the enriching possibilities of cultural transmission through creative engagement. "It opened my eyes," she wrote, "to the vitality and poignance of 'impure' art. Mine is an African view of Las Vegas."[46]

In her usage, "African" denotes an acknowledgment, recognition, and valuing of the objects, places, and spaces that exist in one's everyday life and condition, rather than racial and ethnic connotations relating to black South Africans or indigenous African cultures. However, as a white South African, her lived experience in Johannesburg intersected with black South Africans and indigenous cultures in a way that informed her use of "African" as an operative term. This multivalent "African view" as a way of seeing was present, for example, in her experience with the local and folk architecture of the Mapoch Ndebele people, who built mud houses with thatch roofs and painted the exteriors in colorful geometric patterns based on both indigenous and adopted motifs. Scott Brown admired their complex incorporation of traditional residential typologies, response to forced planning ordinances, and hybrid "Gillette razor blade" graphics.[47] The Mapoch houses and the African vernacular connected her to contemporary research and the larger world of architectural publishing. She knew Betty Spence, a white South African, whose research program at Wits led to numerous studies and articles, such as the July 1954 *Architectural Review* cover article, "M'Pogga," which featured these dwellings and validated her own experience in South Africa, a moment that for Scott Brown represented the "is" and the "ought" as the same.[48] This visual and social acuity to culture—popular, local, folk, and vernacular—would continue to occupy Scott Brown as part of her "African view."

Furthermore, in an oral history conducted in 1990–1991, Scott Brown explained the importance of her "African view of Las Vegas" in her intellectual formation.[49] She has continued to reiterate this phrase in her writings and interviews in the past decade during a period of retrospection, setting the record straight on her career, and in the wake of an increasing interest in her position as a pioneering architect who is a woman. The critical perspective of her "African view" for America and elsewhere has long been important to her thinking, but likely overshadowed by issues such as sexism.[50]

Learning in London, Europe, and Back

In 1952 Scott Brown went to London for the purposes of a fourth-year practicum at Wits. She worked with modernist architect Frederick Gibberd and then enrolled at the Architectural Association School of Architecture (AA). She completed her AA diploma in 1955 and registration as an architect in Britain one year later, so that it was no longer necessary for her to return to Wits. While Scott Brown's decision to go abroad was part of a colonial system of education that transferred cosmopolitan knowledge from the center of the Commonwealth, London, back to the periphery of South Africa,[51] she also needed direction and guidance: "When I was a very young student, I was totally lost.

That was part of the reason why I left for England, because I didn't know what architecture was about."[52] In London, she found an active and engaging architectural culture that she described as follows: "For a neophyte European with an African background, this strange mixture of CIAM, [Arthur] Korn, postwar socialism and New Brutalism was a wonderful elixir. I think it formed the foundation for most of my subsequent thinking about architecture."[53] Her African background, so conscious of "is" and "ought," found a parallel in London in two different ways: aesthetic and social. Scott Brown found, in the New Brutalism and "urban re-identification" of Peter and Alison Smithson, a sympathetic method of looking at what's around as they focused their attention to the street life of London's East End: the "is" of the working class and the "ought" of the upper-middle-class.[54]

In 1954 Robert Scott Brown joined her in London at the AA and they married on July 21, 1955. Both were equally driven towards the same goals. He was the son of a Scottish immigrant, lawyer, and Presbyterian father and half-Jewish mother, who grew up on a farm in Natal and spoke English, Zulu, and German, and later added French, Italian, and a little Serbian, as Scott Brown recounts—"A real Central European reared Anglican but in revolt." She was the Jewish granddaughter of ethnic Latvians and Lithuanians, immigrants to Rhodesian "lion country" and South Africa, who grew up well-to-do in suburban Johannesburg, near where Robert lived.[55] Together they shared a "fervent idealism about architecture and South Africa" with the goal to return and "give something back."[56]

Upon returning to South Africa in 1957, Denise and Robert Scott Brown turned their attention to survey the vast, multicultural, and diverse country in which they planned to work: "Our photographs from that time are of Cape Dutch, Natal English, and urban vernacular architecture; African housing, rural and urban; and folk and popular culture" (fig. 6).[57] This photographic practice of close observation and documentation of architecture and the built environment was instructive, providing a rich index of the dwellings, landscapes, and patterns of living in South Africa that would inform their intended practice.[58] However, despite education, travel, work abroad, and a return home, the Scott Browns still wanted more training to equip them for their future

Figure 6: Denise Scott Brown and Robert Scott Brown exploring the natural landscape in South Africa, 1952.

work as architects in South Africa: "It seemed obvious to us, when leaving the AA, that the best direction for committed architects, and particularly African ones, was toward 'town planning.'"[59] In 1958, the Scott Browns set off for Philadelphia to begin their master's degrees in city planning at the University of Pennsylvania.[60]

There they had a clear intent to gain "training to make us useful in building a better South Africa."[61] Their advisor at Penn, David A. Crane, ensured that they would learn the necessary skills. Scott Brown recalled him saying, "Don't worry ... coming from Africa and talking as you do, you should have city planning training. You need that for where you're going."[62] Crane, who was born in the Belgian Congo to parents who were Presbyterian missionaries, elaborated, "To work usefully in Africa, you'll need an understanding of how economies develop and grow, and how trade routes give rise to cities."[63] For the Scott Browns, their eventual direction and purpose were plain: "We were going back to work in Africa as Africans."[64]

Learning in America

Scott Brown thrived at the University of Pennsylvania through intellectual circumstance and, eventually, practical necessity. At Penn, Herbert Gans, a sociologist and urban thinker, had a powerful impact on Scott Brown's processing of cultural valences. In his work on social planning and critique, he became a participant in order to understand the lived dynamics of people and their environment. For example, to research *The Levittowners* (1967) he moved to the suburb in New Jersey and observed and experienced the community from within. On one level, this approach resonated with Scott Brown's own approach and background. She described the connection between New Brutalism and Gans: "What they shared was the idea I had found intriguing as a cultural colonial in Africa: that you should look as open-mindedly as you could at real patterns and try to build from them—for both moral and aesthetic reasons."[65] On another level, Gans and his ideas discarded everything the Scott Browns had learned up to that point: "To a pair of young idealists out of Africa and the AA it was some sort of killing lifeline. Although parts of it sounded like Team 10 and more like Paul Kriesis, it was basically different from anything we had learned as architects in Europe and Africa."[66] Most importantly, Gans's approach synthesized her previous experience into a new outlook: "His cultural relativism and his focus on popular culture helped take our African and English experiences into an American context and provided a knowledge base for the studies I would later make of the American 'everyday landscape.'"[67]

In June 1959, Robert Scott Brown died in a car accident. This tragedy upended Denise Scott Brown's life, and uncertain of her future, she immersed herself in her work: "I returned to school in the fall because no alternative seemed better."[68] She received her city planning degree in 1960. Though she had always intended to return with Robert Scott Brown to South Africa, instead she stayed on at Penn and joined the faculty as an assistant professor. She simultaneously taught and studied for a master's degree in architecture, also at Penn, which she received in 1965.[69]

That year was a watershed for her, thanks to her travel schedule through the United States. She visited Birmingham, New Orleans, Houston, San Antonio,

Figure 7: Mojave Desert, California, circa 1966. Photograph by Denise Scott Brown.

Dallas, Phoenix, and Los Angeles en route to teaching positions that spring at the University of California at Berkeley and later that fall at the University of California at Los Angeles.[70] During two trips to Phoenix, she visited the architect Paolo Soleri, and while driving out to visit him at Arcosanti, she remarked upon the resemblance of the desert landscape to the veld in South Africa: "What to me felt like *real* countryside, i.e. wild and gaunt like the Northern Transvaal" (fig. 7).[71] The towns in Death Valley also piqued her interest. In a letter written to friends at the time, she described their features and effects:

> All you notice is a series of bright billboards, neon signs + TV antennae + then you're through it + into the aged desert again. The buildings are nondescript + sunk into the landscape. The towns appear, then, as nothing other than communication, a brief, syncopated pixie land, soon gone. They are, I'm sure like no other towns anywhere, + would be fascinating to study.[72]

In this quasi-familiar landscape, American development in the desert Southwest prompted her to consider how architecture appears and makes itself known. This attention to the communicative role of architecture continued as she revisited Las Vegas on the return trip. In the same letter, she wrote about some further observations of the city and posed an important question: "Delightful discovery: the Dunes, grandest hotel in town, has faculty rates. Could Las V. be educational? I took a bus at 10pm down the 'strip.' Photographing neon signs. Found one which said 'Wedding chapel—credit cards accepted.'"[73] Later that summer, while still living in Berkeley, she continued exploring the cities and landscapes of the American West, traveling throughout New Mexico, Colorado, and Oregon.[74] Armed with her impressions, photographs, and questions of architectural and urban development in this region of the country, she invited Robert Venturi to be a critic at her UCLA studio jury. She decided that the first place he needed to see—a place she had already been to a total of four times—was Las Vegas. Off they went on a four-day trip in November 1966.[75]

Learning and Las Vegas

Venturi stressed Scott Brown's critical role in exposing him to the city and the ideas they later explored together: "Denise was very influential in pointing out the significance of the ordinary and in introducing me to Las Vegas and Pop culture. I can say she corrupted me."[76] They first met in 1960 as colleagues at a Penn faculty meeting; from 1961 to 1964 they each taught a course in a two-semester sequence on architectural theories, and they co-taught it in spring 1964.[77] The year 1967 was momentous: Scott Brown received tenure at UCLA and married Venturi on July 23 in Santa Monica, before moving back to Philadelphia, when she joined Venturi and Rauch (fig. 8). However, Scott Brown had worked with the architectural firm as early as 1964, becoming a partner in the office in 1969; it was renamed Venturi, Rauch, and Scott Brown in 1980 and Venturi, Scott Brown and Associates in 1987.

In their close, early, and formative collaboration, Scott Brown and Venturi recognized that issues of credit and attribution would cause confusion—prompting notable, preemptive disclaimers in their work.[78] The first edition of *Learning from Las Vegas* included a "Note on Authorship and Attribution" following the preface, which Venturi wrote "to make clear that the name 'Robert Venturi' when used to describe the written and architectural output of the firm Venturi and Rauch ... is unfair to the people who have added their thought and creativity to our office, especially to the three other partners."[79] He went on to credit Scott Brown as the designer of the Las Vegas studio at Yale, while also noting the entangled thinking that produced the book and was involved in the formation of his, her, and their ideas since they first met in 1960: "Denise Scott Brown, my collaborator for twelve years, has been so intertwined in our joint development that it is impossible to define where her thought leaves off and mine begins. She is as responsible as I am for the theoretical content of this book."[80] While Venturi's "Note on Authorship and Attribution" in the first edition of *Learning from Las Vegas* "was virtually ignored by almost all reviewers," as Scott Brown wrote in the preface to the revised edition, their intellectual exchange developed in tandem from the beginning.[81]

In 1968 at the Yale School of Art and Architecture, where Robert Venturi was Charlotte Shepherd Davenport Visiting Professor of Architecture and Scott Brown was a Visiting Professor in Urban Design, with the help of a graduate assistant, Steven Izenour, they conducted the studio "Learning from Las Vegas, or Form Analysis as Design Research." Among the many special qualities of the city that made it a compelling case study, Scott Brown recalled: "We were impressed by the bright signs against a very blue sky. There's an almost Greek clarity of light and color there. It's simple-minded to consider Las Vegas only at night. Also we thought that the city's chaos was an order we had not yet understood."[82] In the starkness between the dusty ground and blue sky, this daytime appreciation of the desert horizon recalled her childhood experience in the veld, a familiar sight, just one now marked with signs. Even the connections between the dazzling quality of signage under the mantle of darkness and the wonders of American entertainment reached Scott Brown when she was young. Visiting the Johannesburg Jubilee in 1936 with her family, she recalled the "marvelous" nighttime lighting across the grounds and also knew about Coney Island from the stories and souvenirs from her grandparents' travels, which she imagined as "fairyland."[83]

Figure 8: Denise Scott Brown and Robert Venturi at their wedding reception at Denise's cottage in Ocean Park, Santa Monica, July 23, 1967.

For Scott Brown the Las Vegas project—that is, the urban sprawl and commercial development of the automobile city—reflected an approach she had taken all her life, except that it was now aimed at America. She recalled how her various experiences informed her inclusive outlook and its potential value:

> I brought from Africa my xenophobia of things non African, and from London my Brutalist sensibility and applied them to America. Looking at Las Vegas, I said to myself, "This thing you hate could be the seed of your creativity. Learn to understand it the way it is, suspend judgment briefly, be a little less rigid, you may find the Strip exciting, even beautiful, and perhaps artistically inspiring."[84]

Scott Brown exercised the lessons from her home country and was in this way uniquely qualified to see Las Vegas in a way that others hadn't—or couldn't. Venturi acknowledged as much in an interview profile of his wife: "Venturi concedes that as an outsider, as a South African, Scott Brown helped him 're-see' the American landscape."[85] Further stressing the point, in his 1991 Pritzker Prize acceptance speech thanking the people, places, and institutions influential in his career, Venturi named "Las Vegas" as one such place, clarifying: "which I learned via the perspective of Rome and through the eyes of Denise Scott Brown ..."[86] Scott Brown had a natural disposition to appreciate and see the strong correspondence between the boomtown desert urbanism of both Johannesburg and Las Vegas. Just as her childhood trips to the veld allowed her to see the complex laws and shared relationships between the rural and urban, there, in Las Vegas, she found a similar, rich contrast—and the same urge to understand it.

The Publication, 1972 and 1977

If Scott Brown "corrupted" Venturi to "resee" the American landscape because of her South African viewpoint, and if, as Izenour noted, she provided the "intellectual rigor" to the project, then the change between the 1972 edition and the 1977 revised edition comes into relief—a realignment towards

Figure 9: Car view of the Strip with Robert Venturi and Denise Scott Brown,
Las Vegas, 1968.

Scott Brown's critical role.[87] Indeed, she led its graphic design.[88] For example, the first figure in the 1977 revised edition is a photograph of the signs on
the Las Vegas Strip taken through an automobile windshield by Scott Brown,
which replaced an illustration of nineteenth-century eclecticism from Loud-
on's *Encyclopedia* in the 1972 edition. This brings the revised edition closer
to their original project intent, laid out in the 1968 article, "A Significance for
A&P Parking Lots or Learning from Las Vegas," which featured a similar Las
Vegas Strip photograph by Scott Brown. It also reorients the project to Scott
Brown's mode of seeing that first began with her mother driving her and her
sister around Johannesburg. In Las Vegas too, Scott Brown was a passenger,
now with camera in hand, as Venturi drove them through the streets (fig. 9).[89]
While a photo credit line may read as firm in terms of authorship, a practice
of photography—a way of looking together—is not. That is to say, Venturi steering the vehicle is as contingent as Scott Brown shooting the target—a dual co-
incident; one cannot happen without the other.

The change in the book cover, too, suggests the repositioning of the revised edition back towards Scott Brown's original vision and intent undergirding the study. In the preface to the revised edition, Scott Brown heavily critiqued Muriel Cooper's "Bauhaus design" for the first edition: "The 'interesting' Modern styling of the first edition, we felt, belied our subject matter, and the triple spacing of the lines made the text hard to read."[90] More than just reconciling form and content, the revised edition also orients the visual experience of the cover to better match Scott Brown's impression of the unique qualities of the Las Vegas commercial landscape. Apart from a much smaller size in paperback, the revised edition's cover was now light blue and elevated the billboard-proportioned "Tanya" suntan lotion photograph on the page, unencumbered by a dust jacket full of words.[91] These changes make the cover itself mirror the visual experience of "bright signs against a very blue sky" that so appealed to her sensibilities.

Finally, the revised edition doesn't just bear her imprint in terms of the layout, image sequence, and cover design, but also in its dedication: the first edition is dedicated to Cecilia and George, Robert Scott Brown's mother and stepfather; the revised edition is dedicated to Robert Scott Brown.[92] For all the publication's initial impact and subsequent influence, *Learning from Las Vegas* was deeply personal for Scott Brown. In this way, South Africa is at the heart of the study because it was guiding, and after the tragic loss of Robert Scott Brown, it was a geography that led in new directions. The book, then, can be seen as a testament to Denise Scott Brown's talent and determination to still succeed in carving out a life and career in architecture that she had imagined otherwise.

•

Reflecting on how significant going to study abroad at the AA in London was, Scott Brown recalled, "In this way, at twenty, I left home, family and country for good without actually realizing it."[93] In 2011, she received an honorary degree from Wits—a university she had unintentionally left so many years before. In her Commencement Address, she noted, "Ironically, I have used what I learned for South Africa, in France, England, Japan, Morocco, China, and America, but I have not taken it to you." Her initial publishing record suggests

Figure 10: Andy Warhol, Denise Scott Brown, 1971. Dye diffusion transfer print
(Polaroid Polacolor Type 108). 4¼ × 3⅜ in.

the transnational perspective she has always had. In 1962, her first article reviewed the planning model for Philadelphia.[94] Two years later, her second article reviewed a planning model for Natal in South Africa.[95] As an outsider, on different margins, she has been able to move between worlds and use this experience to create new ones. Though she is so self-aware of these multiple cultures and identities as she has traversed them, the lens through which she looks—and is seen—can still surprise: "My intimacy with several cultures, while young, helped me to do my work in these places—though the African in me still asks, 'What am I doing here?'" (fig. 10).[96]

Notes

1   Scott Brown, "Worm's Eye," 77.

2   See Scott Brown, Oral History Interview with Denise Scott Brown, 1990 October 25–1991 November 9, Archives of American Art, Smithsonian Institution; Scott Brown, "Some Ideas," 105; and Scott Brown, "Invention and Tradition," in *Having Words*, 6.

3   For an important essay that grounds Scott Brown's biography and "African view" within apartheid-era South Africa and ethnographic techniques of study, see Levin, "Learning from Johannesburg."

4   The Las Vegas project took on many forms that evolved and fed into one another. The first article, Venturi and Scott Brown, "A Significance for A&P Parking Lots, or Learning from Las Vegas" (1968), provided information about the studio and opened Part I of the publication. A second article, Scott Brown and Venturi, "On Ducks and Decoration" (1968), explained the idea of the "duck" in their architectural theory. The Fall 1968 architecture studio was titled "Learning from Las Vegas, or Form Analysis as Design Research," later renamed by the students "Learning from Las Vegas: The Great Proletarian Cultural Locomotive." The first edition of the book, Venturi, Scott Brown, and Izenour, *Learning from Las Vegas* (1972) was revised five years later with an added subtitle, *Learning from Las Vegas: The Forgotten Symbolism of Architectural Form* (1977); A facsimile edition of the first edition was republished in 2017. Some recent studies include von Moos and Stierli, eds., *Eyes That Saw* (2020); Stadler, Stierli, and Fischli, eds., *Las Vegas Studio* (2015); Stierli, *Las Vegas* (2013); Vinegar and Golec, eds., *Relearning from Las Vegas* (2009); Vinegar, *I am a monument* (2008); and Rattenbury and Hardingham, *Robert Venturi and Denise Scott Brown* (2007).

5   Venturi, Scott Brown, and Izenour, *Learning from Las Vegas* (1972), xviii.

6   Venturi, Scott Brown, and Izenour, *Learning from Las Vegas* (1972), xviii and Venturi, Scott Brown, and Izenour, *Learning from Las Vegas* (1977), 73.

7   Gabor, *Einstein's Wife*, 195.

8   Denise Scott Brown, email to author, April 9, 2022 and Scott Brown, *A View from the Campidoglio*, 9; and see McLeod, "Wrestling with Meaning," 67n2,

Stierli, *Las Vegas*, 32–33, and Gabor, *Einstein's Wife*, 195 for more on authorship and ordering.

9   In this vein, a study of Steven Izenour's role and contribution warrants consideration.

10   Waite, "Call for Denise Scott Brown" (2013).

11   Denise Scott Brown's family name was Lakofski; she was known as Denise Lakofski until she married Robert Scott Brown in 1955.

12   Scott Brown recalled being bullied in primary school, and a headmistress, D.V. Thompson, who provided important support; see Tenenbaum, *Your Guide*, 118–120.

13   Scott Brown, Oral History Interview and Tenenbaum, *Your Guide*, 118.

14   Denise Scott Brown, email to author, March 28, 2022; Scott Brown, Oral History Interview; and Chipkin, *Johannesburg Style*, 118; see Monte Carlo and Unitas buildings designed by Bernard Janks in Pevsner, "Development," 373.

15   Denise Scott Brown, Commencement Address, University of the Witwatersrand, July 21, 2011.

16   Gilbert and Moore, *Particular Passions*, 311.

17   Venturi and Scott Brown, *Architecture as Signs and Systems*, 106–107.

18   Scott Brown, "Towards an Active Socioplastics," 24.

19   See Herbert, *Martienssen*, 18–22, 29–35 and Chipkin, *Johannesburg Style*, 157–158.

20   Denise Scott Brown, telephone conversation with author, April 9, 2022 and Scott Brown, Oral History Interview.

21   The firm of Hanson, Tomkin, and Finkelstein was among the key proponents and builders of modernist architecture in South Africa during the 1930s and 1940s; see Herbert, *Martienssen*, 50–53, 86–89, 136; Chipkin, *Johannesburg Style*, 164–169; and van der Waal, *Mining Camp to Metropolis*, 239–242.

22   Scott Brown, Oral History Interview.

23   Scott Brown, "Some Ideas and Their History," 106.

24   Scott Brown, "Questions of Style," 264.

25   Scott Brown, "Changing Family Forms" (1992), 108. First published in *Journal of the American Planning Association*, Spring 1983, 133–137.

26   Scott Brown recounts her first team research studio focused on hospital kitchens and including looking at hotels, including the Grant Hotel in Johannesburg; see Tenenbaum, *Your Guide*, 128.

27 Gabor, *Einstein's Wife*, 166 and Denise Scott Brown, email to author, April 9, 2022.

28 For more on "Man Made Johannesburg," see Robin Middleton's essay in this volume, with an introduction by Mary McLeod. My thanks to Mary McLeod for sharing critical insights and research on this and other matters, especially note 8.

29 Scott Brown, Oral History Interview.

30 Gabor, *Einstein's Wife*, 167.

31 Denise and her sister Ruth started an archaeological society at Kingsmead College in Johannesburg in 1946, and in 1950 were appointed Associate members of the South African Archaeological Society, on the basis of many successful finds from their field work. See *Kingsmead College Magazine*, Kingsmead College (1950), 34.

32 Evelina Francia, "Learning from Africa," 27.

33 Scott Brown, commencement address (see note 15).

34 Venturi and Scott Brown, *Architecture as Signs and Systems*, 108.

35 Denise Scott Brown, email to author, April 9, 2022.

36 Scott Brown, "Towards an Active Socioplastics," 24.

37 Venturi and Scott Brown, *Architecture as Signs and Systems*, 107.

38 Tenenbaum, *Your Guide*, 128.

39 Tenenbaum, *Your Guide*, 118 and Orazi, "Building Arguments," 157.

40 Tenenbaum, *Your Guide*, 123.

41 Scott Brown, "Invention and Tradition," in *American Architecture*, 168; originally a symposium paper delivered at the Buell Center for the Study of American Architecture, Columbia University, April 21–24, 1983.

42 Scott Brown, "Invention and Tradition," in *American Architecture*, 159.

43 Denise Scott Brown, email to author, April 9, 2022.

44 Scott Brown, "Invention and Tradition," in *Having Words*, 6.

45 Scott Brown, "Worm's Eye," 69–81.

46 Scott Brown, "Worm's Eye," 77.

47 Scott Brown, "Some Ideas," 108, fig. 181.

48 Spence and Bierman, "M'Pogga," 35–40 and Chipkin, *Johannesburg Style*, 316. *Architectural Review*, a decade earlier in 1944, had included "Native housing traditions" in an issue about the architectural development and contemporary buildings of South Africa: see Anon., *Architectural Review* 96, no. 574 (1944), 93–128; and again focused on the country

with a feature on Johannesburg in 1953: Pevsner, "Development," 360–382. For more on publications and exchanges on indigenous South African architecture in professional journals, see Dainese, "Histories of Exchange," 443–463.

49 Scott Brown, Oral History Interview.

50 See Scott Brown, "Room at the Top?" 237–246, originally delivered as a talk at the West Coast Women's Design Conference in Oregon, written in 1974. Even in this essay, while she points out "the social trivia (what Africans call *petty apartheid*)" of sexism, her sensibility as a South African is present, 239.

51 While at the AA, however, she visited Norman Hanson to borrow photographs of his early work in South Africa to exhibit in London, see Scott Brown, "Worm's Eye," 71.

52 Miranda, "Architect Interview."

53 Scott Brown, "Between Three Stools," 9.

54 Venturi and Scott Brown, *Architecture as Signs and Systems*, 107.

55 Denise Scott Brown, email to author, April 9, 2022.

56 Gabor, *Einstein's Wife*, 169, 177.

57 Venturi and Scott Brown, *Architecture as Signs and Systems*, 112.

58 For further discussion, see Stierli, *Las Vegas*, 109–113.

59 Scott Brown, "Between Three Stools," 10.

60 The Scott Browns are a prime example of the connection between Johannesburg and Philadelphia, and in the 1950s and 1960s, a group of South Africans went to graduate school in America, especially Penn, many returning home to practice. See Chipkin, *Johannesburg Style*, 316–319. Although not mentioned in Chipkin, Adèle Naudé Santos (Master of Architecture and Master of City Planning, Penn, 1968), former Dean of the School of Architecture and Planning at MIT from 2004 to 2015, is another such figure.

61 Scott Brown, commencement address (see note 15).

62 Venturi and Scott Brown, *Architecture as Signs and Systems*, 113.

63 Scott Brown, commencement address (see note 15).

64 Scott Brown, "Some Ideas," 113.

65 Scott Brown, "The Rise and Fall of Community Architecture," 32.

66 Scott Brown, "Between Three Stools," 11.

67 Scott Brown, "Towards an Active Socioplastics," 29–30.

68 Scott Brown, "Between Three Stools," 12.

69 Her early teaching reflected her transnational experience, drawing upon African references. A Fall 1960 studio focused on the design for a tropical African market and a 1962 course on urban housing prompted students to look to Mapoch villages and African kraals, along with Philadelphia row houses and apartment blocks in Sheffield, England, for typological models. For more on Scott Brown's teaching at Penn, see Lee Ann Custer and James Yellin's essay in this volume.

70 Scott Brown, "Letter to Friends, Fine Arts, January 31, 1965," 83–86. See also Sylvia Lavin's essay in this volume.

71 Scott Brown, "Letter to Friends," 85.

72 Scott Brown, "Letter to Friends," 88.

73 Scott Brown, "Letter to Friends," 88.

74 Scott Brown, "Letter to Friends," 90.

75 Minnite, "Chronology," 248 and Miranda, "Architect Interview."

76 Belogolovsky, "Learning," 122 and similar sentiment in Scott Brown, "Preface," in Venturi and Scott Brown, *Architecture as Signs and Systems*, ix.

77 See Lee Ann Custer's essay in this volume and Custer, "Teaching Complexity and Contradiction." My thanks to Lee Ann Custer for her help.

78 In their extensive bibliography, Scott Brown and Venturi are scrupulous about the way in which authorship is ordered. For coauthored pieces, the primary author is listed first; *Learning from Las Vegas* is a notable exception. For more on how ideas and influences from others can inform and complicate authorship, see Mary McLeod, "Venturi's Acknowledgments."

79 Venturi, Scott Brown, and Izenour, *Learning from Las Vegas* (1972), xii.

80 Venturi, Scott Brown, and Izenour, *Learning from Las Vegas* (1972), xii.

81 Scott Brown, preface to Venturi, Scott Brown, and Izenour, *Learning from Las Vegas* (1977), xv.

82 Belogolovsky, "Learning," 123.

83 Rockwell and Mau, *Spectacle*, 64.

84 Francia, "Learning from Africa," 28.

85 Gabor, *Einstein's Wife*, 195.

86 Venturi, Acceptance Speech, Pritzker Prize. For more on Venturi and Rome, see Stierli, "Academy's Garden," 42–63 and *Venturi's Grand Tour* and Costanzo, "Truly Liberal Orientation," 223–247 and "I Will Try," 269–283.

87 For more on the graphic design of *Learning from Las Vegas*, see Stierli, *Las Vegas*, 23–68; Vinegar, *I Am a Monument*, 111–171; and Golec, "Format and Layout," 31–47.

88 Scott Brown, "The Tyranny of the Template: The Graphic Design of the First Edition of *Learning from Las Vegas*" in *Learning from Las Vegas* (2017) and email with author, April 9, 2022; Stierli, 60–64; and Vinegar, 146–148 and especially 223, note 88 for Sylvia Steiner, Mario Furtado, and Cynthia Ware's role at the firm.

89 Though Venturi had previously taken photographs, Scott Brown recounted that after they met, he mostly stopped, Denise Scott Brown, telephone conversation with author, March 16, 2022.

90 Scott Brown, preface to Venturi, Scott Brown, and Izenour, *Learning from Las Vegas* (1977), xv. In another quirk of the first edition, the text for Part I begins on page xviii and continues onto page 1.

91 Scott Brown likened the cover of the revised edition to "an old-fashioned 19th century book [that] would have a picture set in: billboard of 'Tanya'." See Stierli, *Las Vegas*, 37, 62. For more on the book covers and Scott Brown's dissatisfaction with shade of blue, see Vinegar, 120–122 and 223, note 93.

92 *Learning from Las Vegas* (1972), iv and *Learning from Las Vegas* (1977), v.

93 Gilbert and Moore, *Particular Passions*, 312.

94 Scott Brown, "Form, Design and the City—Reviews," 293–299.

95 Scott Brown, "Natal Plans," 161–166.

96 Scott Brown, foreword to *Having Words*, 3. Scott Brown established a scholarship at Kingsmead College, her primary and secondary school, in the name of Robert Scott Brown that connects important threads of people, education, and South Africa in her life; see Tenenbaum, *Your Guide*, 136–137.

Recollections I: Man Made Johannesburg

Robin Middleton with an introduction by Mary McLeod

Denise Scott Brown has described Robin Middleton, whom she first met when they were architecture students at the University of Witwatersrand, as one of her oldest friends, someone who became "like a sibling in our household." They met during Robin's fourth year in the architecture department, and Denise's third year; although they are the same age, Denise had begun her university studies as a liberal arts student before switching to architecture. As Robin describes in the account below, they often went on camping trips to Makapan and Sterkfontein with a group of friends, including Denise's sister Ruth Lakofski (who would later live with Robin for fifty years until her death in 2008) and Robert Scott Brown (who would become Denise's first husband). During these trips, the camping group would sometimes work with biologist Sidney Brenner excavating fossils and archeological remains.

While at Wits, Denise headed a student subcommittee on exhibitions. In a 1990–91 oral history, she recalled: "We spent most of our third year doing very little schoolwork indeed, and making a very big exhibition. It was called 'Man Made Johannesburg.' I co-opted Robert onto my committee, and we two worked mostly together, because he had a motorbike. We had to go collect the photographs on this motorbike from all the architects in town. We made lists of the buildings we wanted, helped by our professors. And then we had to collect them. There was another very good and close friend—Robin Middleton ... He designed the exhibition. It was really great, but it was a huge amount of work for us. I used to ride the back of the motorbike, carrying these photographs— some of them big, like this—on the back. And that was our exhibition vehicle." She remembers Robin in his student years as already being recognized for his superb work as an exhibition designer, starting with a show of paper sculptures in the University of Witwatersrand's main lobby.[1]

MMcL

Figure 1: Denise Scott Brown and Robin Middleton talking at a reception given in honor of Denise Scott Brown and Robert Venturi on the occasion of receiving their American Institute of Architects Gold Medal. Fisher Fine Arts Library (architect: Frank Furness, 1888–90; renovation: Venturi, Scott Brown and Associates, 1986–91), University of Pennsylvania, Philadelphia, June 2016. Photograph by Diana Murphy.

Man Made Johannesburg

One of my first encounters with Denise was when we worked together as students on the exhibition "Man Made Johannesburg," which was staged at the Johannesburg Public Library at the end of 1951. The *South African Architectural Record*, which published an account of the show in its January 1952 issue, credits the Transvaal Provincial Institute of Architects and the Council of Architectural Students of the University of the Witwatersrand.[2] I can recall no such "Council." The students who might have assembled on occasion to make a demand or to organize an event were a haphazard assembly, always, usually, myself. I was an inveterate busybody. I organized lectures and promoted the exhibiting of paintings, and it is possible even that I promoted the idea of the exhibition, quite evidently inspired by the "Man Made America" issue of the *Architectural Review*, in December 1950.

The basic organization, the finding of funds, establishing the venue, determining the themes and the vetting of all the exhibits was, however, clearly in the hands of the Institute of Architects, represented by four of our own professors, John Fassler (the Dean), Jacques Morgenstern, Gilbert Herbert, and Duncan Howie. They set the parameters of the exhibition—a historical introduction, the development of the Johannesburg suburbs, from mansions to low-cost housing, including churches, schools, and hospitals, then to industrial development, to locations for black workers, to finally a focus on the city center itself and its townscape, with an analysis of traffic problems and plans for the future. The students, however, were allowed to select the images for the historical introduction and to write the accompanying texts (no doubt well vetted). I was given complete freedom in designing the exhibition—overtly influenced by Le Corbusier's Pavillon des Temps Nouveaux of 1937, Albini's and Rogers's exhibitions as published in those years in *Casabella* (Richard Lohse's *New Design in Exhibitions* had not yet appeared) and, all too evidently, the graphics of the *Architectural Review*. Not too bad a mix.

I was then in my fourth year of studies, which meant that I was working in an office, that of Fleming and Cooke, thus out of contact with my year mates. I was abetted from the start by Jean Humphries, who worked alongside me.

Figure 2: Cover of the issue of *South African Architectural Record* devoted to the "Man Made Johannesburg" exhibition, January 1952. The photo shows the entrance area to the exhibition, with the wrapped scaffolding.

She introduced me to a group of her camping companions, Denise Lakofski and her sister Ruth, Robert Scott Brown, Liza (Elizabeth) MacCrone and her brother Robert. Denise and Robert Scott Brown were then in the year behind me, Ruth was studying geology, Liza and her brother something other. Together some of us prepared the exhibition and we all continued camping.

The setting for the show was a large hall in the Johannesburg Public Library. The floors were of cork tiles, the walls immaculate white plaster. Nothing could be affixed to any of the surfaces. The framework for the entire exhibition was thus constructed of scaffolding poles, which supported scaffolding boards that enveloped the room and provided surfaces for the displays. One could bash nails or pins into them as required. Moreover, they cost nothing; they were borrowed and could be returned.

Given a free hand in the Historical Section, we concentrated on that. We found three Gothic window frames from a building that was being demolished in the center of town and designed some frilly wire frames to be inserted within as supports for photographs. These were chosen with much care from the collections of the Africana Museum and our professors.

Figure 3: The Historical Section of the exhibition, displayed in Gothic window frames from a building that was being demolished in Johannesburg.

Our school was still in thrall to the Bauhaus. The history of architecture was firmly marginalized. There was a nod to ancient Greece, with the emphasis on the thought rather than the architecture (our text book was surprisingly up to date, H.D.F. Kitto's *The Greeks*, of 1951), skipping thence to the Italian Renaissance. These buildings we had to know. We were expected to memorize the plans, sections, and elevations of a number of the key buildings, as illustrated by Banister and Fletcher, and to reproduce them in exams. Names and dates were also required. This acknowledgment of Greece and Rome was the legacy of Rex Martienssen.

On our own, we had begun to probe the history of architecture in England, though there was not much to be read—Sacheverell Sitwell's somewhat ludicrous *British Architects and Craftsmen,* of 1945 (though I did discover Lees Court in Kent there) and Donald Pilcher's *The Regency Style,* of 1947; Pilcher, in fact, taught us, but we got nothing from him. These books were overtaken by John Summerson's *Georgian London,* in the seductive Pleiades edition, of 1945, and his stirring essays in *Heavenly Mansions,* of 1949. His *Sir John Soane* was yet to come, in 1952. This last set us forming discussion groups and writing papers. But that was a year ahead.

Figure 4: The Industrial Section of the exhibition, showing the string "cooling towers" erected by Robert Scott Brown and Robin Middleton.

We were taught nothing of local history, whether of the nineteenth century or modern, though the school, as already noted, was headed by Fassler, architect with Cooke and Martienssen of a handful of remarkably adept houses and small blocks of flats in the Corbusian manner, dating from the 1930s. By the late 1940s, however, Fassler had turned to Perret.

But the late Victorian cast-iron galleries that littered the downtown streets and the robust stone houses of Sir Herbert Baker (Fleming's father's partner) that followed had stirred our interest. There was no question of our adherence to Le Corbusier; however, we wanted something of beginnings. An outline was offered in an issue of the *Architectural Review*, of October 1944, that ranged from the tribal huts of Pondoland, through Cape Dutch architecture to the early buildings of Johannesburg (skipping the cast-iron galleries) and on to the works of Baker and Fleming, and so to Fassler, Martienssen, and Cooke; Hanson, Tomkin, and Finkelstein; and on to H.H. Le Roith, the current favorite. There was, in addition, a rich series of articles, "The Historic Buildings of Johannesburg," by C.A. Stoloff, published in the *South African Architectural Record* in 1947 and early 1948. We were thus, though uninstructed, well equipped to choose the pictures not only for the opening

13

11

TRADITIONAL

10. "NORTHWARDS," PARKTOWN.
11. HOUSE LEITH, HOUGHTON.
12. HOUSE KENNEDY, LINKSFIELD.
13. THE LODGE, "NORTHWARDS."
14. JOHANNESBURG PUBLIC LIBRARY.
15. INSTITUTE OF MEDICAL RESEARCH.
16. "HOUSE HARRIS," LOWER HOUGHTON.
17. "HOUSE HANSON," LOWER HOUGHTON.
18. "HOUSE STERN," LOWER HOUGHTON.
19. "HOUSE MARTIENSSEN," GREENSIDE.

12

16

MODERN

Figures 5 and 6: A spread in the *South African Architectural Record,* January 1952, showing images from the Traditional and Modern Sections of the "Man Made Johannesburg" exhibition. The photos in the Modern Section include Denise Scott Brown's childhood home, the Lakofski house (right page: middle,

14

15

MAN - MADE JOHANNESBURG

16

18

19

17

17

far left), designed by Norman Hansen in 1936; the Stern House (right page: middle, far right) designed by Martienssen, Fassler, and Cooke in 1934 and considered at the time to be one of the most radically modern houses in Johannesburg; and, below it, the Martienssen House, designed by Rex Martienssen for himself and his wife in 1939.

of the exhibition but also for the main section, which we did. We were, happily, well trusted.

I drew the backgrounds for a few of the displays long beforehand; the lettering panels arduously composed in earlier weeks by Jean Humphries and anyone she could get to help, each letter being cut separately. They were also easily mounted when the time came, as were the photographs and drawings, though much care was needed in positioning them. I don't think that we erected the scaffolding, but we certainly wrapped white paper around the scaffolding to simulate the exhibitions of Persico and Albini. The trickiest assembly was that of the three string "cooling towers," echoing those of the gold mines. They were suspended, boards above and below, unsupported, which meant that the strings of all three had to be very, very carefully adjusted to provide a clearcut image. Robert Scott Brown and I did that together, Robert instructing.

Although several other architectural students were involved in the making of panels and letters, I can recall only Diana Evenary.[3] The mounting of the pieces and adding the finishing touches to the exhibition was mostly the work of the group with whom I went camping—most of all, Denise, Robert Scott Brown, and myself. The exhibition looked quite professional.

Notes

1   Denise Scott Brown, Oral History Interview with
     Peter Reed, Archives of American Art, October 25,
     1990–November 9, 1991. In the interview, she said,
     "I was put in charge of the Student Exhibition
     Sub-Committee, and then I set up my own commit-
     tee." Robin Middleton does not remember the stu-
     dent exhibition committee, perhaps because he was
     working in an office as part of his fourth-year train-
     ing. Other information in this note comes from Mary
     McLeod's conversations with Robin Middleton in
     New York City, February 18 and March 10, 2022
     and her telephone conversations with Denise Scott
     Brown, March 10 and 20, 2022.

2   See the scan of the issue, provided by the library of
     the University of Witwatersrand https://wiredspace.
     wits.ac.za/bitstream/handle/10539/22925/Jour-
     nal%20of%20SAAI-January-1952-001.pdf?se-
     quence=1&isAllowed=y.

3   Diana Evenary (who now uses the last name Gold-
     stein), however, has no memory of working on the
     exhibition, although she remembers recruiting
     Denise to the exhibitions committee (Diana Gold-
     stein, email to Mary McLeod, March 17, 2022).
     Denise Scott Brown remembers that at least two
     other architecture students helped on the exhibition,
     Denys Greene and Fay Thompson. Denise Scott
     Brown, telephone conversation with Mary McLeod,
     March 11, 2022.

Encountering Architectural History in 1950s London

Andrew Leach

The '60s were an era of relentless questioning, and breaking the rules was, you might say, the rule of the day. We certainly shared this interest, and perhaps it made us philosophize about stylistic change and how it happens. An interest in Mannerism helped. Although its first historians interpreted its architectural twists as creativity run amok, neurosis, or the bored doodling of spoiled-brat aristocrats, we came to see Mannerist rule breaking as a means of accommodating functional and other conflicts in a complex world. It encourages us, as designers, to bend certain rules and allow others to hold so that the overall pattern of systems and desires can hang together. Mannerism can be seen as the art and science of rule breaking, a result of complexity, and an engine of style change.
—Denise Scott Brown, "Questions of Style"

In an interview with Rosa Sessa in 2016, Denise Scott Brown recalled that in contrast to the "scholarly environment" in which Venturi's Italian experience was staged, she "was learning about Mannerism in England because Colin Rowe and Rudolf Wittkower['s] books came out. All the Brutalists," she recalled, "were keen on Mannerism. Robert Scott Brown and I went from London to Italy using a list of mannerist architecture and mannerist paintings as a guide for where we wanted to go."[1] While they were in Venice, she said, "[w]e were talking about the early Modern Movement but also reading about Mannerism, looking at all the things Pevsner showed us."[2] At a memorial service for Robert Venturi, she likewise attributed her attention to mannerism to her early teachers:

I was very interested in scale jumps, and the Mannerism they were part of. Seen as aberrant, Mannerism was reappraised in England in the 1940s. [Nikolaus] Pevsner, its rediscoverer, and one of his students, here tonight, and also John Summerson, guided me through Mannerism. I listened for

Figure 1: Alison and Peter Smithson, Sugden House, Devereux Drive, Watford (completed 1956).

two years running to Summerson's [Architectural Association] lectures on Classicism, travelled in England, France and Italy, with Pevsner's book and Robin Middleton's itinerary, and learned a great deal.[3]

Later in her remarks she repeats the point, in essence: "I had had two years of lectures on Mannerism with Summerson, and had travelled to Venice using Robin Middleton's list of buildings and paintings to see on the way to Venice and then on to Rome. And, though we had a lot to share, Bob had not seen those books."[4]

"Those books" comprised a library and, by extension, a corpus of architectural works, distinct to the time and setting in which the young Denise Scott Brown first encountered them, shaping a landscape of architecture and ideas that we can, with the benefit of distance, now historicize; and in doing so offer a portrait of mannerist architecture that is, in her hands, as distinct as the painting of any court of the sixteenth century. This is clearly distinguishable from the library of books and buildings that sits behind the idea of a Venturian mannerism, anchored as it is to the New Criticism and the Roman encounter.[5] The latter has been widely regarded as the principal "mannerism" of the practice of Venturi, Scott Brown and Associates and its antecedents, not least because of Venturi's own agency in foregrounding the term's instrumentality in the firm's architecture. Closer attention, though, to Scott Brown's graduate formation in London—the scholars whose courses she followed, the sources she later recalled as important, as cited above—shows the conflicts inherent in this shared reference. Her ("British") mannerism, still lodged in the study of art and mediated by Summerson and Pevsner, bears the clearly recognizable origins of the *Manierismus* of the interwar *Kunstwissenschaftler*, even as it became something entirely different as it reached London, en route to Philadelphia (and *its* intellectual ties to Princeton and Yale). Writes Scott Brown: "If you're a Mannerist, you love things that bend rules and clash with each other."[6] Working against orthodoxies, scale, and any tactic that pits architecture against life's "messy vitality" owes something to a form of mannerism that complements and is yet distinct from the intellectual, compositional ironies celebrated in American literary criticism. Scott Brown wrote in 1990 of the British brutalists in terms that resonate with her own ideas: "[They] were interested in uncomfortably *indirect* solutions, as well as in uncomfortably direct ones. They had moved from eyes which do not see to facing the unfaceable, to enjoying the aesthetic shiver."[7]

To the extent that an idea of mannerism is central to the shared practice of Scott Brown and Venturi, the drawing together of these distinct libraries and the spheres of architectural production on which they variously rested, each with roots in the early twentieth-century German-language "discovery" of the mannerist decades, likely made their common invocation of this moment in their architecture and writing particularly compelling. Scott Brown has been vocal about what she herself introduced to this common ground, but these assertions have largely been overlooked by historians of her practice.

A correction is warranted: testing the habit among critics of privileging the mannerism found in *Complexity and Contradiction* as the operative concept of their early practice. We can turn instead to the clues—indeed, instructions—offered by Scott Brown decades after this first encounter with the term and all it was made to mean in the 1950s to better locate something of her enduring definition of mannerism, captured in the phrases above, in her formation as an architect.

This is not to invoke "his" and "hers" mannerisms, but rather to acknowledge that the mannerism of this firm is a pairing (and negotiation) of two distinct sets of lessons derived, in part, from this moment in the history of architecture. Through the force of modernist historiography, these are erroneously assumed to be more consistent and straightforward (to the point of caricature in later decades) than they ever were in their formation.[8]

Denise Scott Brown had studied (as Denise Lakofski) at the University of Witwatersrand before traveling to London to work and there taking up studies at the Architectural Association (AA) in 1952, graduating in the diploma course in 1954. The AA in the early 1950s was an important setting for the reconciliation of newly secured knowledge on tropical and subtropical climate; the late or postcolonial projects of those territories that had, for the most part, spent time under British rule; and the trajectory into the postwar era of modern architecture and planning itself—conceived, in this moment and at that institution, as a singular field.[9] Students followed lecture courses on architectural history, but the architectural design studio was at the center of their experience. More broadly, though, London was, in these years, home to numerous scholars whose early lives and careers had taken place in central Europe, and whose lectures could be encountered in various settings throughout Bloomsbury and beyond. Ernst Gombrich and Rudolf Wittkower taught at the Warburg; Pevsner was at Birkbeck and delivered the Slade lectures at the Warburg; and Johannes Wilde was deputy director of the Courtauld. Alongside them, Anthony Blunt (a product of the Warburg) had taken up Kenneth Clark's role as Keeper of the Queen's Pictures; and John Summerson, who had studied on Gordon Square, taught on Bedford Square, where Scott Brown had been, herself, a student, following lectures he distilled into the BBC radio lectures delivered in 1963 and published soon thereafter, on architecture's "classical language."[10] There was much processing, in these years, of the work of art historians from between the wars, separating the wheat from the chaff, as it were, in extracting the disciplinary project of modern art history, born in central Europe, from the reactionary ideology that had come to inflect the work of many of its practitioners.[11]

Scott Brown's recollection that mannerism was "rediscovered and written about by Pevsner in the 1940s in London"[12] is informative for the centrality she accords the German art historian in that setting.

It is true that Pevsner's depiction of mannerist architecture for his neighbor Geoffrey Grigson's *Mint* (1946—the circles of direct discussion tend to be very small) was among the first English-language accounts of mannerism in the sense that it had been used by Pevsner and his contemporaries between the two world wars. It lays out for a novice reader the characteristics of the sixteenth-century architecture that bridges the so-called high Renaissance and the baroque. Through a series of examples—works by Donato Bramante, Giulio Romano, Baldassare Peruzzi, Michelangelo, Pirro Ligorio, Bartolommeo Ammannati, Giacomo Barozzi da Vignola, among a larger cast of incidental actors—mannerism is laid out as an architecture of irony, exaggeration, irreverence, bullheadedness, and artifice. It is, to quote Pevsner, "a clearly circumscribed style." It is "cheerless ..., aloof and austere where it wants to show dignity, precious where it wants to be playful." It "has no faith in mankind and no faith in matter." It "scorns" all that one might praise of the period styles that precede and supplant it.[13] For an Anglophone reader who had not yet encountered Blunt's account of Italian artistic theory, it may well have been the entry point to Wittkower's essay on Michelangelo's Laurentian Library (fig. 2), or have been crucial preparation for understanding Blunt's lecture on mannerism to the RIBA and the discussion that followed.[14] (The interventions by Summerson and Wittkower that follow Blunt's RIBA address make the novelty of the idea of mannerism to this British audience completely clear: Wittkower in his reinforcement of the basic lines of interwar scholarship; Summerson in his live pondering of the British corollaries to Blunt's Italian referents.[15]) As Scott Brown recalls, Wittkower's student Rowe had located mannerism in

Figure 2: Half-elevation of a doorway flanked by a rusticated Doric pilaster with curved pediment; half-elevation of a doorway with triangular pediment; half-elevation front view and two profiles of Michelangelo's door from the vestibule to the reading room in the Laurentian Library (Michelangelo).

the *Architectural Review* for a modernist readership; and his teacher's *Principles* had set the (Italian) sixteenth century in a humanistic epoch.[16] Both were widely read by architects and students of architecture and fuelled discussions on the trajectory of the modern movement—another kind of orthodoxy, as Scott Brown notes in her quotation of Le Corbusier above, akin to that of classicism.

Pevsner's contribution to the *Mint* may well have had the character of a fresh discovery of the term to a readership that had not, to this point, had much use for it. But his European contemporaries and those Britons alert to discussions on the continent between the wars will have rightly recognized it as a summary of more than two decades' analysis of the art and architecture of the sixteenth century, to which he himself had contributed.

Pevsner's own youthful scholarship was, of course, at the center of the work he had (in Scott Brown's terms) "rediscovered." His "Gegenreformation und Manierismus" (1925) appeared in the same issue of *Repertorium für Kunstwissenschaft* as one of the seminal essays by Walter Friedlaender that would be folded into *Mannerism and Anti-Mannerism in Italian Painting* (1957). Pevsner's early writing on this subject argues the imbrications of style and situation in the wake of the Trentine Council; his English-language essay is, though, something of a sanitized counterpoint to the pricklier "Gegenreformation—Manierismus—Barock," published as a contribution to that same journal by Werner Weisbach in 1928. Pevsner's own teacher, Wilhelm Pinder, had also penned an essay, "Zur Physiognomik des Manierismus," in a *liber amicorum* for Ludwig Klages (1932), and it is conceivable that its claims were already familiar to Pevsner. Beyond these "local" relationships is a lengthy list of books and articles that explored the idea of a "mannerist" art (and later architecture) across the 1920s and 1930s. A piece as short as this cannot rehearse it adequately; it may be enough, however, to say that there was, from the end of the 1910s through to the end of the 1930s, a thoroughgoing and vibrant study of the art and architecture of the sixteenth century that took the "late Renaissance" as a period of change that seemed to resonate, in different ways for different authors, with the circumstances in which they themselves wrote. To consider this another way: as a student, Scott Brown encountered as a "rediscovery" a body of ideas and examples through Pevsner's distillation of the interwar art history landscape that her exact contemporary John Shearman, who studied with Wilde at the Courtauld, found necessary to rectify and historicize in his own *Mannerism* (1967). In 1946, Pevsner himself appeared to draw a line under the German-language discourse, defining as closed, established, even settled, a complex field of competing ideas in which he had jostled for a place, and which was in many ambits seen as ready for fresh eyes from the start of the 1940s. What Shearman read as evidence of an ideologically distorted historiographical field in need of correction, Scott Brown had in her youth seen as a singular and fresh stimulus for thinking about the mannerist decades in architecture's history and the lessons for postwar architecture they contained.

We have no reason for treating this as anything other than the common reaction to Pevsner's essay and the postwar "rediscovery" of mannerism it seemed to herald. Indeed, in an autobiographical passage from 1990, Summerson writes that "'[m]annerism,' introduced in Germany in the twenties, was almost unheard of in England before 1946."[17] It is hardly a stretch to imagine that Scott Brown heard this sentiment in the classes she took (twice) with

Figure 3: Sir Edwin Lutyens, Country Life Building, Tavistock Street, London (1905).

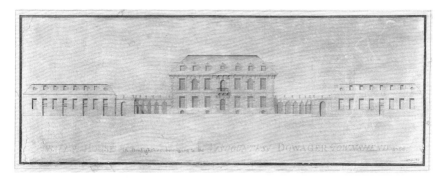

Figure 4: An example of Summerson's "artisan mannerism." Survey drawing
of Balls Park, Hertford (1637–40), front elevation.

Summerson at the AA, even as works like Sir Edwin Lutyens's Country Life
Building (fig. 3) were in direct conversation with the architecture of the Italian sixteenth century.

What precisely one could say of mannerism at this or any other moment is
a question of ground planes. How did Scott Brown first encounter mannerism, and what did that encounter allow? The concept of mannerism itself
was bound up, in the 1940s and 1950s, with the task of reconciling the distinct
(English) study of British architectural history with the working methods
of the central European scholars who had read the history of Italian architecture as a problem of change over time. Its meaning for Scott Brown and
her contemporaries was shaped through a direct experience of architectural
works—what one should know, or could know—that was in turn informed by
that same task. This list was partly driven by her (their) own interests, and
partly by the lectures and lists noted at the outset. The methodological migration of the 1930s changed the scenes of both British and American scholarship
entirely, if in quite distinct ways, and imbued each scene with a complexity
it could not have earlier boasted. A "scientific" approach to the history of art
and architecture, developed in conversations between scholars and institutions in central Europe (and Italy), in London met and melded with British
erudition. Its lessons were explored for their value in understanding the path
of British architecture.

The line Summerson followed through the centuries extended to the present in which he taught and wrote, which made this idea of mannerism (or, more broadly, of a classical tradition) particularly available to those architects and students exploring the field's guiding principles in these years. His idea of the classical tradition was wide-ranging and alert to processes of transmission and change; it extended from the end of the scholastic era to deep into the age of modernism; and its historiography was driven by the preoccupations of architecture rather than the questions of history.[18] He understood that the "study of the architecture of the past has, in this academic world of art history, been raised to a much higher level than that to which we are accustomed in our schools of architecture."[19] Favoring provocation, his sense of mannerism aligned with the easy judgment one might find in Burckhardt a century earlier, even as he moved to reconcile this loose invocation of the term with the rigor with which it had been injected between the wars. His opposition of Palladianism to an "artisan mannerism" (fig. 4) in the seventeenth, eighteenth, and nineteenth centuries is a product of this, and even plays into the differentiation of style from methods of making (akin to Vasari's *maniera*) that would be important to Shearman's thinking in the 1960s.[20] The tension Summerson recognized between the Germanic rigor of Pevsner, Wilde, Wittkower, and their various contemporaries and the open search for lessons in the history of architecture was something he was doubtless still working out across the 1950s as these new ideas were being distilled, reformed, and tested in the London in which Scott Brown then studied. The exploration of architecture's classical tradition was, for Summerson, a study of its path to the present as a reservoir of ideas, values, techniques, and models. That Scott Brown appreciated it as such is notable; as is what she made of that tradition in her architecture and thinking.

The mannerism she encountered in London and which had enlivened the discussion on architecture among her contemporaries was less the *ex novo* discovery she later suggested it to be than a process of introducing to London long established lines of investigation developed in continental Europe over several decades. This made it something new, of course, but covered over the complexities of both that knowledge and the circumstances in which it found a new footing in England. In rehearsing what was familiar ground for many, scholars like Pevsner and Blunt moved questions of change, agency, complexity, and invention into a moment in which architecture's history fed the sensibilities of a generation of British architects. And so, when Denise Scott Brown traveled with her husband Robert to Venice, armed with Summerson's lectures, Pevsner's essay, Middleton's list of things to see, and (above all) currency as designers, she was beginning to formulate a response to the question posed by Summerson back in 1949, and which has extended throughout her career, inflecting *their* career: "That [writing] suggests to me certain things which should be done, but I do not quite know what those things are."[21] Beyond the specific claims that Scott Brown makes in her invocation of mannerism in accounts of her work and thought, perhaps we can see in Scott Brown's career as an academic, critic, and architect an enduring effort to respond to this quandary in the face of history.

Notes

1 Sessa, "By Means of Rome," 363, referring to Rowe's essay "Mannerism and Modern Architecture" and Wittkower's *Architectural Principles in the Age of Humanism*, published in 1950 and 1949, respectively. My essay was written in a moment when travel from Australia was not possible, and so I wish to note here my gratitude for the generous assistance offered by Edward Bottom, Head of Archives at the Architectural Association, London; and William Whittaker, Barton and Victoria Myers Director of the Architectural Archives of the University of Pennsylvania Weitzman School of Design.

2 Sessa, "By Means of Rome," 364.

3 Hilburg, "Well Lived." In an oral history with Peter Reed conducted for the Smithsonian Archives of American Art, Scott Brown makes this same point concerning Summerson's lectures on classicism. As a matter of proximity, it deserves noting that Middleton was for many years the partner of Scott Brown's younger sister, Ruth Lakofski, who also studied at the AA (Scott Brown, Oral History Interview, 1990–91, 17, 23).

4 Hilburg, "Well Lived." Scott Brown concludes a sustained account of the relative depth and complexity of her encounter with mannerism over that of Venturi with this observation: "In Europe, everyone was using the word 'Mannerism'; in America, no one was using it. That word didn't just come out of Bob. He'll say it did" ("Manierismuseum," 99).

5 Costanzo, "Text, Lies and Architecture"; Leach, "Dilemmas without Solutions."

6 Scott Brown, "Manierismuseum," 96.

7 Scott Brown, "Between Three Stools," 9.

8 Common to mid-century scholarship on mannerism, in all its diversity, is an assurance that there is a consistent idea of what the term means and contains. This, arguably, is the seed of exactly the kind of discord we encounter in this example. I will explore the history of this problem in a book provisionally entitled *Unstylish Style*.

9 Patrick Zamarian (*The Architectural Association in the Postwar Years*, 68–119) presents a close reading of the institution's contested history in the 1950s. Scott Brown went on to study with Maxwell Fry and Jane Drew in this dedicated program (Scott Brown, "The Petition is My Prize").

10 Summerson, *The Classical Language of Architecture*; see also Critchley, "Mannerism and Method."

11 Although her book concerns a later style, Levy's insights into this problem in her *Baroque and the Political Language of Formalism* are valuable.

12 Scott Brown, "The Petition is My Prize."

13 Pevsner, "The Architecture of Mannerism," 135.

14 Blunt, *Artistic Theory in Italy 1400–1650*; Wittkower, "Michelangelo's Biblioteca Laurenziana"; Blunt, "Mannerism in Architecture."

15 Blunt, "Mannerism in Architecture," 199–200.

16 Rowe, "Mannerism and Modern Architecture"; Wittkower, *Architectural Principles in the Age of Humanism*.

17 Summerson, quoted in Salmon (ed.), *Summerson and Hitchcock*, xxii.

18 There are no records of Summerson's lectures in the AA Archives, nor among Scott Brown's papers at the Penn Architectural Archives. His stance is, however, consistent from *Heavenly Mansions* (1949) to *The Classical Language of Architecture* (1966), and this spans the period in which Scott Brown (as Lakofski) attended these courses.

19 Blunt, *Artistic Theory in Italy 1400–1650*, 200.

20 Van Eck, "Sir John Summerson on Artisan Mannerism."

21 Blunt, *Artistic Theory in Italy 1400–1650*, 200.

Figure 1: Denise Scott Brown at *Das Pathos des Funktionalismus*
("The Pathos of Functionalism"), Berlin, 1974.

The Function of Functionalism for Denise Scott Brown[1]

Denise Costanzo

The April 1967 issue of *Architectural Design* included a brief article—only 354 words—by Denise Scott Brown, then teaching at the University of California, Los Angeles. "The Function of a Table" efficiently unpacked this object's complexities:

> What is the function of a table? I may eat off it, write at it, hold a party, dance on it, or drink myself under it. A child may throw a cloth over it to make a house or turn it on end to make a boat. I am lord at its head, serf at its foot, equal if it is round, a humble supplicant if I kneel before it.

The author describes a matrix of uses that can unfold over time: "Breakfast for four in the morning, navigation for two in the afternoon, and, with extensions, dinner for ten in the evening; and two hundred years later, a museum piece." They are so "many and various" that "it would not be possible to list all the functions which could be served by a simple table over the course of a single day or many centuries."[2] Scott Brown asks: "What, then, is the meaning of the phrase 'form follows function'?" This raises the theoretical stakes, invoking an architectural credo widely enthroned by the 1950s.[3]

The logic of this ethos was undercut by Scott Brown's example. Many possibilities she lists "were not considered in the making of the table; but rather, the form of the table itself, through its own visible possibilities, evoked them." Thoroughly identifying any structure's future uses is impossible because "the functions ... ascribed to a form lie in the mind of the user and are based on his needs." Form preceded function, and even generated it in unanticipated ways. Scott Brown's scale then expands from the object to the urban: "When one considers the many complex and often contradictory functions of the city, is there much meaning to Matthew Nowicki's statement, 'form and function are one'?"—crediting Nowicki with a phrase he quoted from Frank Lloyd Wright in 1949.[4] She concludes by describing her piece as "an extract from a forthcoming book on environmental meaning."

This teaser provocatively challenges a truism as a hook. Unfortunately for intrigued readers, the promised book never materialized, but the function–form issue persisted in her later writings. It figures in Scott Brown's sole-authored essays and her joint works with Robert Venturi, including their book *Learning from Las Vegas* of 1972 with Steven Izenour, and "Functionalism, Yes, But …" which she and Venturi presented at a 1974 symposium in Berlin (*Das Pathos des Funktionalismus*, "The Pathos of Functionalism") and later published (fig. 1).[5] Three decades later, Scott Brown returned to the topic with a lengthy essay on functionalism, illustrated with a matrix of photos enacting each of the table uses described in 1967 (fig. 2). She even called herself and Venturi "dour functionalists" in 2004.[6] Her unabated commitment to this theme conflicts with their reputation as critics of functionalism, characterized in *Learning from Las Vegas* as a repudiation of the design symbolism they embraced.[7] The contradiction is (perhaps) resolved by their insistence, from the 1970s on, that communication is one of architecture's essential functions.[8]

If these discussions of function make the trajectory of Scott Brown's views an open book after 1967, her preceding journey into the topic is more obscure. My aim is to untangle this prehistory, thereby clarifying the genesis of one conceptual anchor in Scott Brown's career. As indicated, the immediate context for "The Function of a Table" was a book project entitled "Determinants of Urban Form" that survives as a collection of partial drafts and proposals.[9] Her article's first three paragraphs are identical to an introductory chapter's opening section. Consistently titled "Form and Function," this text remains unchanged, down to the last comma, from the earliest (twenty-six-page) draft of September 1964 through a compressed four-page version of 1965–66.[10] She was unwaveringly committed to the ideas in her 1967 article, and their precise articulation.[11]

The chapter manuscripts hold Scott Brown's answer to the question of whether "form and function are one." While her table analysis critiques form's dependency on function, she also posits "that function is the *only true basis* for the art of city building" (emphasis added). Yet this linkage is qualified, noting

"... that the nature of the relation between form and function in the city is complex indeed, and susceptible to no grand oversimplification."[12] In her later, much-shortened version of the chapter, this is one sentence she extends, adding: "as we broaden our consideration from the single building to the city and from a time scale of the few years to the long-span time scale of city building so we need additional ways of looking at the making of form."[13] This shows that her 1967 article was not a rejection, but a problematization of the form and function dynamic.[14] The enemy is "oversimplification."

A sequence of declarative assertions underscores this relationship's complexity: "each form is determined by functions, forces, and technics, as well as the inner worlds of its makers—though in no very simple way."[15] In her distilled chapter, she summarizes the book as fundamentally

> concerned with the physical system of the city and its form, and with the ways in which this form is determined, not only by "functions," or by the inner worlds of its makers, but by "forces" within the other environing systems, as well as within the physical system itself, and through the technical means available to the society.[16]

This passage demonstrates two significant points. First is her study's ambitiously conceived scope: Scott Brown intended to address urban design methods with both conceptual precision (hence the definitions) and across an expansive range of variables (symbolism, technology, transportation, demography, economics, and politics) with complex interactions.[17] Second, her discussion of form and function transformed the form–function dyad into a triad by adding a third "f": forces. Having problematized the duo's causal relations, she places it in dynamic tension with a range of factors in the physical and social world. The result is her modified axiom: "Form, therefore, follows function (though possibly at a distance) and is determined by forces," further inflected by creative agency through "the talents and temperaments of its makers."[18]

The conceptual triad of form, function, and forces was also prominent in Scott Brown's teaching at the University of Pennsylvania (Penn) and UCLA during these same years. Between 1963 and 1966, as she wrote her chapter drafts and submitted an extract to *Architectural Design*, she taught three urban planning studios entitled "Form, Forces and Function" at Penn in fall 1963, fall 1964 ("FFF2"), and at UCLA in fall 1966 ("FFF SM," centered on Santa Monica).[19] Furthermore, the photos dramatizing "the Functions of a Table" (fig. 2) were taken for her course at UC Berkeley in spring 1965, which included a lecture on "Concepts of the City: Form, Forces and Function."[20] Scott Brown's course materials not only illuminate her pedagogy (see Lee Ann Custer and Sylvia Lavin in this volume), but also bring her early thinking on "function" into further focus. Records of her three FFF courses include an extensive collection of lengthy syllabi, typewritten lecture texts, and detailed assignments. One lacuna is the session presenting definitions of concepts, including function, with no corresponding material in the files.[21] The book manuscripts fill this void: the longest early chapter draft was her lecture. Its title ("The Definition of City Form") was that of the first section of the course, and it ends with a carousel-ready list of illustrative slides.

Scott Brown's syllabi also illustrate the panorama of sources informing her approach to function. Assigned readings for her "definitions" lecture include the Smithsons' "Team X Primer," which challenged the urtext of functionalist urbanism: "a hierarchy of human associations should replace the functional hierarchy of the Charte d'Athènes."[22] Her course introduction also invokes "Team 10's revolt against the rigidities of CIAM" and the planning norms established in the Athens Charter, along with Louis "Kahn's redefinition of 'function.'"[23] This is consistent with familiar aspects of Scott Brown's formation: her encounter with Peter Smithson at the Architectural Association in London from 1952 to 1955, and a reverence for Kahn that, along with Smithson's advice, brought her and Robert Scott Brown to Penn for graduate study in 1958.

A broad conception of functional relationships as expressed by the "form, forces, and function" triad, along with the challenging task of coordinating them through planning, was central to the FFF courses. Her syllabus describes the planner's role as guiding a city's built form "to enable it to perform stated functions and to fulfill stated goals." This straightforward idea is also complicated; the latter involve "the social, economic, cultural, psychological,

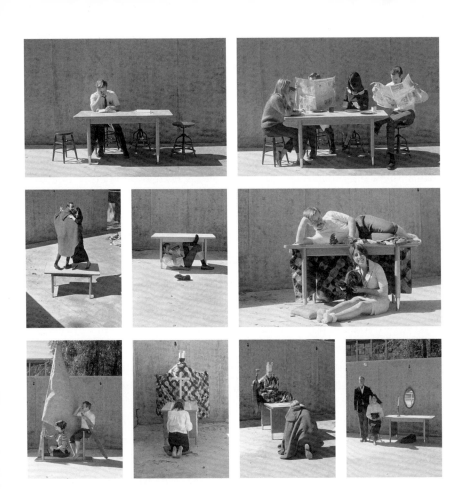

Figure 2: The functions of a table: table for work; for reading; for dance, for drink; as house; as boat; as religion; as authority; as antique.

physiological, and other needs of the society and the individuals which compose it," along with formal considerations—a broad and contentious set of variables.[24]

Scott Brown likely began thinking through the form–function dynamic during the first (and most reading-intensive) 1963 FFF course offering.[25] Her earliest chapter draft is dated one day before the FFF2 class session on definitions in September 1964.[26] The space of teaching provided a platform for her conceptual exploration of function and form, synthesizing many intellectual influences.[27]

Among these was an event that took place between Scott Brown's time in London and her 1958 move to Philadelphia for graduate study: the 1956 CIAM summer school held at the Istituto Universitario di Architettura in Venice (IUAV). She has associated both periods bracketing this event with influencing her views on function: the New Brutalists upheld "the early modern 'functionalist' revolution, the one I had identified with," and at Penn she read sociologist Robert Merton on functionalism.[28] While Scott Brown has not related the summer school to this topic, function was a critical theme. She and Robert Scott Brown were among participants from fifteen countries engaged in a month of intensive study and design work.[29] The 1956 summer school, like prior ones held at IUAV in 1952, 1953, and 1954, was led by four prominent Italian architects—Franco Albini, Ignazio Gardella, Ernesto Rogers, and Giuseppe Samonà—and managed by the younger Giancarlo De Carlo. A slate of Italian lecturers included the industrialist and modernist patron Adriano Olivetti, the event's main financial sponsor.[30] The final reviewers were Italian architects Gino Valle and Ludovico Quaroni, and Jaap Bakema of the Netherlands.

All CIAM summer schools focused on urban planning and architecture as integrated endeavors, a natural extension of the organization's decades-old philosophy.[31] Work and discussion centered on the development of Venice ("an inexhaustible source of problematic prompts") and its environs, in 1956 specifically the industrializing port cities of Mestre and Marghera.[32] A report in *Casabella* describes the event and illustrates several team projects, including one on transportation systems by the (hyphenated) Scott-Browns' group (fig. 3).

Tema: gli insediamenti di Venezia in terraferma

1. *Una critica delle soluzioni proposte dalla teorica urbanistica classica mette in luce le caratteristiche differenziali di Venezia, con i suoi pregi ed i suoi svantaggi. Per una efficienza delle relazioni umane è necessario assicurare la massima possibilità di contatto sia tra entità aventi diverso " grado " (casa individuale, piazza, neighborhood, città) sia tra diverse entità dello stesso grado (casa con casa, neighborhood con neighborhood, etc.). Venezia, a differenza della città-giardino e delle " Ville radieuse " sembra rappresentare un tipo di soluzione completo nei due sensi.* ★ 1. *Une critique des solutions proposées par la théorie classique de l'urbanisme met en lumière les caractéristiques différentielles de Venise, avec ses avantages et ses désavantages. Pour que les relations humaines soient efficientes, il est nécessaire d'assurer la possibilité maximum de contact soit entre des entités ayant un " degré " divers (maison individuelle, place, neighborhood, ville), soit entre diverses entités de même degré (maison avec maison, neighborhood avec neighborhood, etc.). Venise, à l'encontre de la ville-jardin et de la " Ville radieuse ", semble représenter un type de solution complète sous ses deux points de vue.* ★ 1. *A criticism of the solutions suggested by classic theoretical town-planning shows up the differential characteristics of Venice with its advantages and disadvantages. For efficient human relationships it is necessary to ensure maximum opportunities for contacts whether among entities having different " grades " (individual house, square, neighborhood, town) or among different entities of the same " grade " (house with house, neighborhood with neighborhood, etc.). Venice, quite differently from the " Garden-City " or the " Ville Radieuse " seems to represent one type of solution which would be complete under both view-points.*

2. *Un sistema di trasporto rapido suburbano costituisce la spina dorsale del complesso Mestre-Venezia-industria-nuovi insediamenti. Questi ultimi assumono conformazione lineare da una sola parte del sistema del traffico: dall'altra, la campagna agricola.* ★ 2. *Un système de transport rapide sub-urbain constitue l'épine dorsale de l'ensemble Mestre-Venise-industrie-nouvelles installations. Ces dernières assument une configuration linéaire d'un seul côté du système du trafic; de l'autre, il y a la campagne agricole.* ★ 2. *A fast suburban transport network forms the backbone of the new plan for " Mestre-Venice-industry-new settlements ". The latter assume a linear form as a single side of the traffic system is concerned; on the other side we have agricultural land.*

3. *Gli attacchi della progettata arteria di traffico veloce influenzano la determinazione dei centri di vita. La posizione dell'arteria stessa rispetto alle fasce residenziali può dar luogo a varie configurazioni di cui l'ultima (soluzione mista a traffico principale e secondario lungo i bordi dell'insediamento) sembra la migliore.* ★ 3. *Les points de jonction de l'artère de trafic rapide projetée influencent la détermination des centres de vie. La position de l'artère elle-même par rapport aux bandes résidentielles peut donner lieu à des configurations variées dont la dernière (solution mixte à trafic principal et secondaire le long des bords des installations) semble être la meilleure.* ★ 3. *The joining points of the planned fast traffic arterial road affect the choice or positions of living centres. The position of the arterial road itself as compared to the residential strips, may lead to different forms of which the last (a mixture of main and secondary traffic along the outskirts of the settlements) seems to be the best.*

4. *La via di trasporto rapido crea sempre nuove " teste di ponte " attorno alle quali gradualmente sorgono gli insediamenti. La struttura si completa con delle forme di " riempimento " tra un attacco e l'altro.* ★ 4. *La voie de transport rapide crée toujours de nouvelles " têtes de pont " autour desquelles les installations s'élèvent graduellement. La structure est complétée par des formes de " remplissage " entre une jonction et l'autre.* ★ 4. *The fast traffic highway originates always new " bridge-heads " around which settlements form gradually. The layout is completed by a " filling in " form between one joining and the other.*

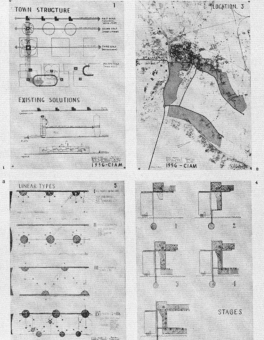

TOWN STRUCTURE

EXISTING SOLUTIONS

1956 - CIAM

1956 - CIAM

LINEAR TYPES

LOCATION. 3

STAGES

1956 - CIAM

Gruppo: Campbell, Chipkin, Heinemann, Hultberg, Jackson, McKay, Paredes, D. e R. Scott - Brown, Townsend.   71

Figure 3: Group project by Campbell, Chipkin, Heinemann, Hultbert, Jackson, McKay, Paredes, D and R Scott-Brown, Townsend, "Tema: gli insediamenti di Venezia di terraferma," *Casabella* 213 (November–December 1956).

The 1956 event departed from its predecessors when participants rejected CIAM urban planning orthodoxy. They declared the Athens Charter "an overly simplified instrument in the planning process," and "in contrast therefore to what happened in previous courses, it was not adopted systematically by any of the studio groups."[33] Although Lorenzo Mingardi discerns "traces of the arguments against the Athens Charter" in projects from 1954, he mentions no public stance taken on the document in prior events (notably, Le Corbusier delivered a lecture at the 1952 school).[34] A debate over CIAM planning principles became their repudiation, and the Athens Charter was repeatedly invoked as an antagonist during the 1956 event.[35]

The summer school participants' position was consistent with crystallizing critiques of CIAM urbanism that generated Team 10 (in which De Carlo and Bakema were active).[36] The Athens Charter's call to design cities around "four functions" (work, dwelling, recreation, and transportation) meant 1950s conflicts over urban doctrine were also about function as an idea. It was invoked critically and often during the 1956 summer school. In one lecture, Ludovico Quaroni called Le Corbusier's mechanistic notion of function "mistaken," and presented the formulation of a better understanding of this concept as an important concern. He noted "we are now carefully examining this idea of function," adding, when "we start considering the concrete functions, as the life persons live, and the spirit of those persons, the functions of a building multiply and complicate themselves." He associated a vast spectrum of issues with function, seen as "a compound of physical, spacial [sic], psychological moral factors … it is aimless to study the reality of the man himself, without considering him as part of a superior reality, such as the family, the neighborhood, the community, the society, the collectivity."[37] Quaroni's ideas prefigured Scott Brown's later views in his insistence on both a conceptual clarification of function, and engagement with its complex human dimensions.[38]

Scott Brown's framework is also anticipated in Ignazio Gardella's statements that "classical town planning does not take into account the Time element and is therefore idealistic." He insisted that planners, "instead of starting on the scale of a master plan—to be imposed on an existing situation regardless of time … must start by finding and resolving the forces in separate and tangible

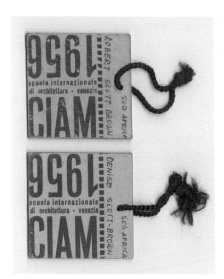

Figure 4: Denise and Robert Scott Brown's name tags, CIAM Summer School, 1956.

phenomena of the problem." His reference to time as a variable is notable, as is his call to find and resolve "forces," the third leg of Scott Brown's later triad.[39] Other remarks from the summer school show efforts to reclaim "functionalism." Ernesto Rogers, having identified two prevailing attitudes (Platonic and Aristotelian), described functionalism as "the synthesis of these two positions in architecture," suggesting it could be valid.[40] Similarly, Carlo Melograni wanted to resume the functionalists' "rational" method—understood properly—but insisted: "we must go beyond what we can call 'pure' functionalism" and also consider "the 'spurious' functions of every day's [sic] life."[41] Like Quaroni, Rogers, and Gardella, Melograni called on architects and urban planners to embed ideas of function not in theoretical abstractions, but in a wider, empirical, and complex view of reality.

Scott Brown kept transcripts of these lectures (and her and Robert Scott Brown's name tags; fig. 4). The 1956 summer school was one chapter in her tri-continental formation, an episode that repeated and reinforced themes from many sources over many years, including the graduate studies she began two years after Venice under social planner Herbert Gans. Yet positions articulated by summer school participants clearly foreshadowed her persistent, even obsessive relationship with function, including her insistent adoption of the "functionalist" label for herself and, later, Venturi. Shortly before "The Function of a Table" appeared in 1967, Scott Brown published a similarly provocative, much longer essay challenging functionalist logic (and leveraging her self-awareness as a still-rare woman in architecture). In "Planning the Powder Room," Scott Brown calls herself "a confirmed and unrecalcitrant functionalist of the 1930s type," wielding the title proudly, even defiantly.[42] Her proclamations echo heated debates, and a determination to redefine, reclaim, and redirect the modernist heritage, from an intense month in Venice a decade earlier.

The year 1967 was pivotal in Scott Brown's career. Both articles augmented a list of publications which, with her book project, she compiled into a dossier for tenure at UCLA, where she had been co-chair of a new Urban Design Program since 1965.[43] The book was a priority, and she had sought funding for leave to write "Determinants of Urban Form" since 1964. In February 1967, after rejection by the Institute for Creative Arts at UC Berkeley and discouraging news from the Twentieth Century Fund, she informed her dean that she would take a year's leave of absence starting June 1967: "I must write this book next year, with or without support."[44] Her ICA application letter makes her case poignantly, describing twelve-hour workdays during the academic year and full-time work during the summer.

Unstated is how larger professional and personal decisions must have added urgency to Scott Brown's book project. She declared it more imperative for her career than her academic position a month before the release of another volume in which she had considerable involvement: Robert Venturi's *Complexity and Contradiction in Architecture*.[45] While this book's impact unfolded over many years, she knew well Vincent Scully's prophecies on the impact of a provocative book exploring conceptual questions and the challenges of designing in a non-straightforward world.[46] The summer Scott Brown began her writing leave, she made another major decision: to marry Venturi.[47] That fall, the newlyweds would teach together at Yale, inaugurating history-making joint work on the rationality of functional yet maligned

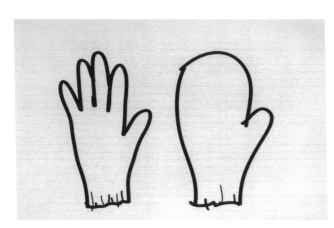

forms in Las Vegas, Levittown, and beyond.[48] In 1968, Scott Brown resigned her UCLA position, and after 1970, their priority was professional practice, not academia.

While "Determinants of Urban Form" remained unfinished, this interface of teaching and writing was a productive space where Scott Brown formulated rigorous views on function. Ideas from Scott Brown's drafts and the FFF courses reverberated through her next four decades of work. The Decorated Shed and its progeny—generic loft and mitten-glove analogy (fig. 5)— were already in evidence:

> City form tailored too specifically to the special needs of one population at one time may become functionally obsolete long before the end of its structural life, whereas form designed to suit "functions" more generally defined may prove less efficient for any one specific need, but over the span of its structural life more useful to more people.[49]

So was Scott Brown's persistent engagement with another conceptual triad. Regarding urban form, she insisted: "The city should be answerable to the Vitruvian requirements of Firmness, Commodity and Delight. Further … it should be expressive of and meaningful to the society to which it pertains." Those producing forms need "an understanding of the relation between firmness, commodity and delight in our day." Hints of exchanges with Venturi are also present: "A knowledge of and feeling for the city-making functions and forces within the physical environment and within the society and its institutions" requires "an understanding of the possibilities for form-making at different levels in the society and the role of the form-maker in a complex and contradictory society." Scott Brown's triad and Venturi's titular duality appear together in one sentence on "principles and theories of form, forces and function, but also the possibilities of form-making and the place of creativity in a complex and contradictory society."[50]

This melding of ideas, more than clear-cut individual contributions, defines the shared corpus of Venturi and Scott Brown; her name first appeared alone on a book cover in 1990.[51] The choice to redirect her intellectual energy away from a solo book project to invest in a partnership had far-reaching implications intensified by gender. In Venturi's case, this same decision's impact was dampened by his male identity and individual credit for his first manifesto. For Scott Brown, the question remains open: what if she had spent 1967–68 completing "Determinants of Urban Form" instead of practicing and teaching with Venturi? Whether or not this book could have been her *Complexity and Contradiction,* it would have certainly solidified her individual disciplinary voice.[52]

One legacy of this critical juncture is clear: forty years after Scott Brown's 1967 article, her views on function were rooted in the same soil. In 2008, she remained a defiant functionalist:

> Early modern architects believed that beauty would result from looking straight at a problem, avoiding preconceptions, and letting functional demands lead directly to form. Am I the last architect alive who believes that this philosophy of functionalism was a glory of Modern architecture and that the challenge of grappling with the client's brief or program is still a joy of our profession?[53]

She further articulated her ideas in 2016: "Form follows forces long before we get there to define functions or set guidelines. But the form-function thesis is challenged by activities that change much faster than the structures that hold them."[54] To be a functionalist in a way that holds up to both logic and reality, designers must—paradoxically—stop trying to control what structures will do. Even as they bring needs, aesthetics, and principles into the problem, they must also recognize and respond to where they are and what impinges on that world. As she urges, be prepared "to face the ugly result of doing the right thing," finding "an agonized beauty" that "is the kind I like—and it can change aesthetic sensibilities. That is my view of functionalism."[55]

For Scott Brown, functional design accepts the ways dynamic systems of forms and forces inflect each other. This is an apt lens for her conceptual engagement with function, shaped by ideas and realities she encountered in London, Venice, Philadelphia, and Los Angeles. She saw how theory could establish the professional authority she needed far more than her male counterparts in the 1960s. Scott Brown pursued an assertive strategy to think boldly, broadly, and incisively about core design issues, leveraging her sharp intellect to position herself against simplistic certitudes and facile thinking. Functionalism was her foil—both opponent and weapon—in this duel with her own discipline. A few paragraphs in *Architectural Design* offer a window into her early career before she became part of a duo rather than a soloist. This *leitmotiv*'s persistence in her work was not only a function of conviction, but necessity. Much like a table, Scott Brown's relationship with function is not as simple as it first appears.

Notes

1   I extend deepest thanks to Rosa Sessa, who generously shared materials from the CIAM summer school archives at IUAV, and to Frida Grahn for sharing archival materials on the 1974 functionalism symposium in Berlin.

2   Scott Brown, "The Function of a Table," 154.

3   Louis Sullivan's 1896 proclamation that "form ever follows function" was, if not the first, the most famous assertion of this idea. For its trajectory, see Poerschke, *Architectural Theory of Modernism.*

4   Wright's original passage reads: "Form follows function is but a statement of fact. When we say 'form and function are one,' only then do we take mere fact into the realm of creative thought." Matthew Nowicki, "Composition in Modern Architecture," in *Writings and Sketches of Matthew Nowicki*, ed. Bruce H. Schäfer, 3.

5   Venturi and Scott Brown's essay "Functionalism Yes, But ..." appeared in *A+U: Architecture and Urbanism* in 1974 and was reprinted in *A View from the Campidoglio*. A German translation ("Funktionalismus ja, aber ...") was published in *Werk-Archithese* in 1977.

6   The passage continues, "We see the Modern Movement's belief in functionalism as one of its glories. While Postmodern and Neomodern architects have departed from early Modern doctrines on function, we have remained functionalists for both moral and aesthetic reasons." Scott Brown, "The Redefinition of Functionalism," in Venturi and Scott Brown, *Architecture as Signs and Systems*, 142.

7   Venturi, Scott Brown, and Izenour, *Learning from Las Vegas*, 134.

8   I explore this issue in my article "Venturi and Scott Brown as Functionalists."

9   Materials on Scott Brown's book are with her teaching records in the Venturi Scott Brown Collection at the Architectural Archives at the University of Pennsylvania (hereafter DSBTR, VSBC, AAUP). These include the ten-page "Determinants of City Form: A Study Proposal," June 1, 1964; "DVSB Proposal." Manuscript chapters and a "Revised Outline of Contents, December 28, 1965," are with her materials for promotion and tenure at UCLA, "C.2 Manuscript: Determinants of Urban Form;" DSBTR, VSBC, AAUP.

While her descriptions of the book's scope and structure varied, preserved chapters represented around one-third of the manuscript as intended.

10   See the 26-page typescript "The Definition of City Form, First Draft," September 6, 1964; "DVSB Misc. Writings 1964–65." A revised version of the chapter ("Chapter 2: Form, Function and Forces") is accompanied by the first few pages of her earlier chapter draft in "Chap 2 Form Function and Forces"; DSBTR, VSBC, AAUP. My discussion of this book project parallels points made by Lee Ann Custer elsewhere in this volume.

11   Scott Brown's distinctive phasing echoes in an article by Reyner Banham appearing shortly before hers, with her drafts proving who got there first; "Chairs as Art," 568.

12   "The Definition of City Form: Form & Function," 1964, 1.

13   "Ch. 2: Form, Function and Forces," 1.2.2.

14   Scott Brown's view aligns with Nowicki's on the interdependence Wright posits over unidirectional dependence: "If we accept the mutual dependence of form and function, then the problems of form in modern architecture might well be studied as the problems of function." Matthew Nowicki, "Composition in Modern Architecture," in *Writings and Sketches of Matthew Nowicki*, ed. Bruce H. Schäfer, 3.

15   "The Definition of City Form: Form & Function," 1964, 5. The phase "in no very simple way" recurs throughout the early draft.

16   "Ch. 2: Form, Function and Forces," 1.2.4.

17   "Revised Outline of Contents, December 28, 1965." Folder "C.2 Manuscript: Determinants of Urban Form;" DSBTR, VSBC, AAUP.

18   "Ch. 2: Form, Function and Forces," 1.2.3.

19   The title of Kulić and Stanić's article "Form, Forces and Functions," based on the authors' interview with Scott Brown, mentions the course, her thoughts on function and form, and illustrates two student projects from 1964.

20   "Concepts of the City: Form, Forces and Function; environments and systems; determinants;" Course outline, C.P. 100 City Planning for Architects & Landscape Architects, Spring 1965, UC Berkeley; DSBTR, VSBC, AAUP. Scott Brown identified the photographer, Dan Brewer, as her teaching assistant; conversation with author, March 29, 2022.

21 Multiple binders hold duplicate copies of materials for these courses. The second lecture of the semester for C.P 503, Fall 1963, is described on page 8 of the course introduction: "DEFINITIONS — form, forces and functions; city form; physical form; activity and structure; determinants and disciplines; causes and correlates; laws and rules; is and ought; ideal, idealised and real; abstract, general and particular; form and design; aims for form and form makers."

22 Allison and Peter Smithson, CIAM 9, Aix-en-Provence, 24 July 1953, quoted in Smithson, *Team 10 Primer*, Cambridge, MIT Press, 1968, 78.

23 "Form, Forces & Function: Toward a Philosophy for Studio FFF," course syllabus p. 3; Binder 1: "C.P. 503, FA 1963, Studio FFF Inc.," Box 5: City Planning 503: Studio FFF: Form, Forces & Function – Fall 1963. DSBTR, VSBC, AAUP. I thank Lee Ann Custer for alerting me to these courses prior to archival research on this topic.

24 "City Planning and What It Means to Me to be a City Planner," course syllabus pp. 13–17, Studio FFF (C.P. 503), 1963.

25 Scott Brown describes this course and its context in *Urban Concepts*, 13–17. When Kulić and Stanić noted, "You started expanding the idea of what functionalism is as soon as you began teaching the *Form, Forces and Functions* course at Penn," Scott Brown replied: "Yes, that was an early part of it, but I have found further ways to describe it;" "Form, Forces and Functions," 66.

26 The 1963 course schedule has the Definitions lecture on September 9, 1963, a Monday. The manuscript date was Sunday, 6 September 1964; she likely refined her first year's lecture for Monday's class.

27 For more on Scott Brown's teaching at Penn, including related statements on function in prior courses, and the relationship between her book manuscript and teaching, see Lee Ann Custer in this volume.

28 Scott Brown, "Some Ideas and Their History," in Venturi and Scott Brown, *Architecture as Signs and Systems*, 110, 113.

29 Mingardi provides an overview in "Reweaving the City." He mentions the Scott Browns' attendance in 1956 but does not discuss their experience in detail. He notes that sixty-eight "young architects and graduating students" attended in 1952 (114). In 1956 there were only thirty, less than half. Another helpful account appears in Marchi, *The Heart of the City*.

30 Marchi, *Heart of the City*, passim, and Mingardi, "Reweaving the City," 119. A report on the school was published by one of the managing architects, Gabriele Scimemi, in "La quarta scuola estiva del CIAM a Venezia." The participant list shows only two other women participants, both Italian.

31 The first was in 1949 at the Architectural Association in London, with heavy involvement from architects affiliated with the MARS group; Mingardi, "Reweaving the City," 107–109.

32 "Venezia, fonte inesauribile di spunti problematici, esprime oggi con particulare drammaticità una istanza vivissima nella cultura architettonica ed urbanistica contemporanea;" Scimemi, "La quarta scuola estiva del CIAM a Venezia," 69.

33 "La quarta scuola estiva del CIAM a Venezia," 70 (translation by author). A summary of discussion on the evening of Wednesday September 15 states: "The 4 functions of CIAM were suggested as a means of studying the bridgehead as a whole. This was rejected as being too analytical a method." Five-page discussion summary beginning "Monday AM," p. 3; "Ricordi Venezia e CIAM;" VSBC, AAUP.

34 Mingardi, "Reweaving the City," 115–116, 118. He compares the 1954 summer school projects with those of 1953, whose project on the Biennale campus (also the event's sponsor) was less social and urban than the 1952 and 1954 projects on connections between Venice and the mainland.

35 For instance, "New proposals emerged like that of the 'central street' (in open contradiction to the Athens Charter)." Scimemi, "La quarta scuola estiva del CIAM a Venezia," 70.

36 Mingardi summarizes the tension between the Athens Charter's affirmation at the CIAM meetings in Bridgewater (1947) and Bergamo (1949), and a questioning of the "results" of the principles' application and calls for their "reform." He notes that at Hoddeston (1953; "The Heart of the City") "the problems of the modern city could not be considered according to the four functionalist categories," 111, 113–114.

37 "'The Architect and Town Planning,' lecture given by Arch. Ludovico Quaroni at the International School of Architecture of CIAM, Venice, Sept. 14, 1956," p. 7; "Ricordi Venezia e CIAM;" VSBC, AAUP.

Reprinted by van Bergeijk (with a Dutch translation) in "CIAM Summer School 1956."

38 On Quaroni's obscurity outside Italy, see van Bergeijk, "CIAM Summer School 1956," 115–117.

39 Gardella's comments in summary of discussion on Tuesday, September 14, PM, 1956 (beginning "Monday AM"), page 3 of 5; "Ricordi Venezia e CIAM;" VSBC, AAUP.

40 For Rogers, the Platonic view was one "that tries to examine problems impartially and rather mechanically," the Aristotelian "that regards problems from a fixed ethical standpoint without enough consideration of means." Summary of discussion on Tuesday, September 14, PM, 1956 (beginning "Monday AM"), page 3 of 5; "Ricordi Venezia e CIAM;" VSBC, AAUP.

41 "'Some Aspects of Building in Italy' by arch. Melograni, 26 settembre 1956," p. 3; "Ricordi Venezia e CIAM;" VSBC, AAUP.

42 Scott Brown, "Planning the Powder Room," 81.

43 Brownlee et al., editors, Out of the Ordinary, 248. A summary of her dossier's contents shows seven published writings (including the Powder Room article), and "The Function of a Table" as "not yet in hand," although both are dated April 1967. It lists two book projects in process: "Determinants of Urban Form" and "Notes on the Present State of Architecture." Her tenure materials include her letter to the ICA describing the demands of teaching while building a new program (twelve-hour days during the semester, full time even during the summer). Scott Brown to Executive Committee, Institute for Creative Arts, October 27, 1966, included in compilation document ("Support for and Attempt to Fund Book"), DSBTR, VSBC, AAUP.

44 Scott Brown to Dean George A. Dudley, February 20, 1967, included in "Support for and Attempt to Fund Book." The compilation document includes Dudley's letter of support for her ICA application, in which he urged approval "despite the fact that Ms. Scott Brown already plays a vital role in the newly established small faculty we have in our urban design program at UCLA;" Dudley to Clark Kerr, November 18, 1965. Letters from two publishers express only cautious interest. A proposal, dated June 1, 1964, also requested funding for one year's leave to write the book; folder "DVSB Proposal;" DSBTR, VSBC, AAUP.

45 The book was publicly released in March 1967; Scott Brown has said she and Venturi "read each other's manuscripts;" Kulić and Stanić, "Form, Forces and Functions," 73, and McLeod, "Venturi's Acknowledgments."

46 Scully famously declared Venturi's book "probably the most important writing on the making of architecture since Le Corbusier's Vers une architecture." Venturi, Complexity and Contradiction in Architectures, 11.

47 Scott Brown married Venturi shortly before she turned thirty-six years old in October. She and Venturi later adopted their son James, born in 1971; Brownlee et al., editors, Out of the Ordinary, 248.

48 Urban anthropologist Elizabeth Greenspan recently restated this connection: "Learning from Las Vegas' essential insight was that communication was an architectural function too." Greenspan, "Star System," 2.

49 "The Definition of City Form: Form and the Designer," 1964, 18.

50 "The Definition of City Form: A Conceptual Framework for Considering the Relation of Form, Forces & Function," 1964, 23.

51 Urban Concepts presents four essays and a portfolio of six "Urban Design Reports," part of a special series of publications by a journal ("An Architectural Design Profile"). Its scale approximates a special issue. Scott Brown's next sole-authored volume was the essay collection Having Words of 2009.

52 She wrote of the book in 1990, "It was never funded. The social science foundations said 'Interesting but not our field'. The architectural ones said 'Wonderful but we have no money'." Urban Concepts, 18.

53 Scott Brown, "Functionalism, Yes Yes," 22.

54 Kulić and Stanić, "Form, Forces and Functions," 66.

55 Kulić and Stanić, "Form, Forces and Functions," 67.

Figure 1: Denise and Robert Scott Brown in Venice in the mid-1950s.

Recollections II: The Mutual Experience—in Giuseppe Vaccaro's Office in Rome

Carolina Vaccaro

> When direct communication begins, mutual regard and a sense of a common work allows influence both ways; the elder using and learning and borrowing from the younger—as well as the other way round—across generations who are at work at the same time.[1]
>
> —Alison and Peter Smithson, *Changing the Art of Inhabitation*

Learning is a mutual exchange.[2]

When Denise and Robert Scott Brown arrived in Rome looking for a job in 1956, architecture in Italy was still in the throes of postwar liberation from the long and oppressive years of the Fascist regime. For Italian architects of that time, typological and linguistic experiments reflected urgent social issues in the wake of postwar urbanization. The growth of the outskirts and reconstruction required adaptation to new technologies and research to develop a new architectural language, one more related to the people's own figurative imagery. The 1950s also provided an opportunity to finally take part in the international debate. European architectural culture was greatly influenced by the social engagement of the British architects Alison and Peter Smithson, particularly in their research in housing and participatory architecture. The Smithsons, also known as the New Brutalists, who were members of Team 10, had a new way of looking at the ordinary, related to growing social concerns in architecture. Their recognition of reality and their holistic line of research rooted architecture in people's functional and symbolic needs. The New Brutalists believed "that beauty could emerge from designing and building straightforwardly, for community life as it is and not for some sentimentalized version of how it should be."[3]

Their views matched what Denise Scott Brown had experienced during her youth in South Africa: the polarity of reality and ideals—what she called "the

Is and the Ought"—and the urgency to relate architecture to people's social reality. Denise and Robert Scott Brown had encountered the New Brutalists in London, just before arriving in Italy, and were therefore well equipped to meet this prevailing sentiment in Europe. But they would also benefit, as South Africans, from the gaze of those who have the advantage of being outside traditional culture. During their time in Rome, working in the office of Giuseppe Vaccaro, the young couple concretely represented the common perception of "a free place to be in," as Peter Smithson put it.[4] The natural and "unfiltered gaze" of Denise and Robert Scott Brown corresponded to the search for a similar new gaze in the European—and Italian—architectural culture of the time.

The Roman architect Ludovico Quaroni, whom the young architects had met during their previous stay in Venice at the CIAM Summer School (fig. 1), directed them to Vaccaro, "who required two assistants immediately to help for a few weeks in drawing up a project."[5] Denise and Robert Scott Brown's time in Rome working for Vaccaro became a starting point for sharing ideas:

> The INA Casa housing was a project Robert and I could immediately identify with. Out of South Africa of the early 1950s and England of the mid 1950s, we were idealistic about the housing mission of architecture and demanded a high degree of functional and structural probity in architectural design. Most architects in practice could not meet our youthful demands for moral correctness. Here was a project that (almost!) could.[6]

At the time, Vaccaro was working on the Ponte Mammolo social housing project. The aim of the project, part of the Italian INA Casa reconstruction program of the 1950s, was to integrate the population that was moving into the city from rural areas. The neighborhood at Via Tiburtina, designed by Vaccaro (the south core), established a remote dialogue with other eccentric projects under the auspices of the INA Casa Plan, such as Adalberto Libera's horizontal housing unit in Rome's Tuscolano district. This eccentricity represents a constant in Vaccaro's work; he was more inclined to be a member of the family who "design-by-thinking-of-the-making."[7] This attitude was akin to northern European examples such as Aldo van Eyck and Team X, or even to more empirical inspiration in overseas culture, in the United States. The

Figure 2: Ponte Mammolo social housing, model view.

project team, coordinated by Vaccaro, was joined by Denise and Robert Scott Brown. The open-minded attitude of the working group suited their outsider's view and their young South African gaze well.

The site of Ponte Mammolo was an irregular area on the outskirts of Rome, characterized by the monumental presence of concentrated tufa stone outcrops, typical of the Roman countryside (figs. 2 and 3). This topography informed the residential-type solutions that were used: to avoid competing with the morphology of the landscape, the choice fell on two-story buildings. The project made use of the typological solution *Unità di buon vicinato* (good neighborhood unit), organized around a central pedestrian area and reminiscent of northern European projects of the time (figs. 4–6). This typology, "carefully tied to the lives of [its] users,"[8] is assembled around a pedestrian area, with a group of families small enough to retain a sense of cordiality but large enough to avoid overly frequent meetings among a limited number of people.[9] Denise Scott Brown describes the project as follows: "The basic unit, a two-bedroom apartment, was paired first with another similar unit, then with a second pair via an access stairway. This coupled group, two stories high, made an eight-apartment cluster, which was then linked to its equivalent on either side—linked but set back in plan, to form diagonal streets of rectangular, offset units."[10]

This typological shift and its aggregation variables crystallize the social aim of the *Unità di buon vicinato*. The solution, therefore, considers the space of aggregation— in and between objects—as a social space, an intermediate zone that interacts between communicating spatial areas. This in-between habitable space favors contact and relationships among different and distinct spaces, in tune with Fumihiko Maki's observation, "It seems that creating a

Figure 3: Ponte Mammolo social housing, model view.

place for human encounters involves expanding the territory of the building."[11] Designing by recovering signs and meanings that belong to everyday life and common feeling became the theoretical basis for a dialectical attitude between disciplinary tools and reality. This bottom-up, realistic, and situational approach, in harmony with the idealistic view of the young South African architects, was later widely developed and theorized by Denise Scott Brown in her works, writings, and teaching.[12]

Another topic that featured in the design group's common ground was the issue of scale. The project addressed and resolved the relationship between urban and architectural scale through oversized roofs that gather together more than one housing unit (fig. 4). In the process, it suggests ways of addressing relations between the large scale and the human scale. As Denise Scott Brown writes, using

> one simple unit and a few fairly simple rules for connecting it with others, Vaccaro was able to achieve a surprising complexity and variety in the overall. This was matched against a system of roofs, where a single slope embraced all units of the one couple and attached to a counter-sloping roof beside it, producing a large-scale modulation across the site and setting up a series of varying situations where stairs, units and roofs met—not unique but not mass repeated either.[13]

Figure 4: Building silhouette in the "good neighborhood unit": the slope of the roofs repeats the staggered line of the stories.

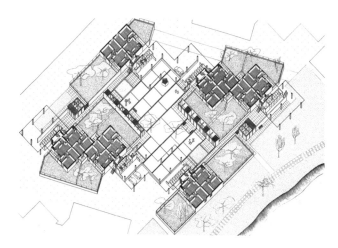

Figure 5: Axonometric ground plan of the "good neighborhood unit," with the equipped courtyard.

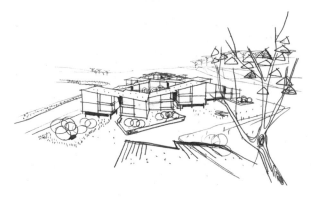

Figure 6: Sketch of the courtyard.

Linking and melding the small scale and large scale is still a topical theme in contemporary architecture and is also a "strategy for bigness."[14] The combination of different scales recurs in Vaccaro's work, and the topic was crucially re-introduced in the work of Denise Scott Brown and Robert Venturi. "Carry urbanism inside the building," Scott Brown theorized, and the principle is seen in their books and projects, as well as in history, as Venturi's *Complexity and Contradiction in Architecture* (1966) shows. We are dealing with "complexity and variety in the overall," as Scott Brown points out. Variation and repetition were central themes for Vaccaro, who regarded change as an organizational principle. According to him, the distribution of houses takes the "human perspective" into account and allows for "the enjoyment of rhythm (order) but avoids the annoyance of non-simultaneous repetition of the same situation (monotony)."[15]

The primary motive for Giuseppe Vaccaro was to create unity from diversity, and vice versa. As Denise Scott Brown explains, "In his design, Vaccaro played with the meshing of several systems. Each was derived within its own logic but, in combination, they made a greater whole."[16] He introduced a strategy that may be termed "open linkage," inherent in Maki's Group Form. Scott Brown mentions this connection in 1996.[17] The basic intention of Group Form or "collective form" was to provide for the individual and the collective, giving expression to both the particular and the general. Collective form is, in the words of Maki, "not a collection of unrelated, separate buildings, but of buildings that have reason to be together."[18] Linking, or "carrying urbanism inside the building," are issues widely theorized by Denise Scott Brown, who considers them as integrated parts both of the system and the unit. Linkage is the glue of the city; it is the act by which we unite all the layers of activity and the resulting physical form of the city. Linking, or disclosing linkage, are constant activities in creating collective form. Historical examples include the thinking of van Eyck, who "finds in vernacular building a substantial clue to the natural process of human association in urban situations. Vernacular units and links are evolved together and appear at the end as a perfectly coordinated physical entity—village or town."[19]

Figure 7: Caltabellotta village in Sicily, the birthplace of Giuseppe Vaccaro's father.

Postwar Italian architecture, and social housing in particular, started to explore vernacular architecture, in a search for a wider sense of context and identity (fig. 7). The intention was to achieve more human growth of the city: a human quality that determines forms concerned with lifestyles, movement, and relations among people in society. These principles are connected to Scott Brown's seminar on "Form, Forces and Function" at the University of Pennsylvania in the early 1960s (see Lee Ann Custer in this volume). In her later essay "Activities as Patterns,"[20] Denise Scott Brown investigates both the geometry of buildings and the nature of use and users. The typological shift that crystallizes the social theme of the *Unità di buon vicinato* seemed to move in the same direction, consistent with Denise Scott Brown's statement, "Working for Vaccaro helped prepare us for urbanism in America."[21]

Following this mutual experience, a lifelong friendship developed out of the time spent in Vaccaro's office. After this brief period working in Rome, Denise

Scott Brown moved on and Giuseppe Vaccaro continued his work by experimenting with other building types. However, both learned not only from each other, but also together. The importance of this "feeling in common" is perhaps the lesson we can draw from a working relationship that began more or less by chance, but which never left those who experienced it.

For my part, I have been lucky enough to inherit and experience a similar precious friendship all through my life, a friendship that has spanned generations. Denise's works and thoughts, as for many, radically influenced my training as an architect, my work as a teacher, and my personal life. Recently, in 2021, I co-curated the exhibition "Learning to See" in Philadelphia.[22] The exhibition examined Denise's work and ideas on architecture and the built environment, primarily through her photographic work and her practice of "learning from what's around you." Once again, through her gaze on the world, I continued to learn intensely. Looking back at all my opportunities to study her works and thoughts, and to the many times we have spent together, I can say that "learning to see" is one of the great lessons I feel I have learned from Denise. She is an example for all of us.

Notes

1 Smithson and Smithson, *Changing the Art of Inhabitation*, 89.

2 These are personal reflections on a moment in time when Denise Scott Brown and her first husband Robert Scott Brown worked in the office of my father, Giuseppe Vaccaro, in Rome.

3 Scott Brown, "Learning from Brutalism," 204.

4 Smithson and Smithson, *Changing the Art of Inhabitation,* 78.

5 Scott Brown, "Working for Giuseppe Vaccaro," 5.

6 Scott Brown, "Working for Giuseppe Vaccaro," 6.

7 Smithson and Smithson, *Changing the Art of Inhabitation*, 30.

8 Venturi and Scott Brown, *Architecture as Signs and Systems*, 112.

9 Vaccaro, "Roma: Quartiere a Ponte Mammolo," 14.

10 Scott Brown, "Working for Giuseppe Vaccaro", 7.

11 Maki, "Thoughts about Plazas; Recollections," 39.

12 Among the many texts on this subject, I would like to highlight the special issue of the journal *Architectural Design* entitled *Urban Concepts: Denise Scott Brown* (London, 1990).

13 Scott Brown, "Working for Giuseppe Vaccaro," 7.

14 Taylor, *Strategy for Bigness: Maki and Group Form*, 316.

15 Vaccaro, Ponte Mammolo's project report manuscript 1957, Archivio Vaccaro, Rome.

16 Venturi and Scott Brown, *Architecture as Signs and Systems*, 112.

17 Scott Brown, "Working for Giuseppe Vaccaro," 12.

18 Maki, *Investigations in Collective Form*, 5.

19 Maki, "Linkage in Collective Form", in *Investigations in Collective Form*, 25.

20 Venturi and Scott Brown, *Architecture as Signs and Systems,* 120.

21 Venturi and Scott Brown, *Architecture as Signs and Systems,* 112.

22 "Learning to See: Denise Scott Brown," an exhibition curated by Carolina Vaccaro and Noa Maliar, Tyler School of Art and Architecture and Temple Contemporary Gallery, Temple University, Philadelphia, May 20–September 18, 2021.

Denise Scott Brown's Nonjudgmental Perspective: Cross-Fertilization between Urban Sociology and Architecture

Marianna Charitonidou

> We tried to switch, but then discovered that we actually liked the planners—among them a new generation of social scientists, like Herb Gans and Paul Davidoff who were advance guards of the New Left, and who endorsed "advocacy planning," where you find out what the people you are designing for really want, rather than imposing architects' oughts on them.
>
> —Denise Scott Brown, *From Soane to the Strip: Soane Medal Lecture 2018*

This essay aims to shed light on the impact of urban sociology on Denise Scott Brown's approach, placing particular emphasis on the affinities between her thought and the perspective of sociologist Herbert Gans. In parallel, it intends to examine the relationship between the New Brutalists' "active socioplastics" and Scott Brown's act of deferring judgment, her so-called "non-judgmental perspective." The point of departure is Scott Brown's remark that architects, instead of trying to adopt the perspective of sociologists, should try "to look at the information of sociology from an architectural viewpoint."[1]

Scott Brown resettled in London in 1952 to work as an architect, but eventually enrolled at the Architectural Association School of Architecture (AA). During her stay in London, she was particularly interested in the urbanistic ideas of the New Brutalists.[2] In a seminal article entitled "The New Brutalism," the British critic Reyner Banham paid special attention to the exhibition "Parallel of Life and Art," held at the Institute of Contemporary Art (ICA) in London in 1953, curated by Alison and Peter Smithson, Nigel Henderson, and Eduardo Paolozzi. Banham describes New Brutalist aesthetics "as being anti-art, or at any rate anti-beauty in the classical aesthetic sense of the word."[3] According to Scott Brown, the New Brutalists were "a movement of the 1950s and

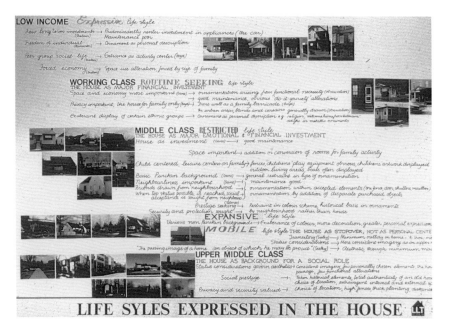

Figure 1: Robert Venturi, Denise Scott Brown, and Steven Izenour, Learning from Levittown Studio, fall 1970: "Life s[t]yles expressed in the house."

1960s that related architecture to social realism."[4] Commenting on the British context, she writes: "I landed in post-World War II England amidst the look-back-in-anger generation, in a society in upheaval, where social activism was part of education."[5] One of the main characteristics of the New Brutalists' ideology, again according to Scott Brown, was the intention to shed light on what happened "in the streets of poor city neighbourhoods." She describes how sociologists such as Michael Young and Peter Willmott invited "planners to understand how people lived in the East End of London, saying that those who had been bombed out of housing could not simply be moved to the suburban environment of the new towns." This helped architects to realize the importance of trying to understand the reasons for which "life on the streets was [for low-income citizens] a support system."[6] Scott Brown has also highlighted that "Before Jane Jacobs, Young and Willmott voiced complaints against the social disruption induced by urban planning."[7] Scott Brown describes Peter Smithson's concept of "active socioplastics" as the idea that "architects should design for the real life of the street and for the way communities actually work, even if the results are not conventionally pleasing."[8] Moreover, she would comment on how this "view evoked a sympathetic response in [her], deriving from [her] childhood and youth in Africa."[9]

Peter Smithson would play a significant role in the decision by Denise Scott Brown and her husband Robert Scott Brown to move to Philadelphia to study city planning at the Graduate School of Fine Arts at the University of Pennsylvania in 1958.[10] Scott Brown has remarked, "Peter Smithson recommended that we apply to the University of Pennsylvania because the architect Louis I. Kahn taught there."[11] The Smithsons, who had met Kahn in the framework of the Team 10 meetings, were influenced by his work, as seen in an essay they devoted to him in 1960.[12] Kahn had been appointed Professor at the University

Figure 2: Robert Venturi, Denise Scott Brown, and Steven Izenour, Learning from Levittown Studio, fall 1970.

100

of Pennsylvania in 1955 and was an important figure within and beyond Philadelphia. When Scott Brown arrived in Philadelphia, the Institute for Urban Studies of the University of Pennsylvania was significantly influenced by the methods of the social sciences, and there were few connections with the dominant models in the Architecture Department. She would study "economics, urban sociology, housing, urban statistics and city planning history and practice" and "could not believe that [she] had lived [her] life until then without the information."[13]

The Critiques of Urban Renewal

To grasp the specificity of the context of Philadelphia during the late 1950s, we should bear in mind the critique of postwar urban renewal.[14] Scott Brown has commented that it "derived from the problem that urban renewal had become 'human removal.'"[15] She has also underscored that architects and urban planners' "leadership had diverted urban renewal from a community support to a socially coercive boondoggle."[16]

In parallel, during this period, several universities in the United Sates launched programs in city planning or urban design—among them Harvard University, which initiated its program in 1956. Social scientists drew upon New Left critiques. Scott Brown remarked concerning the context in Philadelphia in the 1950s and its relationship to the New Left, "Here, long before it was visible in other places, was the elation that comes with the discovery and definition of a problem: poverty. The continued existence of poor people in America was a real discovery for students and faculty in the late 1950s. The social planning movement engulfed Penn's planning department."[17]

The activities and publications of Jane Jacobs are also very important for understanding the social aspects of the ideas of Scott Brown during these years. Among the texts by Jacobs that had an impact on Scott Brown's thought are articles entitled "The City's Threat to Open Land," "Redevelopment Today," and "What is a City?"—all published in *Architectural Forum* in 1958.[18]

New Objectivity as Deferring Judgment

The University of Pennsylvania was one of the universities that hired sociologists to teach in their planning departments, one of the most important being Herbert Gans. Gans had graduated from the University of Chicago[19] and was the first person to receive a doctoral degree from the Department of City Planning at Penn (1957).[20] Scott Brown remarked that she went "from the New Brutalists to Gans," discovering that they shared the idea that "you should look as open-mindedly as you could at real patterns and try to build from them—for both moral and aesthetic reasons."[21] Gans is mentioned in Paul Davidoff's seminal article "Advocacy and Pluralism in Planning"[22] and would, along with his colleagues Davidoff and Thomas A. Reiner, play an important role in the emergence of the advocacy planning movement in the United States. This would influence Scott Brown's later work on the South Street project (see the essays by Sarah Moses and James Yellin in this volume).

Among the books by Gans that influenced Scott Brown was *The Urban Villagers: Group and Class in the Life of Italian-Americans*, which examines the everyday life of the inhabitants of Boston's West End, a slum-cleared area. The book constituted a critique of urban renewal strategies in the area and was based on eight months' *in situ* research conducted in the period preceding its demolition. Gans remarked, "The West End was not really a slum, and although many of its inhabitants did have problems, these did not stem from the neighborhood."[23] In the photographs that Scott Brown took at South Street in Philadelphia, one can discern the impact of Gans's approach on her perspective.

When Scott Brown arrived at the University of Pennsylvania, Gans had "recently moved to Levittown to be a participant-observer of the new society that was forming there."[24] His seminal book *The Levittowners: Ways of Life and Politics in a New Suburban Community* was published in 1967.[25] Three years after its publication, Venturi, Scott Brown, and their collaborator Steven Izenour coordinated the study "Remedial Housing for Architects, or Learning from Levittown," which was conducted with their students at Yale University (figs. 1–3).[26] The study was indebted to Gans's work and went hand in hand

Figure 3: Robert Venturi, Denise Scott Brown, and Steven Izenour, Learning from Levittown Studio, fall 1970.

with what Scott Brown has referred to as her "non-judgmental perspective," regarding which she commented, "But we don't say we don't judge. We say we defer judgement. In deferring it, we let more data into the judgement, we make the judgement more sensitive."[27] This process of deferring judgment is related to her strategies for combining social and aesthetic parameters. As Scott Brown remarks, "Why do we accept certain aspects of the strip and not other aspects? The basis of that judgement is partly social, partly aesthetic."[28] Scott Brown's nonjudgmental viewpoint combines Gans's understanding of urban sociology and her passion for the aesthetics of pop art; as she remarked in 1971, "I like the fact that the influences upon us are the pop artist on one side and the sociologist on the other."[29] She also noted that "The forms of the pop landscape ... speak to our condition not only aesthetically but on many levels of necessity, from the social necessity to rehouse the poor without destroying them to the architectural necessity to produce buildings and environments that others will need and like."[30]

Scott Brown connected "socioplastics and the pop imagery and collage techniques launched by the IG [Independent Group]," stating that they "obviously inform our 'Learning from Las Vegas' and 'Learning from Levittown' research projects."[31] Another crucial tool used in these studios was mapping, which originated from Scott Brown's planning education. Scott Brown has remarked that "In planning school, [she] ... learned to understand complex urban orders by mapping urban systems and studying their patterns," which was crucial, since "patterns of mapped data [can] help us to discover an order emerging from within—from what appears to be the chaos of the city—and to avoid imposing an artificial order from without," thereby distinguishing "what 'ought to be' from what 'is.'"[32]

Toward a Conclusion, or Looking at Sociology from an Architectural Viewpoint

This essay has aimed to render explicit the way in which Scott Brown's "non-judgmental perspective" was influenced by the New Brutalists, Herbert Gans, and her training in urban sociology at the University of Pennsylvania. Her way of looking at architectural and urban forms was shaped by this educational and cultural background.[33] Scott Brown's exposure to and collaboration with social planners made her reflect upon the exchanges between architects, urban planners, and sociologists. She discovered that architects' tools are useful for reshaping sociologists' perspective and could help sociologists extend their framework. She developed a critique not only vis-à-vis "the architects who say there's nothing we can learn from the sociologist," but also vis-à-vis "the sociologists [arguing] that ... architects [should] ... extend [their] ... conceptual framework"[34] in order to be able to grasp the specificities of urban sociology. In other words, she believed that being in between these worlds can help you to learn from both.

Notes

1 Scott Brown, in Cook and Klotz, *Conversations with Architects*, 252.

2 Scott Brown, "Studio: Architecture's Offering to Academe"; Scott Brown, "Learning from Brutalism."

3 Banham, "The New Brutalism," 359.

4 Scott Brown, "Some Ideas and Their History," 109.

5 Scott Brown, "Some Ideas and Their History," 109.

6 Scott Brown, cited in Fontenot, *Non-Design: Architecture, Liberalism, and the Market*, 202; Young and Wilmott, *Family and Kinship in East London.*

7 Scott Brown, "Some Ideas and Their History," 109.

8 Scott Brown, *Urban Concepts*, 35.

9 Scott Brown, "Learning from Brutalism," 203.

10 The advice of Peter Smithson was likely not the only reason for Scott Brown's decision to study urban planning. During the CIAM Summer School in Venice 1956, the Italian architect Ludovico Quaroni gave a lecture entitled "The Architect and Town Planning." At the core of the lecture was an exploration of the ways in which architects could have social responsibilities. Quaroni argued that the key for enhancing architects' impact on society was the dissolution of the boundaries between town planning and architecture, explaining "why ... town planning [should] be the architects' concern" and drawing a distinction between an understanding of function as object and an understanding of function as principle. Quaroni also underlined the importance of the architect's role in revealing the connections between the individual and the collective in society. Scott Brown might have been influenced by Quaroni's lecture, particularly as far as the critique of modernist functionalism and the dissolution of the distinction between architecture and town planning are concerned. Van Bergeijk, "CIAM Summer School 1956."

11 Scott Brown, "Studio: Architecture's Offering to Academe."

12 Smithson and Smithson, "Louis Kahn."

13 Scott Brown, *Urban Concepts*, 10.

14 Charitonidou, "The 1968 Effects and Civic Responsibility in Architecture and Urban Planning in the USA and Italy."; Charitonidou, "Between Urban Renewal and Nuova Dimensione: The 68 Effects vis-à-vis the Real."

15 Scott Brown, "Towards an 'Active Socioplastics,'" 32.

16 Scott Brown, "Towards an 'Active Socioplastics,'" 33; Pacchi, "Epistemological Critiques to the Technocratic Planning Model."

17 Scott Brown, "A Worm's Eye View of Recent Architectural History."

18 Jacobs, "The City's Threat to Open Land"; Jacobs, "Redevelopment Today," and "What is a City?"; Klemek, "Jane Jacobs and the Transatlantic Collapse of Urban Renewal."

19 The work of Martin Meyerson and John Dyckman was important for his approach. Klemek, *The Transatlantic Collapse of Urban Renewal*, 56.

20 Birch, "From CIAM to CNU: the Roots and Thinkers of Modern Urban Design," 24.

21 Scott Brown, *Urban Concepts*, 32.

22 Davidoff remarks that "Planners should be able to engage in the political process as advocates of the interests both of government and of such other groups, organizations, or individuals who are concerned with proposing policies for the future development of the community." Davidoff, "Advocacy and Pluralism in Planning," 332.

23 Gans, *The Urban Villagers: Group and Class in the Life of Italian-Americans.*

24 Scott Brown, *Urban Concepts*, 10.

25 Gans, *The Levittowners: Ways of Life and Politics in a New Suburban Community.*

26 Charitonidou, "Ugliness in architecture in the Australian, American, British and Italian milieus: Subtopia, between the 1950s and the 1970s," 5.

27 Scott Brown, in Cook and Klotz, *Conversations with Architects*, 254.

28 Scott Brown, in Cook and Klotz, *Conversations with Architects*, 254.

29 Scott Brown, in Cook and Klotz, *Conversations with Architects*, 254.

30 Scott Brown, "Learning from Pop," 28.

31 Scott Brown, "Learning from Brutalism, " 205.

32 Scott Brown. "Studio: Architecture's Offering to Academe."

33 Charitonidou, "Denise Scott Brown's active socioplastics and urban sociology: from Learning from West End to Learning from Levittown," 136.

34 Scott Brown, in Cook and Klotz, *Conversations with Architects*, 252.

"In 1965, after ten years of urbanism, my foci were automobile cities of the American Southwest, social change, multiculturalism, action, everyday architecture, 'messy vitality,' iconography, and Pop Art."

—Denise Scott Brown, *Wayward Eye*

Part II
1960s: Teaching

Teaching "Determinants of Urban Form" at the University of Pennsylvania, 1960–1964

Lee Ann Custer

Denise Scott Brown taught at the University of Pennsylvania from 1960 to 1964, when she not only developed her pedagogical approach, but also a formative way of looking at and thinking about buildings, spaces, and urban form.[1] Her focus on multidisciplinary research and analysis in her teaching—as well as in her related writings, including her unpublished book manuscript, "Determinants of Urban Form"—would become a methodological hallmark of her later career and her design practice with Robert Venturi.

Despite the attention generated by the 1972 publication of *Learning from Las Vegas*, which began as a 1968 Yale studio course taught by Scott Brown, Venturi, and Steven Izenour, little scholarship has addressed the environment that fostered her pedagogy: Penn's Graduate School of Fine Arts—with its opportunities and challenges. There Scott Brown developed an approach to studying urban form that emphasized what she termed the "forces"—social, economic, environmental, technological, and so on—that shaped the architecture and open spaces of cities. Scott Brown contended that these factors, and not only the function of a building or space (as the modernists would have had it), determined urban form. She also developed two conceptual foci that would ground later design philosophy: first, that the street is an essential building block of urban form, and second, that urban form has communicative power, which she termed "meaningfulness."[2] These theoretical positions coalesced in 1964, in the second iteration of her studio course, "Studio FFF2: Form, Forces & Function" (FFF2), whose format would motivate the subsequent Las Vegas studio and publication.

The relative inattention accorded to Scott Brown's early teaching and related writing—when viewed alongside similar activities of Venturi, who also taught at Penn and used the classroom as a testing ground for his theoretical positions—brings into relief the sexism that she faced, making her achievements and her daring, wayward eye all the more remarkable.

Learning at Penn

Scott Brown arrived at Penn's School of Fine Arts in 1958, at a time when the curriculum was in flux. G. Holmes Perkins had become dean in 1951 and shifted the school's approach from Beaux Arts to Bauhaus-inspired modernism.[3] He emphasized graduate education, added landscape architecture and city planning, and appointed to his faculty social scientists, including Herbert Gans, under whom Scott Brown studied.[4] Gans was interested in popular culture and critiqued the European modernists' emphasis on form and function by enjoining city planners to look at social concerns.[5] Scott Brown's advisors also included the architect and planner David Crane, whose multidisciplinary planning studios were part of her curriculum.

Crane's spring 1959 studio, "A New City for India," would become an important model for Scott Brown's pedagogy. The course, with assistance by planner and lecturer Britton Harris, focused on the replanning of Chandigarh, the capital of the Indian state of Punjab. Crane's course description emphasized what Scott Brown would come to describe as "forces" in her own teaching and writing. Crane wrote: "The study is to be largely concerned with the physical structure of the city in relation to basic physiographic, technological, social, and economic determinants."[6] The "physical structure" of the city can be understood as "form" and the "physiographic, technological, social, and economic determinants" as the forces that shaped it. Scott Brown's class notes corroborated Crane's interest in the social dimensions of a city or region. According to Scott Brown's student notes, Crane prompted that streets should be seen as "opportunities not as nec[essary] evils ... think of them as buildings," and queried, "Who will read the messages?"[7] These ideas stressed the street as a typology worthy of designers' attention and the power of urban form to communicate, sparking Scott Brown's design philosophy. Moreover, the format of Crane's research-based studio—with its interweaving of law, economics, demography, transportation, and social studies into the first half of the semester, and division of students into teams for design development in the second half of the term—formed a blueprint for Scott Brown's future studio courses, such as her FFF studios.[8]

Teaching at Penn

After completing her master's degree in city planning in 1960, Scott Brown taught an array of courses at Penn over the next four and a half years.[9] Her teaching integrated studio and theory; "All of it went together," she recollected.[10] Former students recalled that Scott Brown was a "demanding and exacting teacher," that she was interested in "how people used the space," and that her "drawing exercises took us out into the city."[11]

Introduction to Urban Design (City Planning 501): Fall Semesters of 1960 (Co-Taught with Crane), 1961, 1962

Scott Brown taught an introduction to urban design for planning students in which she prioritized the street as a design problem and the communicative power of urban form (fig. 1). She developed these ideas alongside Crane in their 1960 co-taught iteration of the course.[12] They spotlighted ideas of "functional efficiency" and "psychic and physiological reaction" in relation to physical forms in the city.[13] Functional efficiency was defined as the ease (or difficulty) with which a city could be used, particularly in terms of movement and legibility. "Should we commute 1 hr., 2 hrs., 4 hrs. a day? Can you find your way without a map in Central Philadelphia? In Levittown?" they wrote.[14] Regarding psychic and physiological reaction, they asked: "Why do some spaces 'feel' peaceful, others insecure? Which table would you choose in an empty restaurant? Why?"[15]

From this early date, Scott Brown's teaching treated the concepts of the street as a space worthy of design and of urban form's capacity to evoke feeling. For instance, in fall 1960, "West Philadelphia Spaces: Design of City Streets" assigned students to redesign portions of Spruce and 38th Streets near Penn's campus—looking to the area that would become the centerpiece of FFF2 in 1964. Students analyzed the existing conditions and proposed a new design with regard to views, circulation, and the siting of buildings.[16] Preparatory design exercises included a collage to "give an impressionistic feeling of 'city.'"[17] The student work unmistakably emphasized the signs, surfaces, and image-ability of the commercial facade—pointing to the interests that would ground

Figure 1: Denise Scott Brown with her planning students at the University of Pennsylvania, fall 1960.

her later work on the commercial strip in cities like Las Vegas (fig. 2). Members of each student team were assigned either to research a particular aspect of the site, such as design standards for intersections, or to prepare an aspect of the final presentation, such as the site model (fig. 3).[18] A former student, James Yellin, recalled this studio's team-based approach as an essential component of Scott Brown's teaching.[19]

Another assignment, "Form and Function in the City," presaged her FFF studios even more directly. The project's first paragraph read:

> You will have heard the slogan "form follows function," and perhaps its counterpart "form evokes function." We hope to show that the relation between form and function, need and shape, goals and means, is a complex and oscillating one, and that the question "Which comes first?" does not make much sense. The important thing to ask is "What are the kinds and 'levels' of goals for which we can plan; and at what scale in the city do they apply?"[20]

This emphasis on forces—the social, economic, and environmental factors—to critique modernist ideas of function, or "Modern Architecture & The Functionalist Tradition," as one of her lectures was titled, would resonate throughout her career.[21]

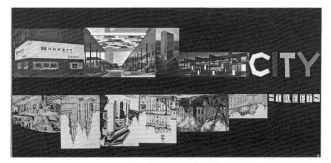

Figure 2: Student work, Exercise #7. Denise Scott Brown and David Crane, City Planning 501 Studio, University of Pennsylvania, fall 1960.

Figure 3: Student work on "West Philadelphia Study." Denise Scott Brown and David Crane, City Planning 501 Studio, University of Pennsylvania, fall 1960.

Theories of Architecture, Landscape Architecture and Planning (Architecture 411/511): Fall Semesters of 1961, 1962, 1963

This course for first-year architecture students was part of a series of four theories courses introduced by Perkins as he shifted the school to graduate-only education.[22] Perkins and Romaldo Giurgola, the Italian-born-and-trained mainstay of what would be called the "Philadelphia School," taught the two upper-level classes on civic design and architecture, respectively; Scott Brown and Venturi taught the pair of introductory courses.[23]

For her course, Scott Brown organized a series of guest lectures by faculty from disciplines across the school. In fall 1961, for instance, Louis Kahn lectured on "Technology and Design," and Ian McHarg spoke on "The Ecology of City and Region, Man + Environment."[24] Scott Brown also led seminars (dubbed the "Laboratory Section") for the discussion of the lectures, readings, and drawing exercises that asked students to observe the world around them—like Penn's campus and nearby Levittown.[25] Scott Brown again addressed the dual concepts of the street as a design problem and of the messages reflected and conjured by urban form—that is, its meanings. For instance, one question on the midterm paper pertained to "redefinition of the use of streets" as articulated in the writings of Le Corbusier, Kahn, and Crane, recalled Richard Bartholomew, who took the course in 1962.[26] Additionally, as part of the faculty lecture series, Scott Brown presented "Theories of City Form and Growth," signaling her interest in the subject.[27] For this section, in fall 1962, she assigned students an early version of her essay "Meaningful City," indicating a flow of ideas between her teaching and writing.[28]

During the academic years 1961–62, 1962–63, and 1963–64, Scott Brown's theory course was paired in sequence with Venturi's "Theories of Architecture," which he taught every spring semester from 1961 to 1965.[29] In spring 1964, Scott Brown co-taught in Venturi's course and led its weekly seminars.[30] This marked the first time Scott Brown and Venturi taught together, cementing their partnership and the combination of research and design that they would implement in their later studios on the New York City subway, Las Vegas, and Levittown.[31] Scott Brown likely brought her interest in the design of the street and her emphasis on the communicative power of the everyday urban environment into their conversations. A note from Venturi, tucked into Scott Brown's teaching records from fall 1962, indicates his willingness to serve on the final jury for the course that semester—an early beginning for their ongoing, lifelong exchange of ideas.[32]

"New City" Studios (City Planning 601): Spring Semesters of 1961, 1962, 1963

Scott Brown also taught, as part of teams of three to four faculty, upper-level studio courses in planning, analogous to "A New City for India," which she had taken with Crane. A "new city"—a prospective place—was a frequent topic for these city planning studios; for instance, in 1962, the studio treated the new town of Reston, west of Washington, D.C.[33] Other sites were global in scope, in keeping with then-recent large-scale city planning efforts around the world, such as Chandigarh and Brasília. In 1961, the subject was "New City Peruvia"—"a new urban frontier for Peru"—and in 1963, the topic was "New City Guayana," a future city in Venezuela.[34] The idea of a "new city," Scott Brown explained, eliminated "the complexity and detail of [the students'] own culture and surroundings," allowing them to "span, in one semester, a wide range of problems that might be difficult to handle close-up."[35] Whereas Scott Brown's other courses generally concentrated on existing built environments, these studios more overtly reinforced the idea of the planner's prerogative to design a city in a place that was relatively unknown to them—a position that could be likened to a colonial gaze.[36]

Form, Forces, and Function (City Planning 503): Fall Semesters of 1963, 1964

In fall 1963, Scott Brown created a new introductory studio course in the city planning department for urban designers, "Studio FFF: Form, Forces & Function" (FFF1). The following fall, she repeated this course as FFF2.[37] Both iterations of the course advanced her concept of the relationship between the titular Fs. She contended that the interdependencies between these elements in existing places could provide critical findings through research and analysis, which form future planning designs.[38] In FFF1, students focused on a wide range of sites and topics, including Duncan Hudson's proposal for the redesign of the shopping center in Cherry Hill, New Jersey, Arlo Braun's study for a "Highway Hotel," Gerry Wolfe's "Street as Space & Shelter Today," and Bill Firth and Michael Menendez's "New Town for Higuerote Venezuela."[39]

By contrast, FFF2 was organized as a single semester-long case study of an urban site with a mix of residential, commercial, institutional, and industrial uses: 40th Street in Philadelphia, then just west of Penn's campus. The area was undergoing great changes; a process under the banner of the federally backed tools of "urban renewal" demolished residences and businesses in order to expand the campuses of Penn, the Drexel Institute of Technology, the Philadelphia College of Pharmacy and Science, and the Presbyterian and Osteopathic hospitals to create "University City"—displacing the predominantly African American neighborhood of Black Bottom and other small businesses in the process.[40] In her course materials, Scott Brown pointed out that Penn's

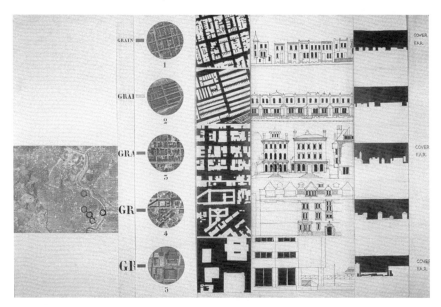

Figure 4: Student work, "Grain Map." Denise Scott Brown, "Studio FFF2: Form,
Forces & Function," University of Pennsylvania, fall 1964.

expansion plans had "nothing to say of the existing and thriving commercial nucleus at 40th and Spruce."[41] By choosing this nearby site, Scott Brown
asked her students to engage the effects of urban renewal that were underway
in their community, and to consider alternatives.

Students' graphic analyses of existing urban conditions laid an important
precedent for Scott Brown, Venturi, and Izenour's later methods for mapping
Las Vegas. For example, a "grain map" recorded the "degree of intimacy with
which different elements are mixed" (fig. 4).[42] Students also mapped existing land use, activity-intensity patterns, and the changing functions of buildings.[43] In their study of "imageability," two students, W. Dennis Childs and
Philip H. Carter, illustrated a map of 40th Street with thumbnail perspective
sketches of its intersections, pairing these views with an assessment of street
activity (fig. 5).[44]

In the design phase, students responded to Scott Brown's guiding question: "What should '40th Street'* be?" That asterisk led to a footnote which

115

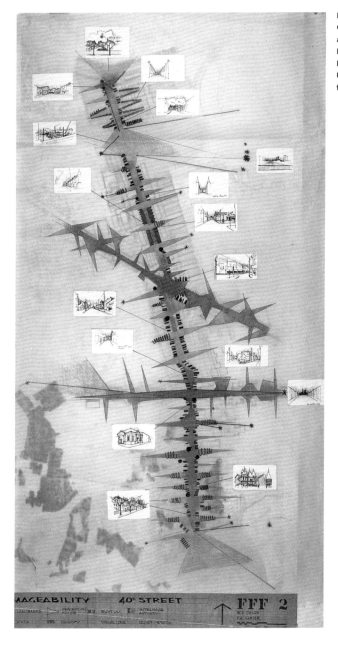

explained that, for Scott Brown, "40th Street" pertained to a zone four blocks wide, "stretching between 38th and 42nd Streets, Woodland Cemetery and Fairmount Park."[45] This "band of change," as she called it, served a variety of residents' needs. Scott Brown asked: "If '40th Street' isn't an 'environmental area' or a 'socio-economic group' or a 'neighborhood unit,' then what is it, and what does it 'want to be'?"[46] The answer may have been encapsulated in the title that Darrel Conybeare, one of her students, adopted for his project: "The 40th Street *Strip.*" Calling West Philadelphia's shopping street a "strip" locates a critical word for Scott Brown's later interest in Ed Ruscha's *Every Building on the Sunset Strip* (1966) and her attention to the quintessential "strip" in Las Vegas.[47]

Crucially, FFF2 advanced Scott Brown's focus on the street as a building block of urban design, sustaining Introduction to Urban Design's assignment on West Philadelphia and reflecting her intensifying teaching concern for the commercial strip.[48] It also crystallized her concept of the meaningfulness of the street—or the communicative power of urban form, which she had been developing in her teaching and writing. In both iterations of the course, Scott Brown again assigned her working manuscript "Meaningful City" and asked students to write a paper on "determinants of urban form," in which they had to address the societal, technological, and environmental determinants of form in West Philadelphia.[49] These assignments concretized the language that she would bring to her book manuscript, "Determinants of Urban Form."

From the Classroom to the Page and Back Again

Scott Brown developed the core tenets of her approach to the design of cities and built form in both her pedagogy and related writings. Her essay "The Meaningful City" (1965) was an analysis of cities' forms of communication, including "heraldry" (graphic and written signs) and "physiognomy" (the shapes and sizes of buildings). As David Brownlee has noted, this terminology translated into the "decorated sheds" and "ducks" in *Learning from Las*

Vegas—and, even more, the language of heraldry and physiognomy came from Crane, tracing back to the framework of the 1960 iteration of Introduction to Urban Design ("Can you find your way without a map in Central Philadelphia?").[50] In a recent interview, Scott Brown corroborated Crane's influence, recounting that he encouraged her to publish "The Meaningful City" when it was not possible for him: "Crane pushed me to do things he couldn't do," she said. "He was going to do it with me ... he stopped writing due to practice at the time."[51] An early manuscript of the essay, stored with records for her "Theories" course, reads: "Let us examine the city as a 'message system' to discover the nature of the messages it can give," emphasizing the communicative potential of urban form and recalling her student notes from Crane's class.[52]

Among the materials Scott Brown included in her application for tenure at the University of California, Los Angeles, in 1967, was an unfinished book manuscript, "Determinants of Urban Form," which she was hoping to publish.[53] Like "The Meaningful City," the book adopted a rhetoric and substance similar to her teaching. Following a section on "the need for the book," the manuscript opened with a definition of form, function, and forces—the central topics of the FFF studios.[54] This included a definition of physical systems and physical form as determined by functions and forces, which echoed the précis for FFF1.[55] The successive sections of the manuscript treated the societal, technological, physical, and natural determinants of urban form, mirroring the topics of the paper assignment in FFF2. Notably, the introduction to the book and the introduction to FFF began with the very same admonition: "As cities have grown to engulf most of the life of the nation, so, through the problems which have resulted, has grown the realisation that city development must be guided, and guided on many fronts."[56] The repetition of text between course and manuscript indicates the crossover of ideas between the classroom and this written articulation of her design philosophy.[57]

Scott Brown thus utilized the classroom, the iterative nature of teaching, and the discursiveness of her written course materials (from studio exercises to assigned readings) to develop the larger philosophy of design thinking that would characterize her and Venturi's work. In fact, the connections between the content of Scott Brown's courses and her "Determinants of Urban Form" manuscript are similar to the connections between Venturi's "Theories of Architecture" course and his 1966 publication *Complexity and Contradiction in Architecture*.[58] Both architects used the classroom to sharpen their thinking.

Unlike Venturi's book, however, Scott Brown's major manuscript from the 1960s remains unpublished. This may have been, in part, due to barriers that Scott Brown faced which Venturi did not: she was an immigrant, she was Jewish, and she was a woman. In all these ways, she was an "outsider" in the elite, white, male-dominated, Ivy League world of architecture and city planning. While Princeton-educated Venturi, whose background as the son of Italian immigrants who had not graduated from college was already atypical in this environment, Scott Brown faced sexism—both explicit and implicit.[59] She has recounted that, as dean, Perkins "thought of me as a T[eaching] A[ssistant]" rather than as a professor.[60] She taught twice as many hours as Venturi for the same pay—leaving her less time to devote to her manuscript.[61] Scott Brown also noted that her book remained unfinished, to an extent, because of the child-rearing duties that she later shouldered.[62]

As Craig Lee recounts in this volume, in 1972, *Learning from Las Vegas* was published with Venturi as the first author. Scott Brown has noted that Venturi's name was listed first because he wrote the majority of the first draft of the manuscript.[63] However, the author order may have also been based on the press's view of Venturi's name recognition (due in no small part to the success of *Complexity and Contradiction*)—even while both he and Izenour attested that Scott Brown was the project's driving force.[64] Although Scott Brown was developing a course-to-book agenda analogous to that of Venturi, she was not able to publish that project. And many of the concepts she developed in her teaching subsequently appeared in the multiauthored *Learning from Las Vegas*—an achievement that she shared collaboratively with Venturi and Izenour, a mode of creative practice that architectural history and the "star system" has historically failed to represent sufficiently.[65]

In her research-based studios and lecture course, Scott Brown refined her concepts of the street as a type of urban space worthy of design and of the communicative power of urban form—with special consideration given to the social forces that shaped it. In the energized environment of Penn in the early 1960s, Scott Brown was able to generate theoretical positions in her teaching that would come to be canonical concepts in postmodern architecture. Many later projects undertaken by the firm she led with Venturi, such as their proposal for the historic Strand district in Galveston, Texas (1975), the Washington Avenue plan for Miami Beach, Florida (1978), and numerous campus plans, including for the University of Michigan (2002), were also clearly manifestations of the methods that she began cultivating in the classroom: survey existing uses, focus on the street as a space in its own right, and strive to make the built environment *mean* to its users. The uplifting nature of artistic forms, the imperative to work with existing forces and not against them, and the necessity of functionality over time—not just its image: these, for Scott Brown, were the determinants of urban form.

Notes

1 This study is based on extensive research on the newly accessioned teaching records of Denise Scott Brown (Denise Scott Brown Teaching Records, hereafter cited as DSBTR), a part of the Venturi Scott Brown Collection, by the gift of Robert Venturi and Denise Scott Brown, at the Architectural Archives of the University of Pennsylvania, Philadelphia (hereafter cited as VSBC, AAUP). It owes much to the support of David Brownlee, Craig Lee, Mary McLeod, Steve Marcus, Allison Rose Olsen, Heather Isbell Schumacher, William Whitaker, and Cynthia Williams. I am also grateful to Nicole and Conrad Person for their support while I was conducting archival research and to Christal Springer and Constance Mood for their help with images. I am indebted to Scott Brown and her former students, cited herein, who spoke with me about this dynamic time at Penn.

2 On the topic of meaning in the theory and architecture of Scott Brown and Venturi, see McLeod, "Wrestling with Meaning," 67–92.

3 Scott, "Origins in Excellence: The Practical Ethos of G. Holmes Perkins and the Philadelphia School," 25–28. See also interview transcript, G. Holmes Perkins, c. 1987, box 3, folder 39, Department of Multimedia and Educational Technology Services Records, UPB 1.9MM, University Archives and Records Center, University of Pennsylvania, Philadelphia (hereafter cited as interview transcript, Perkins, UARC).

4 Scott, "Origins in Excellence," 31–33.

5 Scott Brown, "Towards an Active Socioplastics," 29–31.

6 Course introduction, City Planning 602, taught by David Crane and assisted by Britton Harris, spring 1959, DSBTR, VSBC, AAUP.

7 Scott Brown student notes, City Planning 602, dated "8.4.59," spring 1959, DSBTR, VSBC, AAUP. A separate "Schedule of Events" for the course lists "Urban design discussion by Mr. Crane" for Wednesday, April 8. (Scott Brown likely dated her notes in day-month-year format.)

8 Course introduction, City Planning 602, spring 1959, DSBTR, VSBC, AAUP. See also Scott Brown, "Between Three Stools," 11.

9 For documentation of the course dates, see syllabi and lecture outlines, City Planning 501, fall 1960; Architecture 411, fall 1961; City Planning 501, fall 1961; City Planning 601–2, spring 1962; Architecture 411, fall 1962; and City Planning 501, fall 1962; City Planning 601, spring 1963; Architecture 511, fall 1963; City Planning 503, fall 1963; Architecture 512, spring 1964; and City Planning 503, fall 1964, DSBTR, VSBC, AAUP. See also Penn's Graduate School of Fine Arts course bulletins for academic years 1962–64, copies on file, 277.44–47, University of Pennsylvania Bulletin Collection, AAUP. In spring 1965 and fall 1966, Scott Brown taught a version of City Planning 503 at the University of California, Berkeley (Seminar on City Form) and the University of California, Los Angeles (Urban Design 401: Forms, Forces and Function in Santa Monica), respectively. See DSBTR, VSBC, AAUP.

10 Denise Scott Brown, interview with the author, October 1, 2021.

11 Richard Bartholomew, John Lobell, and Terry Vaughan, respectively, interviews with the author, February 2, 2022.

12 The course description lists "Mr. D. Crane & Mrs. Denise Scott Brown" as critics, although Scott Brown does not explicitly mention co-teaching this course in her essay "Between Three Stools." Either way, it is clear that Crane was an important mentor for her at that time. See course introduction, City Planning 501, fall 1960, DSBTR, VSBC, AAUP; and Scott Brown, "Between Three Stools," 12.

13 Course introduction, 1–2, City Planning 501, fall 1960, DSBTR, VSBC, AAUP.

14 Course introduction, 1, City Planning 501, fall 1960, DSBTR, VSBC, AAUP.

15 Course introduction, 1, City Planning 501, fall 1960, DSBTR, VSBC, AAUP.

16 "West Philadelphia Spaces: Design of City Streets," Planning 501, fall 1960, DSBTR, VSBC, AAUP. Scott Brown likely penned this assignment description, as opposed to Crane, because it refers to Crane in the third person.

17 "Part 1: 'Points,' 'Lines' and 'Areas,' Exercise 7," 2, City Planning 501, fall 1960, DSBTR, VSBC, AAUP.

18 "West Philadelphia Spaces: Design of City Streets," City Planning 501, fall 1960, DSBTR, VSBC, AAUP.

19 James Yellin, interview with the author, September 17, 2021.

20 "Form and Function in the City," dated October 7, 1960, 1, City Planning 501, DSBTR, VSBC, AAUP.

21 For lecture titles, see "Course Schedule," City Planning 501, fall 1960, DSBTR, VSBC, AAUP. For more on function, see Denise Costanzo's essay in this volume.

22 In fall 1961, Scott Brown's theories course was titled "Theories of Architecture"—the same title that was applied to Robert Venturi's theories course in spring 1961. The first two iterations were numbered 411 and subsequently renumbered Architecture 511. In fall 1962 and fall 1963, Scott Brown's course title shifted to "Contemporary Theories of Architecture, City Planning and Landscape Architecture." See syllabi, Architecture 411, fall 1961; Architecture 411, fall 1962; Architecture 511, fall 1963, DSBTR, VSBC, AAUP.

23 On Perkins's curriculum changes, see interview transcript, Perkins, UARC; and Scott Brown, interview with the author, October 29, 2016. On the sequence of theories courses, see Graduate School of Fine Arts course bulletin for academic year 1960–61, dated January 1960, 11, copy on file, 277.43, University of Pennsylvania Bulletin Collection, AAUP.

24 Course schedule, Architecture 411, fall 1961, DSBTR, VSBC, AAUP.

25 Exercises for "Lab Section," Architecture 411, fall 1961, DSBTR, VSBC, AAUP.

26 Bartholomew, interview with the author, February 2, 2022, and "Mid Term Paper," dated October 2, 1962, Architecture 411, DSBTR, VSBC, AAUP.

27 Course schedule, Architecture 411, fall 1961, DSBTR, VSBC, AAUP.

28 List of Required Reading, 4, Architecture 411, fall 1962, DSBTR, VSBC, AAUP.

29 Custer, "Teaching Complexity and Contradiction at the University of Pennsylvania, 1961–65," 30–47.

30 Custer, "Teaching Complexity and Contradiction," 31–32.

31 Custer, "Teaching Complexity and Contradiction," 32.

32 Robert Venturi to Denise Scott Brown, dated November 21, 1962, Architecture 411, DSBTR, VSBC, AAUP.

33 Course introduction, City Planning 601-2, spring 1962, DSBTR, VSBC, AAUP. The 1962 studio was taught with David Wallace and Louis Loewenstein.

34 Course introduction, City Planning 601, spring 1961 and 1963, DSBTR, VSBC, AAUP. Scott Brown, Crane, and Gerald Carrothers taught New City Peruvia in 1961, with Louis Loewenstein as a teaching assistant. Scott Brown, Paul Davidoff, Robert Mitchell, and David Wallace taught New City Guayana in 1963. Paul Hirshorn, interview with the author, February 18, 2022.

35 Scott Brown, "Between Three Stools," 12.

36 While beyond the scope of this essay, this is a topic deserving of future study. See Craig Lee's contribution to this volume and Levin, "Learning from Johannesburg: Unpacking Denise Scott Brown's South African View of Las Vegas."

37 Scott Brown, "Between Three Stools," 13. Although the Graduate School of Fine Arts Bulletin for the 1963–64 academic year shows Scott Brown slated to repeat Introduction to Urban Design in fall 1963, there is not archival evidence that she taught that course a fourth time. See Penn's Graduate School of Fine Arts course bulletin for academic year 1963–64, copy on file, 277.46, University of Pennsylvania Bulletin Collection, AAUP.

38 "Form, Forces & Function: Toward a Philosophy for Studio FFF," 4, September 5, 1963, 5, City Planning 503, DSBTR, VSBC, AAUP.

39 Final Jury Schedule, FFF1, December 11, 1963, City Planning 503, DSBTR, VSBC, AAUP.

40 For more on urban renewal and Penn, see Puckett and Lloyd, Becoming Penn: The Pragmatic American University, 1950–2000. See also "Notes on 40th Street," 1–10, July 3, 1964, City Planning 503, DSBTR, VSBC, AAUP.

41 "Studio FFF2: Notes on 40th Street," dated July 3, 1964, 9, City Planning 503, DSBTR, VSBC, AAUP.

42 "Phase IC3, Grain Map of West Philadelphia," dated October 19, 1964, City Planning 503, DSBTR, VSBC, AAUP. No student name is included on this assignment.

43 Phase 1 Student work, fall 1964, City Planning 503, DSBTR, VSBC, AAUP.

44 Scott Brown Teaching Records, "Imageability of West Philadelphia," Phase 1 Student work, fall 1964, City Planning 503, DSBTR, VSBC, AAUP.

45 "Phase III, Sketch Design I," dated October 21, 1964, 1, City Planning 503, DSBTR, VSBC, AAUP.

46 "Phase III, Sketch Design I," dated October 21, 1964, 3, City Planning 503, DSBTR, VSBC, AAUP.

47   "Sketch Design 1 – 'The 40th Street Strip,'" D. Co-
     nybeare, dated October 26, 1964, City Planning
     503, DSBTR, VSBC, AAUP. Emphasis added. For
     Scott Brown's interest in Ed Ruscha, see Scott
     Brown, "Towards an Active Socioplastics," 39.

48   In her focus on West Philadelphia, Scott Brown may
     have been drawing from the "West Philadelphia
     Spaces" assignment from her and Crane's fall 1960
     studio, City Planning 501, as well as from Crane's
     fall 1959 studio, City Planning 601. The assigned
     reading for the fall 1960 course included: "Crane,
     'City Spaces: West Philadelphia,' C.P. 601 notes,
     November 1959." See course bibliography, fall
     1960, City Planning 501, DSBTR, VSBC, AAUP.

49   For the assignment of "Meaningful City," see
     "Schedule," fall 1963 and 1964, City Planning 503,
     DSBTR, VSBC, AAUP. For the assignment on "deter-
     minants of urban form," see "Paper III: Determinants
     of City Form," dated September 11, 1963, 3–4, City
     Planning 503, a copy of which is included in the re-
     cords for "Phase II Determinants of City Form,"
     dated October 2, 1964, City Planning 503, DSBTR,
     VSBC, AAUP.

50   Scott Brown, "The Meaningful City," 30; and
     Brownlee, De Long, and Hiesinger, *Out of the Ordi-
     nary*, 29.

51   Scott Brown, interview with the author, January 29,
     2022.

52   "Meaningful City," in records for Architecture 411,
     fall 1961, DSBTR, VSBC, AAUP.

53   "C.2 Manuscript: Determinants of Urban Form,"
     dated December 28, 1965, Tenure Package, Univer-
     sity of Pennsylvania, DSBTR, VSBC, AAUP. Notice of
     her promotion with tenure published in *University
     Bulletin: A Weekly Bulletin of the Staff of the Univer-
     sity of California* 15, no. 41 (June 19, 1967): 183.

54   See "Revised Outline of Contents" and "Chapter 2,"
     in "C.2 Manuscript: Determinants of Urban Form,"
     dated December 28, 1965, I.2.1–2, Tenure Pack-
     age, University of Pennsylvania, DSBTR, VSBC,
     AAUP.

55   See "Chapter 2," in "C.2 Manuscript: Determinants
     of Urban Form," dated December 28, 1965, I.2.4,
     Tenure Package, University of Pennsylvania; and
     "Studio FFF," in course introduction, FFF1, fall
     1963, 4, City Planning 503, DSBTR, VSBC, AAUP.

56   See course introduction, FFF1, fall 1963, 2, City
     Planning 503, DSBTR, VSBC, AAUP; and "C.2 Man-
     uscript – Determinants of Urban Form," Study
     Proposal, dated June 1, 1964, 1–2, Tenure Pack-
     age, University of Pennsylvania, DSBTR, VSBC,
     AAUP.

57   For more on the connections between Scott Brown's
     teaching and writing in terms of function, see Denise
     Costanzo's essay in this volume.

58   For more on the connections between Venturi's
     teaching and the book *Complexity and Contradiction
     in Architecture* (1966), see Custer, "Teaching Com-
     plexity and Contradiction at the University of Penn-
     sylvania, 1961–65," 30–47.

59   On Venturi's background, see McLeod, "Venturi's
     Acknowledgments," 57. See also Scott Brown,
     "Room at the Top," 237–246.

60   Scott Brown, interview with the author, October 1,
     2021. The school's annual bulletins listed Scott
     Brown as assistant professor of city planning in both
     the Department of Architecture and the Department
     of City Planning from January 1962 to December
     1964 and listed her as an instructor in city planning
     in January 1961. See Penn's Graduate School of
     Fine Arts course bulletins for academic years 1962–
     64, copies on file, 277.44–47, University of Penn-
     sylvania Bulletin Collection, AAUP.

61   Scott Brown, interview with the author, October 1,
     2021.

62   Scott Brown, interview with the author, October 1,
     2021.

63   McLeod, "Wrestling with Meaning," 67, footnote 2;
     and Venturi and Scott Brown, *A View from the
     Campidoglio*, 9.

64   On the press's interest in Venturi's name recogni-
     tion, see Stierli, *Las Vegas in the Rearview Mirror*,
     32–33; and Gabor, *Einstein's Wife*, 195. On Scott
     Brown as the project's driving force, see Craig Lee's
     contribution to this volume.

65   There are exceptions to this, notably, McLeod,
     "Venturi's Acknowledgments," 50–75.

Recollections III: Learning from Denise Scott Brown and Paul Davidoff

James Yellin

From 1960 to 1962, I was a very undistinguished urban planning student at the University of Pennsylvania, commonly known as Penn. The faculty had many professors with superb credentials, but the two finest teachers were, in my opinion, Denise Scott Brown and Paul Davidoff (1930–1984).[1] The iconic Denise Scott Brown needs no introduction, but some readers may not be familiar with Paul's background. An American urban planner and planning theoretician who received a law degree from Penn, Paul developed the concept of advocacy planning with a colleague at Penn, Thomas A. Reiner.[2] Paul also founded the Urban Policy and Planning Department at Hunter College and taught urban planning at Princeton University as well as at Penn.

Denise told me that she and Paul were "fast friends," but that they were also "fighting friends" whose relationship could be characterized as "constructive conflict."[3] At Penn, Denise and Paul had two small offices separated by a corridor approximately one meter wide. They would, Denise said, lean back in their desk chairs and argue with each other. This would attract a small crowd of students who would stand in the corridor and listen with interest and amusement.

Denise also told me that Paul was "noble" and a "great-hearted activist for social justice."[4] She recalled that she "audited his course on planning theory in 1960 and kibitzed frequently." She criticized him for saying that everything architects do is based on intuition, but he "never suggested that I not attend his class." In hindsight, Denise summed up their relationship: "We made each other wiser."

Where Denise and Paul Disagreed

Paul at first maintained, Denise told me, that planning should be based only on logic and facts, not on intuition. Denise thought that intuition was often a good starting point, but that intuition must be confirmed by logic and facts. In the end, Denise remarked, Paul came to largely agree with her, although Paul still placed less importance on the role of intuition than she did.

And "Whatever our disagreements," Denise noted, "Paul was always encouraging and helped me define myself." In the late 1970s and early 1980s, Denise had as clients the municipalities of Princeton, New Jersey, and Miami Beach, Florida. "And as I believed," Denise continued, "and still believe that clients choose architects that think and look like themselves, I asked Paul: 'But how could I be a Princeton University professor and a Miami retiree at the same time?' Paul replied: 'Isn't that what you are?'"

Where Denise and Paul Agreed

Denise and Paul were both of the New Left, whose goals included racial equality, women's rights, gay rights, the abolition of nuclear weapons, and protection of the environment. But Denise and Paul were of a New Left that thought one must understand the positions of those with whom one disagrees, and that even those with whom one disagrees most strongly may sometimes be right.

They both thought, Denise told me, that the architectural process was more complex than many planners realized. Both also believed that planners should help the disadvantaged and that top-down urban planning does not work, especially for the underprivileged. Both thought that planners should help redress unfairness in society, that they should ask who benefits and who loses because of the planning process, and that in a democracy like the United States urban planning should be part of the political process.

What Denise Learned from Paul

Denise learned many things from Paul. To begin with, Denise said, "I learned about legal reasoning and the Socratic teaching method that goes with it." As a student in Paul's class on planning law in 1958, Denise noted, "I learned about his ideas on advocacy by planners and that planners should represent the interests of disadvantaged people to help rectify inequalities that result in their having insufficient influence."

In his class, Denise said, Paul also convinced her that advocacy is often a good way to proceed in architecture as well as urban planning, and that the focus of urban planners on the long range—often on the year 2020—was "perfect vision planning" and allowed them to avoid the gritty problems of everyday life.

Paul was on Denise's jury in 1964 for a team project on West Philadelphia in a class that Denise was teaching in the Department of City Planning at Penn. Denise recounted that he asked her, "Why do you have to change everything? What's wrong with amelioration? Isn't West Philadelphia almost all right?" Paul and Denise agreed that it was. And her future husband Robert Venturi, who was also a member of the jury, in his book *Complexity and Contradiction in Architecture*, translated Paul's question into, "Is not Main Street almost all right?"

The Philosophy of Denise Scott Brown: "On Analysis and Design"

Some of the ideas Denise shared with students at Penn are laid out in her essay "On Analysis and Design." This essay was, as Denise wrote, a response to Paul's "confusion" regarding the role intuition plays for architects and planners, and it can serve as an introduction to "my effort to counter the belief held in planning circles" that architects who are urban planners do "design," while everyone else does "analysis." This is bad for both planners and architects. Planners suffer because their work includes not only analysis but also synthesis and recommendations. It's bad for architects because the hostility of planners to the "presumed totally intuitive and aesthetically-based activity" of architects "makes collaboration difficult." And the "holier-than-thou outlook" of planners and their presumption that architects totally lack rigor makes the planners "a bore."

Moreover, Denise also wrote, "the Davidoffian planning sequence of eliciting goals, surveying means and posing alternative syntheses for criticism and then choice is one well known to architects." Buildings would collapse "if architects did not think holistically."

It's not "the intuitiveness of the creative process but the rationality of the testing process that should concern the planners." Another approach "would be to start with the uncertainty and try to be scientific about that." Long-range planning would thus become a "scientific endeavour" rather than "a branch of astrology." She further wrote that she was "anxious to see the analyst-designer squabble settled" and hoped that "in the bigger battle between 'scientists' and 'humanists' in planning, architects, sitting as they do in both camps, can serve as a mediating influence."[5]

The Philosophy of Denise Scott Brown: *Learning from Las Vegas*

Denise introduced her students at Penn to a range of ideas, many of which were articulated later in the iconic book *Learning from Las* Vegas, coauthored by Denise, her husband Robert Venturi, and their long-term associate Steven Izenour.[6] According to *Learning from Las Vegas*, the Las Vegas strip "challenges the architect to take a positive non-chip-on-the shoulder view," and shows again that one can "look downward to go upward." Indeed, gaining "insight from the commonplace is nothing new: Fine art often follows folk art."

Along the Las Vegas Strip as elsewhere, buildings can be classified as "decorated sheds" or "ducks." Both kinds of buildings are valid. A building where the ornament is applied independently of the structure is a "decorated shed," such as a food store with the large letters EAT standing in front of the store (fig. 1).[7] A building where the structure is distorted by an overall symbolic

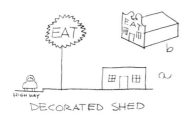

DECORATED SHED

Figure 1: A building on which the ornament is applied independently of the structure is a "decorated shed," such as a food store with the large letters EAT standing in front of the store.

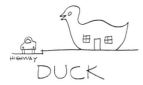

DUCK

Figure 2: A building in which the structure is distorted by an overall symbolic form is a "duck."

form is a "duck." The term "duck" (fig. 2) is in honor of a photograph of a duck-shaped structure in *God's Own Junkyard*, a book by the German-American architect Peter Blake.[8]

As stated in *Learning from Las Vegas*, Modern architects, when they "self-righteously abandoned ornament," unconsciously designed buildings that were ornament. Modern architects are "silly" when they label forms and spaces as functional, when the forms and spaces are really "unacknowledged symbolism." Indeed, Modern architects have been designing "dead ducks."[9]

The Philosophy of Paul Davidoff: "A Choice Theory of Planning"

Students at Penn learned ideas on the structure of planning that appear in "A Choice Theory of Planning" by Paul and Thomas A. Reiner.[10] According to "A Choice Theory of Planning," the ultimate purposes of a plan "cannot be appraised from within a system," but must rely on "outside criteria." That said, planning seems to have three classes of objectives:

1. As a way to promote *efficiency and rational action*, planning is seen as a way to reduce waste or to produce the greatest return from the employment of resources.

2. As a *market aid*, planning may be desired to bring the society closer to a fully competitive market. Alternatively, as a *market replacement*, planning would serve as "a new and controlling system of pricing and distribution" for those who "deny the possibility of a working competitive market."

3. As a way to promote *change or a widening of choice*, a planner should "render explicit the implications of proposals" to help people make informed choices. And a planner should act in accordance with the democratic ethic that "no one has the wisdom or ability to make decisions for the society or for another individual."

Paul and his co-author added, that one may express values as moral statements, as statements of preference, as statements of criteria, or as ends or goals. There is "a philosophical distinction between fact and value," but they are "closely related." Factual statements "invariably reflect the values of their makers." Our values "are colored by our understanding of facts."

The true measures of facts lie on a probabilistic continuum. Therefore, "we cannot be absolutely certain of any assertion." One cannot resolve a "disagreement on a value position by recourse to facts." Values can be verified "only in terms of their consistency with values of a higher level." And there must eventually be reference to "ultimate values which are essentially assumed and asserted as postulates."

Because "facts are probabilistic and values debatable," there are no correct decisions. A decision's merit "can only be appraised by values held individually or in a collectivity."

The ideas in "A Choice Theory of Planning," Denise told me, helped Paul and her develop at Penn from 1959 to 1962 an urban planning process that she called "Mission, Goals Opportunities, Problems, Issues, and Options" (MGOPIO). This process, according to Denise, not only provides a structure for planning, it also "arms people to make decisions that affect them" by making the planning steps explicit.

The Philosophy of Paul Davidoff: "Advocacy and Pluralism in Planning"

Other ideas that students at Penn learned from Paul appear in his essay "Advocacy and Pluralism in Planning." (By "pluralism," Paul meant that the urban planning process should involve competing planning groups and viewpoints.) There are three ways in which advocacy and plural planning could help improve planning practice, according to "Advocacy and Pluralism in Planning":

1. By advocating "alternative plans by interest groups outside of government," which would help better inform the public of the available choices.
2. By forcing public agencies to "compete with other planning groups to win political support."
3. By forcing those critical of establishment plans to "produce superior plans."

Moreover, Paul wrote, the planning commission is a "non-responsible vestigial institution" that is "a major drawback to effective democratic planning." The "failure to place planning decision choices in the hands of elected officials has weakened the ability of professional planners to have their proposals effected." There is, or should be, "a Republican and Democratic way of viewing city development," as well as "conservative and liberal plans, plans to support the private market and plans to support greater government control."

The social group that includes low-income families is "particularly in need of the assistance of planners." In this regard, the racial, social, and economic consequences of "physical decisions" have been "immense," but urban planners "have not sought or trained themselves to understand socio-economic problems."[11]

The ideas in "Advocacy and Pluralism in Planning," Denise said, opened her eyes to ways of implementing advocacy in planning and architecture.

Conclusion

After graduating from Penn, I worked only briefly as an urban planner and served for much of my life as a United States career diplomat. But what I learned from Denise and Paul served me well. In foreign relations as in urban planning, the United States—and other countries—are often doomed to failure when they use a top-down approach to deal with political, economic, and security problems. When a democratic country seeks, for example, to impose its values on another country, even with the aid of military force, the effort is likely doomed to failure.

In addition, as indicated by the philosophies of Denise and Paul, intuition can be a good starting point in analyzing the political, economic and security situation of another country, but intuition must be confirmed by analysis and facts. From personal experience, I know that failure to do so often leads to policy blunders. And like Denise and Paul, a diplomat must be open to dissenting views. Again, I know from personal experience that failure to do so can lead to major missteps.

I consider myself blessed to have known Denise and Paul. They were superb professors and artful urban planners. But above all, they were marvelous human beings. Penn, urban planning, the United States, and the world are better places because of Denise and Paul.

Notes

1   I would like to extend my great appreciation to Denise for taking the time out of her busy schedule to share her experiences with me and to respond patiently to all my questions. I would also like to recognize the insightful suggestions and punctilious proofreading of Joe Rupprecht, an Assistant to Denise and my Executive Assistant. In addition, I would like to thank the following people for their very helpful suggestions: my former United States Department of State colleagues Don Koran and Frederick Ehrenreich, the editor and researcher Adeline Zanchetta, as well as Jeremy Tenenbaum, the Director of Marketing and Graphics at the architectural firm that Denise and Robert Venturi founded. Any mistakes are, of course, my own.

2   Czech-born Thomas A. Reiner (1932–2009) was a leading American regional planning theoretician and practitioner who taught at the University of Pennsylvania from 1958 to 1993, and who was a long-term colleague of Denise and Robert Venturi.

3   If not indicated otherwise, all quotes of Denise are from telephone conversations and email exchanges with James Yellin from September 2021 to April 2022.

4   They had a unique bond. Both lost their first spouses in tragic car accidents, and both remarried into enduring and happy second marriages.

5   Scott Brown, "On Analysis and Design."

6   Scott Brown, Venturi, and Izenour, *Learning from Las Vegas*.

7   The drawings of the duck and the decorated shed are by Robert Venturi.

8   Blake, God's *Own Junkyard*. The structure, which sold roasted ducks, was an example of what Blake called the "systematic uglification" of the United States. Blake (1920 to 2006) studied architecture at the University of Pennsylvania and the Pratt Institute and became editor-in-chief of *Architectural Forum*.

9   Blake wrote in *God's Own Junkyard* that the designs of many 1960s buildings were sterile and thus "dead ducks."

10 Davidoff and Reiner, "A Choice Theory of Planning."

11 Davidoff, "Advocacy and Pluralism in Planning."

Positioning Denise Scott Brown: Los Angeles, 1965–1966

Sylvia Lavin

People have stopped visiting Los Angeles. They know if they wait long enough Los Angeles will come to them. So, watch for Los Angeles, appearing shortly in your neighborhood.

Denise Scott Brown arrived in Los Angeles to join the three-person faculty of UCLA's newly established School of Architecture and Urban Planning in 1965. She included the statement above, by an applicant to the program, in her syllabus for the inaugural planning studio she taught in the fall of 1966.[1] The epigraph proleptically offered a condensed formulation of Scott Brown's aims for the course: to teach students that cities, even apparently formless ones like Los Angeles, were the physical manifestation of what she called "underlying forces" that could be made evident through close and penetrating observation, but that could not be described in the traditional languages of architectural and urban theory and visualization. As the student anticipated, Scott Brown would argue over the course of the semester that an emerging city form was sneaking up on an unsuspecting audience sitting at home, an arrival to be witnessed like an event unfolding on the evening news. No mere metaphor, however, Los Angeles had in fact suddenly appeared on TV screens across the United States at the very moment Scott Brown arrived in the city. The Watts revolt, which began on August 11, 1965, triggered by the impact of "underlying forces"—covenanted neighborhoods and real-estate policies, the divisive and segregating intrusion of freeways, and newly established systems of urban communications—was one of the first such events to be widely televised.[2] Scott Brown came to Los Angeles to teach urban planning at a moment when the failures of urban planning were spectacularly on view.[3] As a result, Scott Brown's method of analytic observation, what she called "town-watching," is best understood as both a deliberately crafted research and pedagogical tool that she actively deployed in her studio and also as evidence of the largely passive and distanced way most inhabitants of the west side of Los Angeles witnessed the violent actualities unfolding across the east side of the city.[4] This conjunction of unrelated phenomena—academic technique and televisual spectatorship—is one of many such meetings and overlaps that shaped her 1966 syllabus. She was a young, white, single, South African woman, an academic trained in new approaches to urban planning informed by the social sciences, a recent arrival to a rapidly developing metropolitan form organized around loosely agglomerated sanctuaries that resisted conventional tools of analysis, and an untenured faculty member teaching for the first time in a public university undergirded by the consolidating forces of the just then dubbed "military, industrial, academic complex."[5] The impact of these markers of position ripple across virtually every one of the remarkable pages of Scott Brown's teaching materials, defining the ways in which the "underlying forces" that determined city form were made visible by her work but also constituted an underlying force that produced the conditions of possibility of her own work as well.[6]

While the fundamental features of Scott Brown's biography are well established, how her biography shaped the relatively unknown work she did in Los Angeles and how that work shaped both her better-known work produced elsewhere and its complex reception warrants attention.[7] Insofar as it has been studied, Los Angeles has been attended to as the place where the Scott Brown and Robert Venturi collaboration was cemented and from which they launched their study of Las Vegas.[8] However, Los Angeles was also where Scott Brown spent a unique period of time during which she was detached from the forms of determination that undergirded her before and after, an interlude between the structures of family and student life that had defined her conditions of possibility before 1965 and the requirements of professional and personal partnerships that structured her life after 1967. Her time in California unfolded during a hairpin turn in a long arc of migration that began in South Africa via the late nineteenth-century pogroms in Latvia and Lithuania, followed a path established by the British Empire to London, paused in Philadelphia attracted to the presence of Louis Kahn, another Eastern

European Jewish immigrant to the US, moved quickly through Birmingham, New Orleans, Houston, Phoenix, and Arcosanti, via Los Angeles to Berkeley, down to Los Angeles again, only to double back to Philadelphia in 1967, after a pit stop or two in Las Vegas.[9] These spatiotemporal coordinates shed light not only on her biography, but more importantly on the forms of authorship and intellection available to a Lithuanian/Latvian/South African/Jewish/woman/ urban planner and architect during those years of both radical and yet unfulfilled possibility in American history.

Architecture operated for Scott Brown as a disciplinary Ellis Island, a structure of entry into the United States but also of assimilation into American liberal democratic culture. For Scott Brown, this process began in South Africa, where she attended a grade school modeled on American progressive education: she still credits the Dewey method of "learning by doing" for her project-based pedagogy, driven by activities rather than by the transfer of traditional forms of knowledge, and for her interest in developing "scientific" methods rather than exercising moral judgment.[10] The school was Christian: although South African Jews were less pressured to divest themselves of Jewish markers than they were elsewhere at the time, Jews were initially "united" with Christian Afrikaners both in their whiteness and in their shared resistance to British imperialism, particularly the British use of concentration camps as tools in their land appropriation campaigns against the Boers. By the time Scott Brown was a university student, however, the rise of Afrikaans nationalism and the arrival of a new generation of Jewish refugees, put this unity into crisis: apartheid linked the Jew and the black in a landscape of violence and trauma.[11] At Witwatersrand, the resistance movement was strong, but it was also largely male. As a result, a student such as "Denise Lakofski" was entangled in a logic determining that to be Jewish was to be white, to be white was to be part of the apartheid state, to be "progressive" was to resist, but to be female was to be, or at least to feel, particularly imperiled by organized action.[12]

The very utopian claims of modern architecture that Scott Brown would come to critique made it appear, in 1952, to be a means of managing these incompatible identities. Its "promise" led Scott Brown away from Johannesburg and

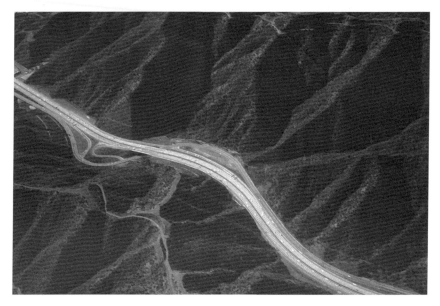

Figure 1: Denise Scott Brown, Los Angeles, 1967.

to London, where postwar reconstruction was in full optimistic swing and where figures such as Alison Smithson made it possible for women to imagine becoming architects who would help build a more just world.[13] At the Architectural Association, Scott Brown discovered a wide interest in architectural developments in the United States, particularly in Louis Kahn's urban design proposals for Philadelphia. As a result, her final step of passage through architecture into American liberal democracy was the completion of her urban planning degree at the University of Pennsylvania. Her professors and mentors included men such as Herbert Gans, whose scholarly innovation was precisely to use "scientific" methods to unmark European immigrants and to argue that despite variations in taste, they too shared in America's democratic values.[14] By 1965, in fact, each of Scott Brown's steps had rendered her markers of identity less and less legible: now married, she no longer had a Jewish name, did not look African to American eyes, and was even instructing architects to view women's bodies, which is to say her body, through the lens of scientific disinterest.[15] It must have seemed that architecture had successfully earned her a place among the American liberal arts.[16]

But of course, the deficiencies of American liberalism were also operative, and the teaching appointment Scott Brown briefly held upon the completion of her degree among the all-male faculty at Penn was not renewed. As a result, she set off on a journey across the United States, spending long hours on the train town-watching, listening to residents of Birmingham tell her that "what you read in the papers about us was exaggerated," to isolated towns in what seemed to her an African desert "communicate," and to students as they mobilized for free speech at Berkeley.[17] She arrived in Los Angeles, unmarried, untenured, and untethered from any of the tribal identities that once might have both marked but also secured her.[18] Her response was to immerse herself in her course preparations, through which she sought to anchor her students and herself within a complete and total intellectual order, a goal she was well aware could not be reached but that she thought should be mustered with the "gaiety of despair."[19] The principal record of this effort was a syllabus that sought to construct an all-inclusive pedagogy that would provide a comprehensive explanatory mechanism for urban life.

Certain components of the course reflect the studio structure she developed at Penn, under the influence not only of Gans, but also of David Crane and William Wheaton: a cartographic understanding of urbanism, a sociological view of urban life, and a teamwork approach to studio production.[20] What changed when she taught in and about Los Angeles was the studio's fullness and intensity, an amplitude derived not only from the syllabus's extraordinary length but also from the course's extensive interdisciplinarity, the large number of participants she included, and the array of techniques designed to capture comprehensive views of the city she presented to students. Where she had previously argued that urban form was legible to those reading underlying determinants, the number of these factors multiplied. Her courses had always been interdisciplinary, but the degree and range of engagement with other disciplines exploded across the academy. And fieldwork modeled on what Gans called the participant/observer technique was not new to her teaching, but the field shifted from what was sometimes a single city block in

Figure 2: Denise Scott Brown, Los Angeles, 1966.

Philadelphia, to the entire region of Los Angeles, ranging from Disneyland, to the beach, downtown, and much in between.[21] In order to help her students "watch" this town, she gave countless lectures illustrated by slides, most of which she had taken herself, that show her stepping back from the focus on individuals and singularities and seeking instead to encompass the widest possible angle of vision: taken from the air or a car, these images show freeways cutting through mountains and neighborhoods, houses precariously perched on canyon edges, and agricultural land paved over for parking lots (figs. 1–3).[22] Challenged by the extreme and radically varied conditions of Los Angeles, what had been a nine-page syllabus when she was teaching at Penn became a hundred-page total-design pedagogy.[23]

Form, Forces and Function in Santa Monica was divided into sections including introduction, bibliography, studio organization, research on "definition and determinants of urban form," and multiple design phases to develop creative suggestions "for emerging forces and forms." Tellingly, Scott Brown felt Los Angeles raised questions about urban rather than civic design, the term used at Penn, and she asked her students "What should an Urban Design

Figure 3: Denise Scott Brown, Los Angeles, c. 1967.

Studio in Los Angeles be? What will become of our theories and philosophies as we match them against this urban extremity?"[24] She focused the studio on Santa Monica because it contained these extremes, from topographical to class and race variation, and because the aviation and information industries had made their headquarters there. Santa Monica thus offered students both "a catalog of typical urban glories and pathologies" and also, particularly because of its growing minority populations, a prototype of future urban trends.[25] She provided students with a history of Santa Monica she wrote herself, from "discovery and settlement" in the sixteenth century to more recent but equally "aggressive" policies, especially the freeway completed just a few months before the start of the semester that had "ravaged the historic Negro settlement in Santa Monica."[26] She expected students to study land use patterns, legal frameworks, demography, economics, governmental forms, technologies and transportation systems. Every one of the 132 class sessions had multiple readings, often guest lecturers, and detailed assignments. She instructed students to begin with various forms of data collection and in situ "town-watching" (finding maps, "discriminately scanning" copious amounts

Figure 4: Denise Scott Brown.
Los Angeles, 1967.

of literature, and conducting interviews) and to conclude with "experimental graphic techniques" designed to move from specific data points to generalized problematics.[27] While some of the assignments were rooted in the practices of urban sociology developed at Penn and MIT, she asked students to be attentive to whether or not forms of analysis like Kevin Lynch's "categories for describing perception and imageability" were useful in the Los Angeles of boulevards and freeways.[28] Instead she encouraged students to "experiment with techniques and methods of drawing and photography which give some feeling of the multiplicity and complexity of patterns of activities and structures in the city and of their changes of intensity in space and time."[29]

Scott Brown's emphasis on the need for students to actively participate in the invention of new modes of urban representation was not merely a way for them to learn by doing, but was itself a performance of Scott Brown's theory of urbanism and of the planner. "The problem, and possibilities of cities are so wide and deep that it is impossible for one man to span them ... We need specialists and their depth of knowledge: what we lack is connection."[30] She conceived of the studio, in other words, as she did an aerial photograph; she considered both tools for revealing epistemic nodes and for constituting connective tissues undergirding networks of disciplines and social groups (fig. 4). She drew an extraordinary number of specialists into this web; no fewer than thirty-eight people passed through the studio as jurors, guest lecturers, critics, and resources. Some were old colleagues from Penn, such as Venturi, Crane, and Gans. Others were newer friends, such as the writer and critic Esther McCoy, Scott Brown's neighbor and the only other woman in the group, and Los Angeles–based architects, like Quincy Jones.[31] Two categories of visitors were among the most consequential for the 1966 studio— one with expertise in representational developments within the architectural profession, and the other engaged in political discourses brought from other disciplines.

Visitors whose work focused on visual strategies included Philip Thiel and Peter Kamnitzer. Thiel, an architect who had spent a short time at Berkeley before taking an appointment in University of Washington, presented graphic techniques that incorporated elements learned while studying under Lynch and György Kepes with notation forms used in dance to capture what he considered to be the time-based character of urban experience. Thiel argued that the rapid and dispersed urbanization of cities like Los Angeles had left designers "embarrassed by the lack of both a theory of form and of tools useful in representing the experience of form."[32] Acknowledging that the motion picture might be such a tool but was still too costly, he offered instead a low-tech system "for the continuous representation of architectural and urban space-sequence experiences" that was "parametrically" adaptable to differences in the rate and direction of movement (fig. 5).[33] While he described this technique as related to Sergei Eisenstein's concept of vertical montage, he also argued that cities, unlike films, could not and should not control the attention of the audience as a film director did and therefore required representational tools that were not predetermined by a single director/planner. His manually calculable system for parametric notation was instead intended to privilege precisely a horizontal approach to urban planning.

Peter Kamnitzer used radically different tools to pursue similar goals (fig. 6). A colleague of Scott Brown's on the small UCLA faculty, Kamnitzer was then just starting work with NASA and GE on what would become "City-Scape,"

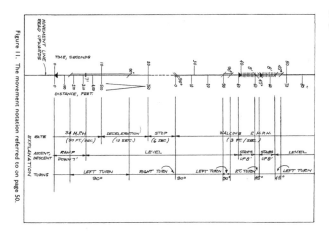

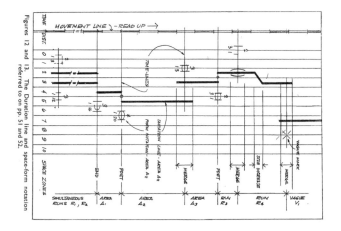

a high-tech digital simulation of urban experience intended to enable planners creatively to manage the complexities of modern buildings and cities.[34] Like Thiel and Scott Brown, Kamnitzer focused on the freeway as the principal means of, in this case digital, participatory "town-watching," deploying a "joystick" rather than camera or pencil as the user's means of navigation. The goal was to enable planners, also conceived of as stand-ins for city-dwellers, to make real-time decisions about urban mobility. Although they each worked

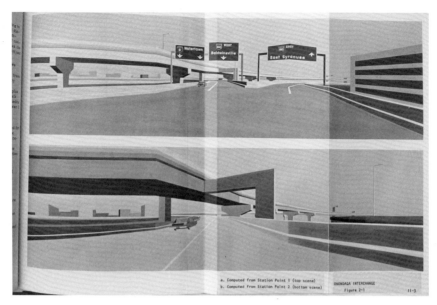

Figure 6: Peter Kamnitzer, *Onandaga Freeway Interchange,* 1969, foldout color plate.

through different visual media (fig. 7), Scott Brown, Thiel, and Kamnitzer all took students on simulated drives through the city, optimistically imagining that these new tools could "provoke the 'next creative leap'" and "offer a new kind of planning process that may one day lead us ... towards a truly participatory form of planning."[35]

The second set of especially consequential participants in the studio were from other departments across the UCLA campus, including law, sociology, and engineering. With them, Scott Brown discussed a range of methodological rather than visual questions. For example, she asked sociologists for feedback on interview techniques, because, as she warned students, some interviewees would be understandably wary of urban planners, having suffered at the hands of urban renewal and its "good intentions." Eventually, treating the syllabus like a manuscript in a prepublication phase, she invited these colleagues to comment on the draft. William Mosher, a transportation engineer—who also focused on participatory planning and freeways, using photography

Figure 7: Denise Scott Brown, Los Angeles, 1967.

to study the impact of movement and individual decision-making in automotive safety—consistently prodded Scott Brown to further expand her point of view and to more explicitly address the politics of good intentions (fig. 8). He pressed her to avoid thinking regionally and to develop what he called a world view. He insisted that the scope of urban consideration should include issues of war, emancipation, and civil rights. He added notes on the growing importance of working mothers and the rights of women to urban planning, and on the problematic nature of planning for public happiness: "this is not necessarily achieved by elimination of public squalor. Some subgroups of society have NO desire to live in the manner those in power plan for. Classic examples are the attempts to change living habits of the American Indians and the attempt to change the living standards in our Appalachian Region."[36] The sociologist Peter Orleans was even more pointed about the need critically to examine the mechanisms controlling things like land use. He underscored that students should consider how "values expressed in physical form [are] constrained by

Figure 8: UCLA Institute for Transportation and Traffic Engineering, collision photograph (undated).

existent *opportunities*," and told Scott Brown that "constraints on market allocation through … racial prejudices make our system more like the tribal one than you suggest."[37] Given that Orleans coedited the monumental volume *Race, Change, and Urban Society* just a few years later, it comes as no surprise that when Scott Brown instructed students to make comparative analyses of Century City and Santa Monica, Orleans asked, "how about Watts?"[38] What is, however, surprising is that not only did Scott Brown solicit this robust feedback, but that she included the most critical comments as marginalia in the final syllabus, making them extra visible with red ink (fig. 9). Her explicit goal in doing so was to avoid presenting "a spurious and dull unity," but it also implicitly transformed the syllabus itself into a demonstration of the multiplicity and complexity of patterns that she was seeking to present as constituting the city and the dialogic and participatory structure of good urban planning.[39] Scott Brown kept her teaching materials in Oxford Pressboard Report binders with metal prongs and multiple tabs, enabling her to add, delete, and reorganize materials and to ensure that the pedagogy was as plastic and performative as the city being taught. Students too were required to produce "reports" containing text and copious photographs and drawings in this same format and to submit them in fifty ditto copies. The studio's entire output was, in effect, a collectively produced, polyvocal publication. Scott Brown's course triggered an expansive debate, identified new channels of discourse, and relied on duplicative media as a mode of dissemination, making the studio output into a "little magazine" of the very kind she wrote about in one of her first published essays.[40] Although her "book" on urban planning was largely written but did not find a publisher, what she could do in the fall of 1966 was clip and ditto her *Form, Forces and Function in Santa Monica* into provisional existence.[41]

What other existences were altered by Scott Brown's year in Los Angeles may never be fully known, because by 1967 she had returned to Pennsylvania, where the university was still committed to civic design and to a rapidly conventionalizing model of planning and its allied disciplines; to Philadelphia, a city that bore the imprint of an urban tradition alien to Los Angeles; and to married life, rooted in both professional and personal partnerships. While this context opened new opportunities for Scott Brown, it also closed others in ways that make clear the specific constraints and possibilities in which she operated during her short but pivotal California sojourn of 1966. For example, the structural differences between her activities as coauthor and informal publisher of *Form, Forces and Function in Santa Monica* and those available to Venturi at the same historical moment are worth underscoring: *Complexity and Contradiction in Architecture* was also published in 1966, but with the support of MoMA, the Graham Foundation, the American Academy in Rome, and a host of assistants. Furthermore, elegantly understated in its self-referential and highly "authored" rhetoric, *Complexity and Contradiction* inserts Venturi's work into a long lineage of famously heroic architects and attends almost exclusively to high culture, despite his later interest in popular tastes.[42] *Form, Forces and Function in Santa Monica*, instead, is participatory and horizontal in its authorship, informal in its modes of production, self-critical, and polysemous in its engagement with different social groups

5. THE ECONOMY
   4 people

The economic form of society as it determines urban form.

Relevance

The economy is a set of interrelated social units through which goods and services are produced, distributed and consumed, and through which a level of material well-being is achieved by the society. The nature of the relation between units is the "form" of the economy and it is apparent that this relation will be different for a subsistence economy, where everything that is consumed by a family is produced by it in and around the home, and an exchange economy, where, in its most complex form, the production and distribution of a single good may be the result of a network of related actions occurring over a vast area, and using a money system to ease the exchanges which occur along the way. Obviously the results for urban form of two such different economic forms as the subsistence economy and the money exchange economy are vastly different.

The concept of the so-called "highest and best use" of land relates to our society's approach; however, what values of society led to this concept? and perhaps the tribal tradition approach offers advantages lost in our present approach. W.M.

??? L.B. and P.O. Government is very much involved in land allocation, "market mechanism" notwithstanding. L.B.

In addition, because, in our society, land is allocated primarily by the operation of a land market, where the highest bidder usually prevails (rather than by, say, tribal tradition or government fiat), there is a good case to be made for the economic determinants as the most broadly pervasive of determinants: the matrix within which other determinants—topography, technology, "sentiment and symbolism," "planning"—appear as "distorting" elements, around which the economic forces reassemble themselves in altered form.   Explain. L.B.

Constraints on market allocation through, for example, racial prejudice, make our system more like the tribal one than you suggest. P.O.

And finally, amongst the social scientists, the urban land economists and their relatives, the regional scientists, have given by far the most rigorous thought to the relation between human behavior and urban form, and are furthest in their attempts to produce "models of rationality" (i.e., systematized mathematical statements on human behavior) which relate human behavior to use of the land. How far are these groups really advanced in their modeling? Most such tools are very limited in their capability and require many simplifying assumptions which reduce their reliability to a very questionable level. W.M.

An old-fashioned term. Leave out "land"—nowadays we're interested more in other aspects of the urban economy than we are in land. L.B.

-20-

Figure 9: Denise Scott Brown, Urban Design 401, *Form, Forces and Function in Santa Monica,* UCLA, Syllabus, 1966.

and cultural forms. Finally, rather than cynically ironic or naively hopeful, what historians now commonly consider pervasive misjudgments made by architects during the 1960s, Scott Brown's text is tinged with the "gaiety of despair" of a woman with much to say and none of the institutional forms of support through which to say it.

Lack of certain kinds of opportunity is only one of the many historical forces that came together to shape Scott Brown's work and that continue to shape its reception. In 1966, she did not receive approbation from Vincent Scully, who wrote the introduction to *Complexity and Contradiction* and became a key force both in maximizing Venturi's identification as the the seminal author of architectural postmodernism and in minimizing Scott Brown's contribution to their collaboration for decades. Instead of receiving their support, Scott Brown was harassed by many of her male colleagues, particularly during the time she spent in Los Angeles.[43] On the one hand, while women are still harassed in the workplace, some have managed to use the institutional power that women like Scott Brown worked to generate in order to make sure that "Venturi" is never again used as a shorthand for their cocreated work. On the other hand, some scholars have argued that because she was South African, she should have done more to address race and blackness in architecture.[44] These revisions are welcome, but also have important limitations. What Scott Brown did in 1966 does not live up to current standards of accountability for the racialized structure of the architectural academy and profession. For example, in a way that would be recognized as objectionable today, she appropriated the language of Martin Luther King when she changed the name of an assignment that had been "personal utopia" when teaching students in 1963 Philadelphia to "I have a dream" when teaching in post–Watts revolt Los Angeles.[45] Nevertheless, assessing this history of appropriation and indirection using only contemporary metrics anachronistically occludes the context informing the actions that were available to her and that she indeed took. Scott Brown made space for male colleagues, less vulnerable (if only by virtue of their gender) than she, to critique both the academy and the profession. She underscored Orleans's explicit address to the racialization of urban planning in her syllabus and embedded the problem in her pedagogy. It is also worth noting, in fact, that Orleans, the most outspoken of her colleagues about the failures of architecture design and planning to produce positive social change, responded to the experience of collaborating with Scott Brown by deciding that the best way he could contribute to the question of race and urban society was to become an architect.[46]

It may, however, not be the critics but those with the very best intention of giving credit where credit is due who risk overwriting the most characteristic, and potentially still transformative, aspect of her work and working method. During this anomalously unfettered period of time, Scott Brown strove tirelessly to be collaborative and polyvocal, to engage critique and to avoid what she feared was the intrinsic vanity of the single architect. She insisted that her students produce workmanlike drawings and avoid over-aestheticized design: "no false art," she exclaimed.[47] And she showed them how to do this by backing away from single objects beautifully represented in order to see the collective terrain in its often-grim reality, to town-watch in ways that inevitably forced the abstraction of visual analysis to bump up against the violence of the nightly news. She was nothing if not workmanlike, as the labor she invested in her teaching materials attests, and she used photography in a similarly workmanlike way. She recognized that her mode of operating through maps, detailed histories, and long conversations would appear to others as *dull*, particularly duller than the spectacular register of TV.[48] She may not have anticipated, however, for how long these deliberately and necessarily unspectacular modes of operating would limit her own visibility to future historians of architecture still looking for spectacle and valuing only "influence."

Although a handful of iconic photographs have been repeatedly extracted from the body of research that they constitute, they prove something self-evident: that Scott Brown was a woman cultivated by progressive education in the liberal arts who could use her well-trained eye to produce images dense with appeal to other similarly well-trained eyes. But this mutually affirming rapport overlooks the fact that, as an archive, her photographic corpus is largely made up of an astonishing number of unformal images taken from a train, on a road, or in a plane; images that move away from framed views of things and that instead seek patterns within the messy overlap of human activity and the surface of the earth. These are images for and of research rather than display, evidence of Scott Brown's commitment to studio as a collective knowledge-producing instrument and of her investment in the broad view that gave rise to interdisciplinarity as a method and a value. Town-watching was a strategy that inevitably entangled the passive academic observer with the violence televised on the evening news and actively risked the appeal of eidetic clarity and singularity in pursuit of comprehensiveness and participation. Though efforts to give credit are certainly overdue, just as are calls for accountability, both risk pressing Scott Brown's work into molds of authorship and artistic value that were simultaneously unavailable to her and that she worked hard to resist. New scrutiny reveals that aspects of her contributions do not meet today's standards, but it also succumbs to ideological overdetermination when it ahistorically turns her into the type of heroic figure she chose not to be and that, given her positioning, she could not have been in 1966 Los Angeles.

Notes

1 More and less complete copies of the syllabus for UCLA course 401, as taught in Fall 1966, are held in the university archives at UCLA, Berkeley, and in the Architectural Archives, University of Pennsylvania. The course title varies within these teaching materials, sometimes appearing as *Form, Forces and Function in Santa Monica* and at others as *Form, Forces and Functions in Santa Monica* ("functions" in plural). The most complete record of the course is located at Penn, where the syllabus is supplemented by binders containing student work and letters evaluating the course, seemingly in support of a tenure review. Because most references to the course title in this larger dossier use the singular, this and all further citations will use the singular and will refer to the binder at Penn, which has not yet been fully incorporated into the finding aid but is held in, and used here by courtesy of, the Denise Scott Brown Teaching Records, Venturi Scott Brown Collection, by the gift of Robert Venturi and Denise Scott Brown, at the Architectural Archives of the University of Pennsylvania, Philadelphia (hereafter cited as DSBTR, VSBC, AAUP).

2 See Wheeler, "More Than the Western Sky," 11–26. On the role of TV in the coverage of the race revolts in Philadelphia and the Guild House, designed by Venturi, before Scott Brown joined the firm, see my "Oh My Aching Antenna."

3 Scott Brown wrote a series of letters to "friends and family" documenting her journey to the West Coast and her time at Berkeley. In one, dated August 21, 1965, she wrote "early in September, I shall be moving to Los Angeles and hope to start work there soon after." She began teaching at UCLA in the fall of 1966. These letters are reproduced in my *Everything Loose Will Land*, 82–90. The letters also include descriptions of her first visits to Las Vegas.

4 "Town-watching" first appears on page 5 of "Introduction," "UCLA 401," DSBTR, VSBC, AAUP, but reappears throughout.

5 Scott Brown describes Los Angeles as in the process of "nucleating," a condition of multicenteredness that Bernard Tschumi, just a few years later and working with similar planning documents but using them to produce a radically more overt political critique, described as organized around bounded sanctuaries. See his "Sanctuaries," 575–90. This quality made Los Angeles the primary exemplar of post-metropolitan urbanism and eventually the shared focus of the so-called postmodern geographers, many of whom, like Edward Soja, also taught at UCLA. Scott Brown's remarks about LA are part of a section entitled City of Change, "Phase III, Part A," 9, "UCLA 401," DSBTR, VSBC, AAUP. Scott Brown was particularly interested in why Douglas Aircraft and the Rand corporation chose Santa Monica for their HQs. On the complex military see Leslie, *The Cold War*.

6 Kimberlé Crenshaw coined the term "intersectionality" to underscore the multiple forms of inequality that operate simultaneously in determining the conditions of possibility for women of color, including the experience of their own identity. Because the conditioning factors of race, immigration status, gender, and class that shaped Scott Brown's possibilities in 1965–66 were not all rooted in oppression and discrimination, I use "positionality" as the better term for situating her within her historical context. See Crenshaw, "Mapping the margins," 1241–1299.

7 Scott Brown has given many interviews on her personal and intellectual history in which she describes her appreciation for Santa Monica, particularly the beach culture and because she and Venturi were married at her Ocean Park home. She has not written about her time at UCLA in particular. While her interviews are scattered among a wide variety of publications and websites, the best source for her account of herself is her collected essays, *Having Words*.

8 Although disentangling their respective contributions to what eventually became a lifetime of collaboration is futile, it does seem to be the case that Venturi's interest in popular culture and Americana grew stronger once they started to work together. Similarly, although they both recognized that contemporary communication systems were transforming American society and architecture, his interest in the early 1960s was more metaphorical, where hers was more operational. For example, while presenting the Guild House in a lecture to students at Yale, he described the windows of the rear elevation as being like an IBM punch card, while Scott Brown described the illuminated signs of small towns in the desert as acts of communication: "Then there were the towns. All you notice is a series of bright billboards, neon

signs & TV antennae ... The buildings are nondescript, sunk into the landscape. The towns appear, then as nothing other than communication." Scott Brown, "Letter to Friends, April 26, 1965," in Lavin, *Everything Loose Will Land*, 88. On Venturi's lecture at Yale, see my *Architecture Itself and Other Postmodernization Effects*, 95–99.

9   The details of this itinerary can be reconstructed through her letters, cited above.

10   Some of the following discussion is based on two extensive interviews I conducted with Scott Brown on July 24 and August 14, 2021. Ayala Levin's essay on Scott Brown and the southern settler-colonial conditions that shaped her views of architecture in the United States appeared after this essay was in press. See Ayala Levin, "Learning from Johannesburg: Unpacking Denise Scott Brown's South African View of Las Vegas," 235–248.

11   On South Africa, see Dubow, *A Commonwealth of Knowledge*; Shimoni, "South African Jews and the Apartheid Crisis," 3–58; Caplan, *South African Jews in London*. On Witwatersrand, see Shear, *WITS: A University in the Apartheid Era*, and Murray, *Wits, the "Open" Years: a History of the University of Witwatersrand, 1939–1959*.

12   When I asked if she had participated in the resistance movement while a university student and if not why, Scott Brown stated, "I was afraid." AnnMarie Wolpe (née Kantor), one of the better-known women activists at Witwatersrand, left South Africa without her children following a particularly terrifying arrest and interrogation. She describes this experience, as well as the links between her activism and that of her husband, Harold Wolpe, in her autobiography, *The Long Way Home*.

13   Scott Brown now describes her early interest in architecture as generated by her desire to participate in "building a just South Africa." This specific vocabulary, now a common descriptor of anti-apartheid goals and used by Scott Brown in *Having Words*, for example, is, as far as I have been able to determine, an *ex post facto* turn of phrase with respect to her move to London. As is well known, interest in American pop culture was widespread among English architects at the time and was particularly strong among the Independent Group and their circle, which of course included the Smithsons and Reyner Banham.

14   See Roediger, *Working Toward Whiteness*. Gans eventually discussed this issue in his own work. See Gans, "Racialization and Racialization Research." For introductions to planning history and to the history of architectural pedagogy, see Rodwin and Sanyal, *The Profession of City Planning*, and Ockman and Williamson, *Architecture School*.

15   In her essay "Planning the Powder Room," published in 1967 but conceived earlier, Scott Brown acknowledges that the design of women's restrooms is a "delicate" subject requiring the "delicacy of a lady." However, and despite the fact that the essay was written in order to invite men to look into such spaces, she assumes what she calls the position of an "unrecalcitrant functionalist of the 1930s type," a type known to be deliberately gender-neutral. The essay is republished in *Having Words*, 128–135. Scott Brown, who had married Robert Scott Brown in 1955, was suddenly widowed when he was killed in a car accident in 1959. The unimaginable trauma of this event was exacerbated by the way becoming unmarried increasingly made her a target of sexual harassment by her colleagues. This appears to have been especially the case in Los Angeles, where few of her colleagues had known her during the first years of her grief and mourning.

16   For her own account of the role of art education in her journey as an immigrant, see her "Invention and Tradition in the Making of American Place" (1986), reprinted in *Having Words*, 5–21.

17   Although her language is typically oblique, I assume that in a letter, written January 31, 1965, she is referring to comments made to her by white architects in Birmingham (she mostly met and was given tours by local architects somehow or other connected to Penn) about the Birmingham confrontation of 1963, part of her repeated rediscovery of apartheid by another name in the United States. For the letter, see Lavin, *Everything Loose Will Land*, 83.

18   Scott Brown often discusses tribal identity as it shaped her childhood in South Africa. Peter Orleans also cites her use of this term. See below.

19   She describes the studio task as certainly impossible and as such requiring a sense of adventure, courage and "gaiety of despair." *Phase II*, 41, "UCLA 401," DSBTR, VSBC, AAUP.

20   There is of course a substantial literature on the history of urban planning: here I mention only Mumford, *Defining Urban Design*; Hein, *The Routledge*

Handbook of Planning History; Banerjee and Loukaitou-Sideris, *Companion to Urban Design; and* Jaynes et al., *"The Chicago School and the Roots of Urban Ethnography."* As she moved farther from Penn, Scott Brown's vocabulary shifted. Not only did she reject the term "civic design" that was used at Penn, but her terms for describing the structure and nature of teamwork also shifted. For example, at Penn, she gave some students the role of "captains" and others "scribes," and defined the overall system as "a limited democracy." This language of hierarchical labor is eliminated in the UCLA syllabus in favor of more neutral terms such as "organizer." See "Studio Organization," 1–3, "UCLA 401," DSBTR, VSBC, AAUP. See also the syllabus for CP503, 7, taught at Penn in 1963.

21 For more on the territorial scope addressed in Scott Brown's teaching, see Lee Ann Custer's essay in this volume.

22 These images are the visual analog to her definition of the planner as the person who is "disillusioned with the single architect working on a single lot," and who endeavors "to overcome our tendency, as architects, to concern ourselves with the isolated building." See CP503, 3 and "II," 51, "UCLA 401," DSBTR, VSBC, AAUP.

23 In fact, some of her visitors found her dogged pursuit of comprehensiveness too much. Leland S. Burns, for example, who would become one of the most influential scholars of modern housing economics and housing policy and would eventually join the UCLA Planning faculty in 1968, wrote a tongue-in-cheek "review" of her course that calculated intellectual output and exhaustion over the course of a day of juries, complete with a chart of the entropic loss of focus. He wrote "By means of a very clever decide, concealed on my person yesterday, I was able to make some rather precise estimate of my 'phase-out rate' and 'productivity rate,'... and have plotted the results on the attached graph ... I recommend holding each presentation to a fixed time period, rigorously enforced (perhaps with a timer equipped with frightening alarm.) It seems to me that this sort of discipline is part of training for the professional world as well." See Lee Burns, letter to Prof. Denise Scott Brown, November 10, 1966, in "Supportive Material," "UCLA 401," DSBTR, VSBC, AAUP.

24 "Introduction," 7, "UCLA 401," DSBTR, AAUP.

25 See Item E, part I, October 3, 1966, "Outline: Introduction to Santa Monica," 2, "UCLA 401," DSBTR, VSBC, AAUP.

26 See Item E, part I, October 3, 1966, "Outline: Introduction to Santa Monica," 6, "UCLA 401," DSBTR, VSBC, AAUP.

27 See Phase I, "The Definition of Urban Form," 2, "UCLA 401," DSBTR, VSBC, AAUP.

28 See Phase I, "The Definition of Urban Form," 4, "UCLA 401," DSBTR, VSBC, AAUP.

29 See Phase I, "The Definition of Urban Form," 10, "UCLA 401," DSBTR, VSBC, AAUP.

30 See "Introduction," 5, "UCLA 401," DSBTR, VSBC, AAUP. This definition is not unique to the UCLA syllabus and appears in most of her teaching materials from 1963 on.

31 Although she and McCoy were neighbors, friends, and colleagues, and although Scott Brown later wrote of their friendship in positive terms, they had a falling out. McCoy wrote a biting letter to Scott Brown in response to Scott Brown's essay about her. Not only did McCoy feel that Scott Brown had falsely represented her as financially dependent on men, in this case specifically on alimony from her ex-husband, but McCoy was deeply upset that Scott Brown, just like the men on the UCLA faculty, had not valued McCoy's work. McCoy wrote that she discovered "soon after we met that you had not read any of my three published books and had no comments on my writing on architecture for American and Italian journals." See the letter from McCoy to Scott Brown, February 6, 1989, Box 14, Folder 4: Denise Scott Brown, "Knowing Esther McCoy" in "Esther McCoy papers, Archives of American Art." On McCoy, see Meyer and Morgan, *Sympathetic Seeing*.

32 See Thiel, "An Experiment in Space Notation," 131, 783, and his "A Sequence-Experience Notation for Architectural and Urban Spaces," 33–52. Thiel would eventually also publish *Visual Awareness and Design*, and *People, Paths, and Purposes*.

33 See "A Sequence-Experience Notation," 34 and 50.

34 On Kamnitzer, see Roth, "Software Epigenetics and Architectures of Life"; de Monchaux, *Spacesuit: Fashioning Apollo*; and my *Everything Loose Will Land*, 309.

35 Kamnitzer, "Computer Aid to Design," 508.

36 See Phase II, "Determinants of Urban Form," Oct. 17, 1966, 26, "UCLA 401," DSBTR, VSBC, AAUP. See also the following note Mosher added: "Perhaps

a resurgence of dwelling in the central city could occur if the needs of the 'modern' family were provided for in parks, recreation, child care, privacy, etc. This relates to the large influx of 'mothers' into the working force." Phase II, 14, "UCLA 401," DSBTR, VSBC, AAUP.

37 See Phase II, "Determinants of Urban Form," October 17, 1966, 9, his emphasis; and 20, "UCLA 401," DSBTR, VSBC, AAUP.

38 Phase II, "Determinants of Urban Form," October 17, 1966, 24, "UCLA 401," DSBTR, VSBC, AAUP. See also, Orleans and Ellis, Race, Change, and Urban Society. It must be noted that most of the photographs taken by Scott Brown in Watts focus on the Watts Tower and not on the neighborhood in general.

39 Phase II, "Determinants of Urban Form," October 17, 1966, 6, "UCLA 401," DSBTR, VSBC, AAUP.

40 See Scott Brown, "Little Magazines in Architecture and Urbanism," 223–233.

41 Departmental records from the School of Architecture and Urban Planning at UCLA contain some material related to Scott Brown's tenure and promotion case that refer to a manuscript. On alternative publications during this period, see Colomina, Buckley, and Grau, Clip, Stamp, Fold: the Radical Architecture of Little Magazines, 196x to 197x, and Buckley, Graphic Assembly.

42 On Venturi and historical privilege, see Massey, "Review: Power and Privilege," 497–498.

43 During my interview with Scott Brown, she carefully and with great detail described the almost constant assault she was under while at UCLA from most of her male colleagues, including her Dean, senior colleagues from other Departments, as well as the members of her own faculty.

44 See for example, Choi, "Black Architectures." For recent discussions of race and its embeddedness in modern architecture, see Cheng, Davis, and Wilson, Race and Modern Architecture and Davis, Building Character.

45 Phase III Part A, 13, "UCLA 401," DSBTR, VSBC, AAUP.

46 Although Orleans was an associate professor at UCLA, he left his position to pursue an architecture degree at the University of Colorado, Denver.

47 In describing the format of student reports, she wrote "this will take two forms, a written-and-illustrated report and a verbal, slide-and-magic-lantern illustrated group lecture [...] It should be in Ditto form

and illustrated copiously by photographs or drawings or both. [...] Drawings should be workman-like affairs designed to inform not evade—no false 'art.' The same with the photographs." Phase III Part A, 40, "UCLA 401," DSBTR, VSBC, AAUP. This requirement and description were consistent across all her teaching at Penn, Berkeley, and UCLA.

48 The "dullness" of the materials needed by the urban planner to non-planners in general, and architects in particular, is something she mentions frequently. To give just one example, she wrote in the introduction to the studio: "if he [the urban designer] continues to find the world of the sociologist 'very dull' ... if the joy of numbers and their uncertainty, or the mechanics of the decision-making processes ... remain foreign to him; if he believes ecology is to do only with plants and flowers, and climate is something we have to overcome with mechanical systems; then I'm afraid he is the one who is stuffy and dull" (her emphasis). "Introduction," 4, "UCLA 401," DSBTR, VSBC, AAUP.

Figure 1: Denise Scott Brown, 1960s. The concertina effect of signage on the active South Street.

With Lots of Love: South Street, 1968–1972

Sarah Moses

In 1946, the Philadelphia Planning Commission Executive Director Robert Mitchell "picked up a pencil and drew a line across a map. That line became the Crosstown Expressway," which was to complete a circuit about Center City, Philadelphia, that the Schuylkill, Delaware, and Vine Street Expressways were otherwise to form.[1] In 1955, the route was drawn as a 2.8-mile, eight-lane depressed highway to supersede South and Bainbridge streets. Erasure of streets on the Crosstown route was almost certain; residents were sent notice from the Department of Highways that cast their eventual ejection as a requirement.[2] In 1967, as the specter of the Crosstown Expressway drove disinvestment in the area that was under threat of obliteration, activist Alice Lipscomb and civic organizer George Dukes, both Black Seventh Ward residents, co-founded the Citizens' Committee to Preserve and Develop the Crosstown Community (CCPDCC) to link disparate constituents—the Crosstown Community—in their opposition to the Crosstown Expressway scheme. In 1968, the Crosstown Community sought to redirect its energies from opposition to active rehabilitation of the corridor and contracted with the office Venturi and Rauch, in the person of Denise Scott Brown, to devise a counterplan to the Expressway.[3]

Scott Brown set her wayward eye on South Street, her camera an instrument to dismantle fictions of the former Seventh Ward as "Hell's Acre."[4] Her photographs capture a streetscape that both invites and gratifies a viewer's repeat glance with vignettes that operate, almost, as metaphors: Half-hidden but ebullient ornamentation laces the underbellies of storefront vaults; signage reassures passersby that imperfect shoes in neat arrangement are "Fine Rejects"; butcher shops advertise chitterlings, pigs' feet, and neck bones and offer discounts to church parties—soul food staples to meet the work of the soul; and a pile of storefront detritus uplifts a poster on which a caricature of Uncle Sam proclaims, in text just visible beneath castoff material: "There's no place just like this place anywhere near this place so this must be *the place*."[5]

That signpost sentiment was not written with reference to South Street but might as well have been. South Street, as Cedar Street, was drawn as the southmost frontier of the City of Philadelphia in 1683, the limen between the cartographer's aspirational gridiron and blank "sylvania."[6] From the 1790s, South Street became home to free Blacks in the province of institutions built to rebut exclusion and discrimination elsewhere; after emancipation and in the Great Migration, influxes of Black migrants came to augment the Black communities in the Seventh Ward.[7] From the 1830s, as immigrants to Philadelphia sought work on the waterfront or in Washington Avenue manufactories, successive enclaves made homes on South Street.[8] From the mid-1910s, South Street was a bastion of Black commerce and entertainment, manifest in iconic venues like the Standard and Royal theaters; the closure of the latter in 1970 was in part a consequence of disinvestment due to the longtime threat of South Street's clearance for construction of the Crosstown Expressway.[9]

Scott Brown's South Street plan was contemporaneous with, and invites comparison to, the better-known work in Las Vegas. In another of her photographs of South Street, the concertina effect of signage—billboards for groceries, patent medicine, watch repairs, hardware, records, and shoes, alongside imperative curbside communiqués to automobile users—offers a glimmer of the fascinations that characterize *Learning from Las Vegas*.[10] The South Street contract for the Venturi and Rauch office came with Crosstown Community advisor Janet Scheff Reiner's incisive remark: "If you can like Las Vegas, we trust you not to neaten up South Street at the expense of its people."[11] In interviews and publications, Scott Brown makes repeat reference to her "African view of Las Vegas," an inducement to "learn from the landscape" as a result of an awareness of a dominant valuation of culture at odds with a homegrown ethos—in her experience of South Africa, "between the polite, England-dominated views of what art, landscape, and culture should be and those derived from what was actually around us, in my case the veld, Johannesburg, and African cultures as they hit the city."[12] As in the Las Vegas work,

Scott Brown's appreciation of what *was* rather than what *ought to be* saturates the minimum intervention strategies of the South Street counterplan. Although Venturi and Scott Brown were then residents of the Society Hill Towers, built as the centerpiece of a slum clearance and redevelopment scheme due north of South Street, their engagement with South Street was intimate; the pair were then dependent on the Venturi Fruit and Produce business at 1430 South Street—an inheritance from Robert Venturi's father—for an income.[13] For their firm, the commission was a potential generator of future business, a milestone as "the first community project we undertook as practitioners not academics," and a test site for theories about Main Street.[14] In reminiscences, Scott Brown frames South Street as "a commercial strip at the scale of Main Street. It could, in fact, be called the main street of Philadelphia's center city black community."[15]

In public testimonies, opponents to the Crosstown Expressway scheme drew attention to its disparate impact on Black residents. Construction of the Crosstown was liable to displace 6,000 or more individuals, 90% of whom were Black.[16] In 1964, the real-estate broker George Scott made repeat reference to the Crosstown Expressway as Philadelphia's "Mason–Dixon Line," a demarcation liable to entrench the abuse of the Black populace to its south.[17] Opposition to the Expressway in public hearings in May 1964 came mere months before a Black citizens' revolt to counter police violence in North Philadelphia—one of the first in the series of actions across the United States that rose to a zenith in the "Long, Hot Summer" of 1967. In 1967, objections to a store owner's discrimination against Black customers on South Street were met with injunctions to obstruct rallies on the street; then-Commissioner of Police Frank Rizzo oversaw the deployment of 500 police officers in riot suits to quash nascent insurgence in the area.[18] In one of Scott Brown's photographs of South Street, the watchwords "Black Power" writhe across a vacant storefront in aerosol paint; a viewer senses that, invisible to the camera, the assertion of Black presence under peril of abuse and obliteration render the air electric (fig. 2). Scott Brown later wrote that, on South Street and in other early appointments, "Social change and the unrest that went with it dogged my steps in every place. Fortuitously the lessons learned in one tied neatly to the next,

Figure 2: Denise Scott Brown, 1960s. An assertion of Black presence in the form of Black Power graffiti.

Figure 3: Denise Scott Brown, 1960s. The commercial character and characteristic vernacular architecture of the South Street "strip" in the late 1960s.

and many questions resolved themselves in planning school ... during the Civil Rights movement."[19]

One aspiration of pro-Crosstown Expressway forces was to have the thoroughfare serve as a conduit for Philadelphia's Bicentennial celebration in 1976.[20] In Scott Brown's prose, a clear conception of the Bicentennial as an occasion to celebrate Black histories in Philadelphia is evident. The first page of her counterplan asserts: "We recommend that [South Street's] importance historically and culturally to immigrant groups and particularly, today, to Negro culture, be spelled out for the Bicentennial in a manner that matches Society Hill."[21] In addition to measures to ensure residents' access to health care, education, recreation, and commerce, the document proposes the institution of a "Museum of Slavery," a "Museum of Immigrant Culture," and "a Promenade of Negro Culture and History."[22] Scott Brown's research shows a consideration of historic preservation tactics and mechanisms to formalize the latter—this before the discipline of heritage conservation was taught in American universities. The plan itself prioritizes the involvement of South Street

161

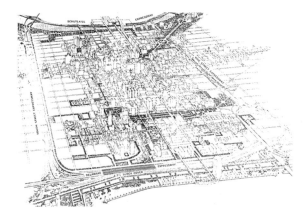

Figure 4: 1961 bird's-eye view of the proposed "ring road" to encircle Center City, Philadelphia. The "South Street Express-way," which became the Crosstown Expressway, is at the left.

residents in rehabilitation efforts, with specific reference to Black business ownership.[23] One reporter's conclusion from Scott Brown's presentation of the plan was that "'conservative surgery' can still save the life of South Street—just in time to give it a major role in the Bicentennial celebration as a model thoroughfare of Negro culture, past and present."[24] Another wrote: "The plan is civic design of such a sensitive and sensible sort that it is radical."[25]

In his iconoclastic sociological work, *The Philadelphia Negro* (1899), W.E.B. Du Bois—then a resident of a settlement house one half block north of South Street—wrote of the Seventh Ward: "On its face this slum is noisy and dissipated, but not brutal ... the stranger can usually walk about here day and night with little fear of being molested, if he be not too inquisitive."[26] Echoes of Du Bois are audible in Scott Brown's characterization of South Street in 1971: "For all its decay and for all the evidence of social and individual distress, South Street is a lively, lovely piece of city, more capable of endearing itself to the imagination than the more famous but less vital Society Hill area bordering it."[27] Scott Brown's reverence for South Street as it was is evident in the qualities of her photographs—comedic or poetic kismet, singular alignments, tenderness made immortal on film—and in her incorporation of design elements then extant on South Street in her parti. Her sketch of West Center, one of the service nodes she proposes at the start of the plan, orients the viewer's vista above a fire hydrant akin to the ones that rise from sidewalks throughout

Figure 5: Counterplan proposal illustration of West Center, a service node. Scott Brown's attention to the South Street context is evident in her rendering of vernacular row houses and inclusion of a then-extant storefront church, the Unity Church.

her photographs; outlines South Street's vernacular row houses with their telltale fire escapes, sills, and cornice brackets; and incorporates, adjacent to the center's entrance, a storefront church—the Unity Church, in fact, that appears in her photographs (fig. 5).[28] Scott Brown later wrote, "Our drawings and maps, although meager because of lack of funds, proved evocative; they were perhaps better than more explicit drawings since people could fill them with their own dreams."[29]

A dreamscape requires imagination to activate; even more so, it requires time, a resource the pragmatic Crosstown Community activists were unable to lavish. The dreamscape became subject to refinement with coalition members' input, as Scott Brown wrote:

> I was surprised when I learned the community did not wish my transportation plan to be shown ... The community vetoed one other scheme: some architects recommended getting donations of paint and painting all the side walls of houses where buildings had been demolished on the street. The community said "If we had enough people with the ability to organize doing that, why would we waste their time on something so futile? We need them for other things such as banging on the mayor's door."[30]

This respectful repartee between the advocates and Scott Brown was the fundament of successive iterations of the work: "So I began to learn interesting and important lessons in planning from the members of this low-income, black community, helped by their brilliant leader Alice Lipscomb and their brilliant and merry Lawyer, Robert Sugarman."[31] Scott Brown came to recognize her value not as an impassive visioner but as a collaborator; rather than dominate the conversation under the aegis of her expertise, Scott Brown put her credentials to use in her role as an interlocutor: "Our value to the committee now was that, as professionals, we could say with authority that the area had architectural value and potential and deserved preservation."[32] In a 2013 interview, Scott Brown reflects on the South Street work: "I got my best lessons in urban planning, I would say, from that low-income community, from the way they thought and the canny way they could see their own needs."[33]

Scott Brown's radical, minimum-intervention, incremental growth proposal can be seen as an embodiment of Jane Jacobs's exhortation: "The least we can do is to respect—in the deepest sense—strips of chaos that have a weird wisdom of their own not yet encompassed in our concept of urban order."[34] From her work on South Street, Scott Brown came to see that "beauty could emerge from the existing fabric and that a not-too-apparent order should be sought from within instead of an easy one imposed from above."[35] For Scott Brown, the work on South Street was a transformative, foundational event in her development as a practitioner.

The South Street counterplan was not built; nonetheless, its development from 1968 to 1972 bespeaks collaboration, communion, and, more than appreciation, celebration. In interviews, Scott Brown repeats that the work was done "with lots of love" and with "heart and soul,"[36] a remarkable throwback to the project lesson she wrote just after its completion: "The architect or planner cannot work 'from the inside' in the city unless he first learns to love it—for the life of its people and for the messy vitality of its body. Without this second love the first will be theoretical indeed."[37]

Notes

1   Berson, "The South Street Insurrection," 91.

2   "When your removal is eventually required …" Levy, "How Philly Neighborhoods Killed the Crosstown Expressway," 12:15–12:17.

3   Reiner, Sugarman, and Scheff Reiner, *The Crosstown Controversy: A Case Study*, 14; Scott Brown, *Urban Concepts*, 34–35.

4   Hunter, *Black Citymakers*, 81, 89, 117, 119.

5   68.12 Philadelphia Crosstown Community Planning Study, South Street, 225.II.A.6812.07, Venturi Scott Brown Collection, by the gift of Robert Venturi and Denise Scott Brown, at the Architectural Archives of the University of Pennsylvania, Philadelphia (hereafter cited as VSBC, AAUP).

6   See Thomas Holme, *A Portraiture of the City of Philadelphia [map]: In the Province of Pennsylvania in America*. (London: Sold by Andrew Sowle in Shoreditch, 1683), Historical Society of Pennsylvania. DAMS #485. This cartographic blankness effaces the presence of indigenous Lenape peoples sometimes known as Lenni-Lenape or Delaware.

7   Du Bois, *The Philadelphia Negro*, 296.

8   See Boonin, *The Jewish Quarter of Philadelphia*.

9   Dillon, "Royal Theatre Closed After 50 Yrs.; Now 'Gravestone' in a 'Dying Era.'"

10   VSBC, AAUP (see note 5).

11   Scott Brown, *Urban Concepts*, 34.

12   Scott Brown, *Having Words*, 6.

13   Scott Brown, Soane Medal Lecture, 11.

14   Scott Brown, *Urban Concepts*, 35.

15   Scott Brown, "An Alternate Proposal That Builds on the Character of South Street," 42.

16   Osborn, "The Crosstown is Dead, Long Live the Crosstown?" 39.

17   Higgins and Weisenbach, "Crosstown Expressway is Denounced as One of the Worst Civic Disasters," 45.

18   Countryman, *Up South: Civil Rights and Black Power in Philadelphia*, 230–232.

19   Scott Brown, *Having Words*, 3.

20   See Alan M. Voorhees and Associates, Inc., "Preliminary Findings and Recommendations Relating to Transportation Needs for Bicentennial prepared for Transportation Task Force," Philadelphia: Philadelphia Bicentennial Corporation, 1969, cited in Reiner, Sugarman, and Scheff Reiner, 112.

21   Denise Scott Brown, Ueland and Junker, Venturi and Rauch, "Report to the Citizens Committee to Preserve and Develop the Crosstown Community," 1, 68.12 Philadelphia Crosstown Community Planning Study, South Street, 225.II.A.6812.17, VSBC, AAUP.

22   Scott Brown et al. (see note 21), 11–12.

23   Scott Brown et al. (see note 21), 14.

24   Donohoe, "Advocacy Planners Put Hope in Ghetto," 6.

25   Osborn, "Saving Picturesque South Street," 225.II.A.102.13, VSBC, AAUP.

26   Du Bois, *The Philadelphia Negro*, 60.

27   Scott Brown, "An Alternate Proposal," 42.

28   VSBC, AAUP.

29   Scott Brown, "An Alternate Proposal," 44.

30   Scott Brown, *Urban Concepts*, 35.

31   Scott Brown, *Urban Concepts*, 35.

32   Scott Brown, "An Alternate Proposal," 44.

33   Scott Brown, interviewed by Jochen Becker, "Denise Scott-Brown: An African Perspective," 1:16:35.

34   Jacobs, *The Death and Life of Great American Cities*, 368.

35   Scott Brown, "An Alternate Proposal," 44.

36   Scott Brown, interviewed by Jochen Becker, 40:32, 40:44.

37   Scott Brown, "An Alternate Proposal," 44.

Learning from Co-op City, or What Price Aesthetics?

Joan Ockman

Among the various "learning from" paradigms put forward by Denise Scott Brown and Robert Venturi starting in the late 1960s, the most famous is "Learning from Las Vegas," the design studio they co-taught with Steven Izenour at Yale School of Architecture in fall 1968, and the book of the same name that resulted four years later. Another studio at Yale, "Remedial Housing for Architects, or Learning from Levittown," followed the one on Las Vegas in spring 1970; and in December 1971 an article by Scott Brown, "Learning from Pop," published in the Italian journal *Casabella*, reprised the theme. This last begins: "Las Vegas, Los Angeles, Levittown, the swinging singles on the Westheimer Strip, golf resorts, boating communities, Co-op City, the residential backgrounds to soap operas, TV commercials and mass mag ads, billboards and Route 66 are sources for a changing architectural sensibility." Co-op City? Related neither to the commercial strip and its signage, nor to pop culture and its media, nor to the ordinary suburban landscape, Co-op City seems an outlier. Yet an article by the two Philadelphia architects published in *Progressive Architecture* magazine in February 1970 titled "Co-op City: Learning to Like It" makes the case for a massive housing project then under construction in New York City as an object lesson in the virtues of ordinariness and popular appeal.[1] Architects should learn "to accept the ordinary on its own terms and do it well," the coauthors write, and "to give the people something they want."[2]

Signed Denise Scott Brown and Robert Venturi, in that order, "Co-op City: Learning to Like It" has the earmarks of having been written principally by Scott Brown. Among the giveaways are a couple of passing references to housing developments in apartheid South Africa. Documents in the Architectural Archives of the University of Pennsylvania confirm our suspicion; more on one of these presently. What the article shares with the Venturis' other exemplars of the "almost all right" is an unorthodox take on a type of built environment vilified by the architectural elite and the press. An early draft of the article dates to December 1968, a couple weeks after the *New York Times* ran a front-page story on the imminent opening of Co-op City's first high-rise apartment block.[3] The milestone was marked by a dedication ceremony attended by such New York notables as Nelson Rockefeller and Robert Moses. Accompanying the news story was a design review by the *Times*'s architecture critic Ada Louise Huxtable, who disparaged the development for lacking both adequate site planning and inspiration.[4] Leading critics in other publications echoed her assessment, describing it as "sterile and blunt" and "fairly hideous."[5] Taking a characteristically contrarian stance, Scott Brown and Venturi arrayed themselves on the side of the giant development, explicitly endorsing the dominant postwar policy ruthlessly implemented by Moses and other power brokers in cities across the country in the name of urban renewal.

Built to house between 55,000 and 60,000 residents in 35 brick towers unadorned save for some concrete "styling," and ranging in height from 24 to 33 stories—some up to two blocks long—the buildings of Co-op City sprawled across a 300-acre site (1.2 km²) located in the northeast reaches of the Bronx at the intersection of Interstate 95 and the Hutchinson River Parkway. Sprinkled among the towers were seven clusters of townhouses, added at the behest of the City Planning Commission to give a modicum of "human scale," plus three shopping centers, a 25-acre education park with schools, a power plant, a credit union, a library and movie house, religious buildings, and eight immense private garages. Laying claim when it opened to being the largest cooperative housing complex in the world, it was a veritable city within the city; had it been an actual municipality, it would have been the thirteenth largest in New York State. A venture of the United Housing Foundation (UHF), a not-for-profit consortium of labor unions, housing cooperatives, and neighborhood associations established in 1951, it was designed by Herman Jessor, a Ukrainian-born architect and long-time veteran of the organization, who began his career as a draftsman in the 1920s and, by the 1970s, completed some 40,000 units of cooperative housing in New York City.[6] The UHF's mission was to provide affordable apartments to its constituency of middle- and moderate-income workers in the garment and other labor unions.

Heavily subsidized by both the state and city, the construction of Co-op City was paid for with a long-term, low-interest mortgage worth a record $330 million and a 30-year tax abatement financed under the Mitchell-Lama Act, an affordable housing program introduced in 1955. To qualify for residency, prospective "co-operators" had to have an income of no more than seven times the annual carrying charges on their apartment, which amounted to $27.50 per room per month, including utilities and air conditioning. They also retained only limited equity in their unit. Jessor and his team kept costs to a minimum through economies of scale, scrupulous budgeting and scheduling, and especially the UHF's practice of serving as its own contractor. Combined with an uncompromisingly no-frills approach to design, this formula enabled the UHF to provide Co-op City's residents with functional and relatively spacious interiors, which even Huxtable had to admit meant "good apartments at unbeatable prices."[7]

Besides its association with organized labor, Co-op City also differed from other urban renewal projects in that it avoided the brutal displacements typically associated with slum clearance. The marshy site on which it stood was previously home to a theme park called Freedomland that went bankrupt in 1964, taking down the famed real-estate mogul and financier William Zeckendorf with it. Brainchild of a former Disney designer, the park was dedicated, as its name suggests, to mythifying American history through creative imagineering.[8] One might have expected Scott Brown and Venturi to have been more enamored of Freedomland than its uningratiating successor. Ironically, at an intensifying moment in the Cold War, early articles on Co-op City did not fail to suggest similarities between the New York behemoth and the mass-produced housing being erected at the same date on the outskirts of Moscow.[9]

Scott Brown and Venturi's brief on behalf of Co-op City was essentially an argument that the urgent demand for affordable housing in American cities necessitated dispensing with architectural niceties. *Contra* the pieties of the design profession, and in contrast to the self-indulgence of both avant-garde formalists and technological utopians, what people basically wanted and needed, they claimed, was a decent place to live. Nor was there any hard evidence that "good design" and "civic beauty" necessarily correlated with social cohesion and community. Channeling a critique made by Scott Brown's teacher Herbert Gans (and indeed years earlier by Adolf Loos), they made the case that the argument for aesthetics rested on a "physical fallacy."[10] While projects of "unique civic importance" might warrant a degree of embellishment, everyday buildings did not: "Our contention is that architects spend too much on decoration. Not decoration in the traditional sense (this might cost less) but in the sense of contorting what should be ordinary building to fit preconceived, high-style models based on the work of Le Corbusier, Kahn, Rudolph, and other admired masters."[11] The issue, in other words—already formulated by Scott Brown in an initial version of the couple's "duck versus decorated shed" thesis[12]—boiled down to simple arithmetic: what price aesthetics?

This *faute de mieux* realism also jived with the philosophy of Jessor, although for the architect of Co-op City the towers-in-the-park typology—a distant trickle-down from the urbanism of Le Corbusier—reflected a firm belief in the latter's inherent superiority to any alternative. For Scott Brown and Venturi it was more a matter of eat-your-spinach: learning to like it, *almost* all-rightness. At the same time, Jessor insisted on taking some distance from the couple's arch attitude toward modernist orthodoxy. A tireless activist on behalf of affordable housing and thin-skinned about criticisms of his work, he bristled at their suggestion that there was a "30's air" overhanging Co-op City. Invited by the editors of *Progressive Architecture* to write a "rebuttal" to their argument, he offered a series of comments that are appended at the end of the article. "New Deal liberalism was a giant step forward in American society," he affirms. "It gave us social security, the minimum wage, welfare relief ... and Government-aided housing.... The final solution to housing for the masses is that it be a government function.... The success of the United Housing Foundation testifies to this need—housing without profit."[13]

Predictably, a very different reaction came from the other end of the professional spectrum. Having brazenly stirred the pot, Scott Brown and Venturi's article elicited outraged letters from a number of *Progressive Architecture*'s readers. The editors chose to publish two of the more indignant ones in the magazine's April issue under the heading "Co-op City Controversy." The first came from Sibyl Moholy-Nagy, who was teaching at the time at Columbia

University. Not mincing words, Moholy-Nagy pointed out the article's contradictions with Venturi's argument in *Complexity and Contradiction in Architecture*, which had appeared four years earlier, declaring it "profoundly shocking that an architect whose 'primary inspiration would seem to have come from the urban facades of Italy ...' should so cleverly ignore the deadly antiurbanism of this project."[14] The second letter came from Ulrich Franzen, who likewise expressed shock. Couching his response in terms of recent political events, he denounced the authors' endorsement of "status quo doctrine," declaring that "one year after the election of the Nixon administration" the defense of "Co-op City's coarsely scaled and lifeless community on grounds of lowest cost and the implied endorsement of existing subsidy policies" raised "the ghost of a silent-majority architecture."[15]

Several months later, Scott Brown responded to both Moholy-Nagy and Franzen with her own broadside. Dated 4 September 1970, the letter, addressed to editor-in-chief Forrest Wilson at *Progressive Architecture*, went unpublished.[16] A carbon copy, conserved in the Penn Archives, begins by complimenting Moholy-Nagy for her previous "sensible and refreshing" critiques of "the latest architectural and planning dogma." But she goes on to castigate her for endorsing "architect-designed ... 'social housing'" that "cannot be afforded by the majority of the urban work force." As to Franzen's "currently fashionable Nixon-silent-majority critique," Scott Brown states, "there seems to be a very fine line between liberalism and class snobbery."

Scott Brown concludes with a pointed comment on "the question of ascription." After initially referring to "Venturi and his wife," Moholy-Nagy had used the masculine pronoun throughout her letter to the editor, while Franzen had ignored Scott Brown's contribution altogether. Scott Brown undertook to set the record straight:

I wrote the article. It contains an inseparable amalgam of our shared opinions, but owes as much to my planning experience and research in housing, here and particularly in development areas, as to either of our architectural theories. For the record, one of us writes the first draft, the other adds, criticizes and edits; whoever is named first wrote the first draft.

This is a fairly standard academic procedure. Missing its implication implies a male chauvinism which can be expected from the Franzens of the profession but hardly from the wife of Laslo [*sic*] Moholy-Nagy."[17]

Clearly "Co-op City: Learning to Like It" touched some hot buttons. Half a century later, at a time when affordable urban housing remains as desperately needed as ever, judgment on Co-op City may still need to be deferred. While the complex has had its share of problems over the years, from construction issues to financial scandals, the pragmatic idealism, or idealistic pragmatism, that originally underwrote its conception cannot altogether be dismissed. One former resident, Supreme Court justice Sonia Sotomayor, who moved to Co-op City as a teenager from a more dangerous and decrepit area in the Bronx, recounts in her autobiography: "We moved into one of the first of thirty buildings for a development planned to house fifty-five thousand ... Yes, Co-op City was the end of the earth, but once I saw the apartment, it made sense. It had parquet floors and a big window in the living room with a long view. All the rooms were twice the size of those cubbyholes in the projects ..."[18] There is probably still a lesson here.

Notes

1   Scott Brown and Venturi, "Co-op City: Learning to Like It." This article has largely been neglected by recent scholars, with the exception of a recent exhibition curated by the Temple Hoyne Buell Center for the Study of American Architecture, *House Housing: An Untimely History of Architecture and Real Estate in 31 Episodes,* which opened at the Venice Biennale in 2014.

2   Scott Brown and Venturi, "Co-op City: Learning to Like It," 70–71.

3   See Farrell, "Vast Co-op City Is Dedicated in Bronx." The article by Scott Brown and Venturi may initially have been solicited by a new publication, *The New York Advocate,* which did not get off the ground. They then offered it to the *New York Times Magazine* and *Architectural Forum,* both of which turned it down.

4   Huxtable, "A Singularly New York Product."

5   These characterizations came from McQuade, "The High-Rising Monotony of World Housing," and Blake, "Co-op City: The High Cost of Hideousness."

6   On Jessor and the cooperative housing movement, see the excellent article by Tony Schuman, "Labor and Housing in New York City: Architect Herman Jessor and the Cooperative Housing Movement."

7   Huxtable, "A Singularly New York Product."

8   See Naish, "Fantasia Bronxiana: Freedomland and Co-op City."

9   See McQuade, "High-Rising Monotony."

10 Gans first made this argument in his review of Jane Jacobs's book *The Death and Life of Great American Cities.* See Gans, "City Planning and Urban Realities."

11 "Co-op City: Learning to Like It," 70. Scott Brown goes on to suggest, however, that it would have been desirable for the architect to have created—without undue expense—vistas from the complex of "something frankly pretty," and to have paid a little more attention to public amenities: "We do feel that the way to finance a fountain or two in the civic landscape may be to sell hot dogs and hamburgers and perhaps even boat rides at the riverside park" (p. 71).

12 See Scott Brown and Venturi, "On Ducks and Decoration."

13 Jessor, "Herman J. Jessor, Co-op City Architect, comments upon the authors' text."

14 Letter from Sibyl Moholy-Nagy, "Co-op City Controversy: Letters to the Editor." Moholy-Nagy cites the phrase in single quotes from Vincent Scully's introduction to *Complexity and Contradiction in Architecture.*

15 Letter from Ulrich Franzen, "Co-op City Controversy: Letters to the Editor."

16 Not surprisingly, the magazine chose not to publish it almost nine months after the original article appeared. Scott Brown also sent a copy directly to Sibyl Moholy-Nagy.

17 Venturi Scott Brown Collection, by the gift of Robert Venturi and Denise Scott Brown, at the Architectural Archives of the University of Pennsylvania, Philadelphia. I am grateful to Allison Olsen at the Penn archives for research assistance.

18 Sotomayor, *My Beloved World,* 99.

On Camp, Revolutionariness, and Architecture

Valéry Didelon

For more than fifty years, Denise Scott Brown has tirelessly contributed to changing the way architects look at themselves—and, quite possibly, changing the way that society looks at architects. Firstly, she challenged the quasi-exclusively male representation of architectural practice, courageously denouncing endemic sexism in the field. She also fought anti-intellectualism in professional circles by promoting the uses of social sciences in the development of urban planning and architectural design. Moreover, she broadened the culture of architects by including popular and commercial buildings and artifacts, long despised by highbrow historians and critics. On the latter point, I will be suggesting here that together with Robert Venturi, Scott Brown demonstrated a "camp" sensibility—an attitude described and theorized by one of her contemporaries, namely the American essayist Susan Sontag. Although there is little indication that Scott Brown was aware of "Notes on 'Camp'" (1964)[1] or that later on Sontag read *Learning from Las Vegas* (1972),[2] it is fruitful to cross-examine these two seminal texts, written and co-written a few years apart by two women who made indelible marks on American intellectual life. Such analysis might in particular shed some light on the way social commitment changed in the field of architecture after 1968.

Taking Notes

Let us begin with the tricky task of defining camp. What one knows about it is mainly what Sontag said through fifty-eight aphorisms published in the mid-1960s.[3] She explained that camp is both a sensibility that concerns an observer and also a quality that applies to the object that he or she observes. On the sensibility side, "It is one way of seeing the world as an aesthetic phenomenon." On the quality side, "the hallmark of Camp is the spirit of extravagance," the excess, the too much. With regard to the observer, "Camp sensibility is disengaged, depoliticized—or at least apolitical." The camp object, on the other hand, is characterized by "a seriousness that fails."

Sontag claimed that true camp lies only in the combination of *sensibility* and *quality*: for example, collecting old Flash Gordon comics, appreciating popular furniture and decoration as a connoisseur, or finding aesthetic qualities in old pornographic movies. Camp implies having a sense of irony to the extent that "behind the 'straight' public sense in which something can be taken, one has found a private zany experience of the thing." Artifacts and people always play a role: "Camp sees everything in quotation marks. It's not a lamp, but a 'lamp'; not a woman, but a 'woman.'" And above all, as Sontag put it, camp affirms that there is "a good taste of bad taste," her ultimate slogan being "it's good *because* it's awful."

Camp sensibility belongs to a historical moment, the mid-1960s, but it clearly has antecedents and successors. Sontag claimed that "Camp is modern dandyism. Camp is the answer to the problem: how to be a dandy in the age of mass culture." The connoisseur of camp indeed shows aristocratic tendencies, even if one takes enjoyment "in the coarsest, commonest pleasures, in the arts of the masses." Camp shares certain attributes with kitsch, but it has more irony and self-awareness. At best, kitsch is "naïve Camp," or "pure Camp." Pop Art also has some similarities, but it lacks for its part an element of love for its object: "Pop Art is more flat and more dry, more serious, more detached, ultimately nihilistic."

As Sontag put it, "there are 'campy' movies, clothes, furniture, popular songs, novels, people, buildings..." In her wake, two authors have discussed camp in architecture, both making the connection to the work of Venturi and Scott Brown—and by the way both failing to acknowledge Scott Brown's specific contribution in the matter. Firstly, Charles Jencks, in *Modern Movements in Architecture*, divided contemporary American architecture into "Camp" and "Non-Camp."[4] From Sontag, he kept the ideas of aestheticization and depoliticization; then he related camp to formalism and to the proponents of the International Style: Walter Gropius, Ludwig Mies van der Rohe, and Philip Johnson. Conversely, Jencks depicted Venturi as a non-camp architect who, although incorporating pop or camp materials, had nothing to do with formalism, and could even be considered "morally hot." Jencks insisted less on camp as a sensibility than as a quality that he associated, for example, with Paul Rudolph's Art and Architecture Building at Yale or Saarinen's TWA terminal—namely, extravagance. With his binary classification, Jencks gave no significance to the irony and second-degree interpretations that Sontag so closely related to camp.

The second author, C. Ray Smith, considered camp in architecture more directly as a matter of sensibility. In *Supermannerism: New Attitudes in Post-Modern Architecture,*[5] he argued that educated people have long been confronted with the spectacle of consumerism, the obscenity of advertising, and the vulgar transformation of the visual environment. As he summarized:

> The situation had gotten so bad by the late 1950s that it could not get worse, it seemed; so it had to get better. But how? Artists, instead of being merely outraged and horrified by all of this, instead of rejecting it all as exclusively as possible, determined (in their hideous fascination) that the way to make those artifacts of our undesigned, uncouth, philistine, everyday culture better was to make fun of them, to make a big, joking, tongue-in-cheek put-down of them. This was Camp—at first.

In *Supermannerism*, Smith refers to the Miami Beach hotels of Morris Lapidus and the Madonna Inn in California by Charles Moore. He gave a prominent role to Venturi, whom he saw as the Andy Warhol of architectural theory. Nonetheless, Smith describes Venturi's writings on Las Vegas as pop, if not camp.

Learning to Like What You Don't Like

With all the flashy casinos and hotels, funny wedding chapels, and glittering giant signs that had sprung up along the Strip, Las Vegas had all it needed to become the mecca of camp. However, few intellectuals granted any importance to the city in the mid-1960s, apart from Tom Wolfe, Reyner Banham, and Denise Scott Brown. Moving to California to take a teaching position at the School of Environmental Design at UC Berkeley, Scott Brown visited Las Vegas as early as 1965. Her background enabled her to take an appreciative approach to the gaudy constructions: firstly, the colorful scenery of the Strip reminded her of South Africa, the country where she had experienced a vibrant vernacular culture in her childhood, namely that of black and white Africans, unduly overshadowed by the aristocratic culture imported from Europe.[6] Secondly, the Las Vegas signs and billboards reminded her of the New Brutalists she had mingled with in England in the 1950s. As a student at the Architectural Association, she had been fond of the architects Alison and Peter Smithson, who championed ordinariness as a source of inspiration. As she recalled,

> ... their appeal, I think, lay in combining the Dadaist found-object aesthetic with an interest in community development. For me, this balance was terribly important. I believed, and still believe, that beauty (albeit an agonized beauty) can be derived from hard reality, and that facing uncomfortable facts can sharpen the eye and refine one's aesthetic ability. The New Brutalism suggested to me that social objectives might be achieved with beauty, if we could only learn to broaden our definition of beauty—and that doing so could make us better artists.[7]

Through several articles published in the late 1960s, Scott Brown theorized her inclinations that had developed successively in Africa, London, and Las Vegas. She assumed that an "objective," or "neutral," if not benevolent, look at the ordinary landscape of suburban America could bring a new vitality to architecture practice. She added that

> ... the shiver that is engendered by trying to like what one does not like has long been known to be a creative one; it rocks the artist from his aesthetic grooves and resensitizes him to the sources of his inspiration. It may be achieved by breaking rules as did the Mannerists. ... This effect might also come from use of a new and shocking source—Le Corbusier's photographs of western grain elevators and tops of ships managed to *épater* the bourgeois, to blow the minds of the citizens of several continents for several years.[8]

Scott Brown, who mentioned Antonioni's cinema and illustrates her article "On Pop Art, Permissiveness and Planning" with photographs by Ed Ruscha, enjoined architects to emulate artists and embrace popular culture. She saw it as a major source of inspiration that could rejuvenate architecture, as she explained: "These new, more receptive, ways of seeing the environment, inspired by other sciences and arts, are almost desperately important to architects or planners who hope to stay relevant; and when the artistic fashions move on, we shall still be here because this pop city, this *here*, is what we have."

Scott Brown's profound interest in the suburban and commercial landscape, awoken in her in Johannesburg, was a sensibility shared by Venturi. Indeed, since his beginnings as an architect he had committed himself to a better consideration of the American context in which he had to design, however unpleasant that context might be. In *Complexity and Contradiction in Architecture*, published in 1966, he asked: "Is not Main Street almost all right?"—illustrating this provocative question with a photograph of a typical American commercial street. Scott Brown summed it up afterward: "Our subsequent collaboration has worked because we both bring a rule-breaking outlook to aesthetic—we like the same 'ugly' things—and we both think that rule-breaking should be not willful but based on the demands of reality."[9] In 1966, they went together to Las Vegas, rented a car, and toured the Strip. Scott Brown later reminisced: "We rode around from casino to casino. Dazed by the desert sun and dazzled by the signs, both loving and hating what we saw, we were jolted clear out of our aesthetic skins."[10]

A Subversive Manifesto

Scott Brown and Venturi shared the disrupting experience of Las Vegas through a series of articles, eventually publishing their controversial book in 1972. I will suggest here that *Learning from Las Vegas* can be read as a striking manifesto of camp sensibility, although it is not entirely explicit. Firstly, the authors considered Las Vegas as a purely visual phenomenon, if not an aesthetic one: "This architecture of styles and signs is antispatial," "it is an architecture of communication over space," and: "The graphic sign in space has become the architecture of this landscape."[11] Henceforth Scott Brown and Venturi's study of the Strip, and more extensively of the commercial boulevard, focused on its more extravagant landmarks. Secondly, the two architects' gaze could be described as camp inasmuch as it seems to be noncommittal, depoliticized, and amoral. Both made it clear on several occasions that they should not be questioned about their lack of social commitment, since "Just as an analysis of the structure of a Gothic cathedral need not include a debate on the morality of medieval religion, so Las Vegas's values are not questioned here." Resolute in keeping the different concerns apart, they insisted that "the morality of commercial advertising, gambling interests, and the competitive instinct is not at issue here."[12] Thirdly, the second part of *Learning from Las Vegas* sounds literally camp, as its authors playfully juggled with good and bad taste. For instance, in describing the Guild House of 1961, built in Philadelphia: "The technologically unadvanced brick, the old-fashioned, double-hung windows, the pretty materials around the entrance, and the ugly antenna not hidden behind the parapet in the accepted fashion, all are distinctively conventional in image as well as substance or, rather, ugly and ordinary." The design of the facade, however, is cleverly elaborated, full of artifice, and above all deeply ironic. They ultimately confess that "this is what makes Guild House an architect's decorated shed—not architecture without architects."[13] One could add: this is what makes Scott Brown and Venturi's approach fully camp and not kitsch at all.

Although both maintained that *Learning from Las Vegas* proceeded from an "open-minded and nonjudgmental investigation"[14] and should only be read as an objective analysis of architectural and urban forms, many of its readers did not understand it that way. The book not only represented an outrage against good taste, but immediately came under political siege.[15] Scott Brown and Venturi were accused of giving up social commitment and embracing the values of capitalism and consumerism. Like Martin Pawley or Tomas Maldonado, the historian Kenneth Frampton was a vigorous and pugnacious detractor of Scott Brown and Venturi's writings on Las Vegas. Years after, Frampton despised the fact that "the camp cult of 'the ugly and the ordinary' becomes indistinguishable from the environmental consequences of the market economy."[16] For him, the celebration of commercial and popular architecture contributed to the reinforcement of alienation, maintaining the status quo in American society. On several occasions Scott Brown took the initiative to counter the criticism of those "armchair academics" or "radical chic architects" who patronized her.[17] At the bottom of their dispute lay a questioning of how to be a revolutionary architect in America in the late 1960s.

At this stage, Sontag's assertion that camp sensibility is "disengaged, depoliticized—or at least apolitical" has to be challenged. In fact, camp has always been used to defend marginal cultural and social forms and behaviors. It flourished as a way of opposing mainstream views of normality. For instance, the gay community has used it to confront heterosexuals with their prejudices. As Judith Butler observed, camp has played a significant political role through its capacity to shake up preconceived ideas, to reverse understandings, and to exaggerate the artificiality of what the dominant cultural players perceived as natural.[18] In the same way, Scott Brown and Venturi challenged the architectural norms that take a cathedral into consideration, but not a bicycle shed, as Nikolaus Pevsner famously put it. They undermined modernist orthodoxy by welcoming extravagant roadside constructions—such as the famous Long Island Duck or the Las Vegas Signs—into the architectural repertoire. They did it too by redeeming the suburban home when, after Las Vegas, they learned from Levittown suburban homes with their Yale students. Scott Brown and Venturi showed a new kind of commitment, as cultural stakes were progressively overriding the traditional arguments of class struggle by the end of the 1960s. By questioning the foundation of good taste, they were taking part in a process of democratization that penetrated American society—despite the election and reelection of Richard Nixon, who championed a return to "law and order."

Laughing So As Not to Cry

As a camp manifesto, *Learning from Las Vegas* shows us how architects could be revolutionary in the rising postmodern era. For Scott Brown and Venturi, it did not mean dreaming of a utopia, but rather showing empathy for people's true expectations and for the existing city as it is—and as they like it. Andrew Ross notes: "Unlike the traditional intellectual, whose function is to legitimize the cultural power of ruling interests, or the organic intellectual, who promotes the interests of a rising class, the marginal, camp intellectual expresses his impotence as the dominated fraction of a ruling bloc as he distances himself from the conventional morality and taste of the ascendant middle class."[19] Scott Brown followed such a narrow and perilous path, as she never recognized herself in the Marxist rhetoric of the European pundits, but rather identified herself as an American architect who was willing to get her hands dirty. For her, as for Venturi, the camp sensibility was a way of dealing with a political, social, and economic context that was less and less favorable to the production of pure architecture in the 1970s. As Scott Brown put it in an interview in 1975: "The artist, in order to make his art, draws his material from the world around him. If that world suits him, the artist uses it as it is; if not, he (or she) uses it ironically. We believe we use it ironically: we use irony as a way to laugh so we don't cry."[20] Scott Brown expressed the melancholy that could be associated with the loss of a better world, but also an awareness that the world we live in can still be enchanting. And to quote the Italian writer Claudio Magris, one might then understand from Scott Brown and Venturi that "disenchantment is an ironic, melancholic and seasoned form of hope."[21] From today's point of view, their camp sensibility still stands as an invitation to show curiosity, empathy, and wit in the way we look at the built environment and envision its transformation.

Notes

1   When asked in 2005, Denise Scott Brown told me
     that she had not read Susan Sontag, whom I unfortu-
     nately did not have the opportunity to meet in the
     course of my research.
2   Venturi, Scott Brown, and Izenour, *Learning from
     Las Vegas.*
3   Sontag, "Notes on 'Camp.'"
4   Jencks, *Modern Movements in Architecture*, 185.
5   Smith, *Supermannerism.*
6   See Scott Brown, "From Soane to the Strip," 10–16.
7   Scott Brown, "Learning from Brutalism," 204.
8   Scott Brown, "On Pop Art, Permissiveness and
     Planning."
9   Scott Brown, "Learning from Brutalism," 203.
10   Scott Brown, quoted in Gilbert and Moore, *Particu-
     lar Passions*, 316.
11   Venturi, Scott Brown, and Izenour, *Learning from
     Las Vegas*, 4.
12   Venturi, Scott Brown, and Izenour, *Learning from
     Las Vegas*, 0.
13   Venturi, Scott Brown, and Izenour, *Learning from
     Las Vegas*, 70.
14   This statement is found in the preface of *Learning
     from Las Vegas*, which is significantly signed by
     Denise Scott Brown and Robert Venturi and not the
     other way round.
15   For an extensive analysis of the heated debate that
     followed the publication of Venturi, Scott Brown, and
     Izenour's book between 1968 and 1978, see Dide-
     lon, *La controverse Learning from Las Vegas.*
16   Frampton, "Place, Production and Architecture."
17   Scott Brown, "On Architectural Formalism and
     Social Concern."
18   See Butler, *Gender Trouble.*
19   Ross, *No Respect*, 146.
20   Von Moos, "Lachen, um nicht zu weinen" (laughing
     so as not to cry).
21   Magris, *Utopie et désenchantement,* 19.

Figure 1: Ken Heyman, Claes Oldenburg with Billboard, New Jersey, c. 1965.

"Strange" Appearances: On Pop Art, Hamburgers, and Urbanists

Katherine Smith

Denise Scott Brown and Robert Venturi's consideration of contemporary art operates at the foundation of their practice. In *Complexity and Contradiction in Architecture* (1966), recent paintings provide meaningful illustrations of formal principles and comparisons to architectural functions; in *Learning from Las Vegas* (1972), works of art are more often allusive examples for popular content, research methods, visual effects, with only one reproduction. Yet pop art is prominent in the latter, where the coauthors establish in opening paragraphs: "For the artist, creating the new may mean choosing the old or the existing. Pop artists have relearned this. Our acknowledgment of existing, commercial architecture at the scale of the highway is within this tradition."[1] We can see similarities in subject matter, between popular images and vernacular cityscapes, and also discern experiential encounters in some pop works, which match the architects' interest in embodied and mobilized perception in their research and design in the 1960s and 1970s.[2] This essay demonstrates the centrality of pop art to the architects' projects during these decades, especially in the thought and writing of Scott Brown. As Venturi confirmed: "Pop art was very important for its strong association with the ordinary. Denise knew this earlier than I did. She understood the relevance of Pop art before I did."[3] While they incorporated two-dimensional works into publications as provocative complements to their ideas on architecture and urbanism, sculpture was equally, if not more, important for their thinking and practice—especially that of Swedish-born American sculptor Claes Oldenburg, identified by Scott Brown as "the closest to us because he deals with objects."[4] While Oldenburg's hamburgers enter *Learning from Las Vegas*, the relevance of his sculpture (fig. 1), and of pop art more generally, becomes increasingly clear in studio notes and exhibition proposals, texts that reveal Scott Brown's perspicacious assessments of his career.

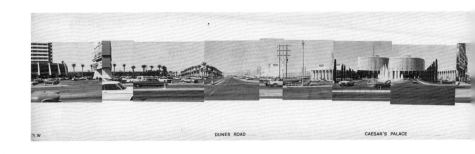

W   DUNES ROAD   CAESAR'S PALACE

"On Pop Art ..."

Scott Brown addressed pop art in an illuminating analysis of urban design, "On Pop Art, Permissiveness, and Planning" (1969), interpreting the recent turn toward objective methods and popular subjects as "permissiveness," as cited in the title. Its synthesis of historical context and openness to diverse sources—from the humanities and social sciences to architecture and urban planning—are characteristic of her trenchant approach to planning. Pop art (and art more generally) guides her broad perspectives on current discourse, as she encourages urbanists to "[look] for new, more receptive ways of seeing the environment," a term applicable to built and media landscapes.[5]

Ed Ruscha's black-and-white photographs illustrate the essay, starting with a Los Angeles parking lot, followed by a Texas gas station. These photographs come from books (*Thirtyfour Parking Lots*, 1967, *Twentysix Gasoline Stations*, 1963) that reiterate the prevalence of vehicular travel and the explosion of highway construction in the US during the postwar period; the final image by Ruscha shows a row of buildings (from *Some Los Angeles Apartments*, 1965), rhetorically monotonous architecture, a complex amalgam of modernist box and applied ornament; its historical allusion (Fountain Blu), recognizable despite the creative spelling, is arguably indicative of the "decorated shed." It epitomizes conclusions about commercial symbolism from Las Vegas in 1968 and anticipates questions about residential architecture in Levittown in 1970.

Scott Brown's focus on Ruscha substantiates her perception of his projects and underscores his influence on the Las Vegas Studio: Yale students visited

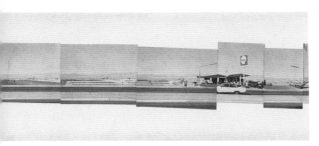

Figure 2: An "Edward Ruscha" elevation of the Strip (detail). Imitation of Ruscha's Sunset Strip map for the Las Vegas Strip, showing the routes lined by palaces like the Grand Canal or the Rhine. Central idea by Denise Scott Brown; executed by Denise Scott Brown, Robert Venturi, and the students of the Learning from Las Vegas Studio, 1968.

the artist in Los Angeles and, in Las Vegas, transferred methods from *Every Building on the Sunset Strip* (1966) to their research agenda. Their photographs (fig. 2) cover four pages in *Learning from Las Vegas*; they retain Ruscha's approach to capturing facades on opposite sides of the street, suturing images together, and reproducing them in rows to recreate their relative positions (and also, as Ruscha, including only minimal textual additions—here casinos and cross-streets).

For Scott Brown, Ruscha functioned as exemplar, for his subject matter and nonjudgmental ("dead-pan") style.[6] The paragraph on Ruscha begins with Robert Rauschenberg and Roy Lichtenstein (whose work had appeared, as she tells us, on the cover of *Time* magazine) and brings in Allan d'Arcangelo, whose paintings of highway signage related to Ruscha's photographs of parking lots and gas stations (his print is the only representation of pop art in *Learning from Las Vegas*).[7] This essay, her most comprehensive analysis of Ruscha's work, clarifies the prominence (and acceptance) of pop artists looking closely at postwar cityscapes (and reflecting current events), as she and her coauthors would repeat in *Learning from Las Vegas*. Her conclusion, as she would reiterate in the seminal essay "Learning from Pop" (1971), which also affirmed this art as an important parallel for the popular—"The urgency of the social situation, and the social critique of urban renewal ... have been as important as the Pop artists in steering us toward the existing American city and its builders"—connects critique to content, as would Oldenburg's art more securely.[8]

On Hamburgers

Like Ruscha, Oldenburg exerted a significant and enduring influence on Scott Brown and Venturi. His artistic strategies, developed during this first decade of his career in direct observation of postwar urbanism, align with approaches of contemporary architects and urban planners, making him an important contemporary. Indeed a photograph of Oldenburg, which shows his literal embrace of exactly the roadside signs and symbols to which Scott Brown and Venturi turned their attention, appeared in John Rublowsky's *Pop Art* (1965).[9] This image stages the correspondences between Oldenburg's commitment to familiar objects and the architects' theorization of commercial landscapes; intersections in their techniques and perspectives also reveal strong affinities.

Oldenburg's early methods of traversing downtown neighborhoods in New York in the 1950s, photographing empty lots, sidewalk moments, and store windows, and translating his perceptions into images and objects and soon into installations requiring physical negotiation by their audience anticipated Venturi and Scott Brown's insistence on studying the casinos and signage of the Strip from a moving car and endowing the resulting publication with experiential qualities. Collapsed buildings, empty lots, rubble piles, collected trash—material remains of ongoing destruction of aging tenements—and storefronts are among the most prevalent subjects, confirming close attention to urban forms and commercial displays. In addition, several examples of sequential images capture pedestrians' movements, trajectories of passersby and the artist's own subtle shifts in location and perspective. Such photographs approximate images in *Learning from Las Vegas,* like the "movie sequence," representing vehicular motion along the Strip.[10]

The Store (1961–62), arguably Oldenburg's first pop art, continued these representations of consumer goods and advertising posters, first in graphite drawings and then in enamel-and-plaster reliefs.[11] Partial, distorted, and overlapping shapes and forms create jumbled accretions; Oldenburg's explanations suggest what he wanted to accomplish: "eyeclusters—formal model for a kind of visual experience: fragmentation, simultaneousness, superimposition,

Figure 3: Caesars Palace centurions, in *Learning from Las Vegas,* 1972.
Photograph by Denise Scott Brown, 1968.

which I wish to recreate in the clusters."[12] If Oldenburg's intent was to elicit
the experience of seeing objects from sidewalk or street—"his glancing in
store windows while passing by," as his late wife and artistic partner Coosje
van Bruggen put it—then we can read these compositions as renderings of embodied, mobilized vision, distinct in style and medium but similar in strategy to Scott Brown and Venturi's deadpan approach to Las Vegas.[13] In fact,
Oldenburg's "eyeclusters" find an analogue in a statement in *Learning from
Las Vegas*:

> The emerging order of the Strip is a complex order. It is not the easy, rigid
> order of the urban renewal project or the fashionable "total design" of the
> megastructure … It is not an order dominated by the expert and made easy
> for the eye. The moving eye in the moving body must work to pick out and
> interpret a variety of changing, juxtaposed orders.[14]

Floor-Burger (Giant Hamburger), 1962
Canvas filled with foam rubber and paper cartons,
painted with Liquitex and latex,
52 inches high x 84 inches diameter
Art Gallery of Ontario, Toronto

142

Figure 4: Claes Oldenburg, page with *Floor Burger,* 1962 in Rose, *Claes Oldenburg,* 1970. Canvas filled with foam rubber and cardboard boxes, painted with acrylic paint, 132.1 × 226.1 cm (52 × 89 in.).

In Scott Brown and Venturi's first published reference to Oldenburg's sculpture, in *Learning from Las Vegas,* brief mention hints at broader influence: Roman centurions on the sign at Caesars Palace (fig. 3) are "lacquered like Oldenburg hamburgers"—an allusion that calls to mind *Two Cheeseburgers, with Everything (Dual Hamburgers); Hamburger, Popsicle, and Price;* and *Floor Burger,* all of which debuted at the Green Gallery in New York, 1962, the latter also exhibited in the artist's retrospective at the Museum of Modern Art in 1969 (fig. 4).[15] This equation of sign and sculpture (and their reference to the artist by last name only) indicates the reach of Oldenburg's practice. It also returns his art to its urban sources; a photograph of a hamburger stand (fig. 5) resembles *Floor Burger* and reinforces the dialogue between Oldenburg's sculptures and the contemporary landscape.[16] Indeed, Oldenburg's inclusion in *Learning from Las Vegas* reflected the critical discourse on his art, which increasingly acknowledged equivalences between his objects and commercial signs, as John

Figure 5: Hamburger stand, Dallas, Texas, in *Learning from Las Vegas,* 1972.

McCoubrey made explicit and relevant to Scott Brown and Venturi: "For miles along the Las Vegas strip ... Oldenburgs of the Young Electric Sign Company and its competitors hold the desert and distant mountains at bay."[17]
This allusion to Oldenburg in *Learning from Las Vegas* implied the similarities in content and scale between signs and sculptures, but it emphasized the surfaces of Oldenburg's objects, painted canvas or plaster. It is surprising, perceptive, even prescient—highlighting an element critical to Oldenburg's notion of and intention toward embodied vision. As he clarified, "The soft sculpture ... [and] enamel sculpture ... are both shiny ... and they change when you walk."[18] Oldenburg's objects—with their soft or hard materials, fluid paint application, and exaggerated scales—promoted tactile engagement and solicited a physical interaction and spatial awareness that Venturi and Scott Brown sought in their projects: books, exhibition designs, and built structures.

While Scott Brown and Venturi would not have known Oldenburg's photographs or drawings, they would have been aware of *The Store*, especially of the soft sculptures, and his monuments, as social critique. Between the Las Vegas and Levittown studios, in 1969, Oldenburg was directly involved in events at the Yale School of Architecture. His monument proposals were featured in *Perspecta*, the school's journal; *Lipstick (Ascending) on Caterpillar Tracks* (1969) was commissioned and installed by the Colossal Keepsake Corporation, a nonprofit organization of graduate students and faculty, who began to introduce revolutionary monuments to college campuses.[19] Oldenburg's *Lipstick* not only presented radical symbolism, but also functioned as a podium for public speeches, not least for the current demands for curricular change and greater social responsibility; they were appeals, like Scott Brown's, in relation to pop art. According to one of the student leaders, they wanted "a more inclusive approach and a greater concern for the street life of the city," criteria for which Oldenburg provided models. It is fitting that one of his objects was central to this moment of sociopolitical agitation at Yale (of which he was an alumnus).[20]

Scott Brown's inclusion of Oldenburg in the Levittown Studio notes constitutes her most incisive analysis and application of his work. Recent publications on his monument proposals and for his retrospective at the Museum of Modern Art were in the bibliography.[21] Statements by the artist in these books presented his current thinking about his monuments. In the latter, Oldenburg claimed,

> A friend who is a student of architecture at Yale told me that the kind of objects I choose are the closest thing to symbols available in our time. Architects find it difficult to design monuments today, he said, because they can't find appropriate symbols ... architects face the problem that whatever is built today is expected to provide some practical civic service—a place to take the baby buggy. My proposals, in keeping with older traditions, do not provide such service.[22]

His large-scale sculptures and his monuments presented, in their resistance toward functionalist precedents, alternative ways to activate spaces, based in vernacular language, a new representational strategy that Scott Brown reflected in Studio notes. And indeed, she and her coauthors implied such consequences in *Learning from Las Vegas*: "The hamburger-shaped hamburger stand is a current, more literal, attempt to express functionalism via association ... for commercial persuasion,"[23] which closely approximates the artist's own statement in the MoMA catalogue: "A monument can be anything. Why isn't this hamburger a monument? Isn't it big enough? A monument is a symbol. I think of a monument as being symbolic and for the people and therefore rhetorical, not honest, not personal."[24] In a photograph of *Floor Burger*, the close cropping of the image, the foreground position of the sculpture, and the inclusion of an observer intensify the sense of space and scale, confining and magnified, encouraging physical sensations in the shift of sculpture toward monument.

Oldenburg also figured in two project descriptions for the Studio. The first required students to gather broad materials on contemporary housing, to:

expand our classification system of ways in which attitudes are determined and comment on those which will be most useful to us in the Studio. Make a bibliography of sources of information on attitudes towards housing and get as many of your sources into the Art and Architecture library as possible. To do this range widely from Madison Avenue to the School of Business to the Survey Research Center (University of Illinois) to local builders and their trade journals, to *Life, Time* and the *New Yorker*, to TV, to Oldenburg and Keinholz [*sic*].[25]

While this inclusion of Oldenburg and Ed Kienholz underscores a desire for plurality in and variety of current contexts, including art, the relevance of these two artists is less clear, though presumably deriving from Kienholz's sculptures and tableaux of found objects and Oldenburg's increasing focus on items related to domesticity, as in *Bedroom Ensemble* (1963) and *The Home* (1964), which represented household furnishings and appliances.

The final research assignment, "The Oldenburg Interpretation," directed students to "[d]o for housing what Oldenburg did for hamburgers":

Oldenburg has essentially made us look at hamburgers in another way because he has portrayed them in an unusual way: big, lacquered and in an art gallery. Does he hate them or love them and should we? Probably he feels some of both, but that doesn't matter—at least, not yet. The first thing is the shift in vision and understanding which an Oldenburg can induce, and the re-interpretation and re-classification of our cultural artifacts which he provides.

Second, in making popular art into high art he legitimises it for the culture vultures. The popular environment, sprawl and strip is drastically in need of a similar service … because Pop is unacceptable until it hangs in the academy and only the artist can put it there.[26]

Scott Brown recognized Oldenburg as a model for his transformations of common objects and his acceptance in New York's art world (as had her comments on Rauschenberg and Lichtenstein in "On Pop, Permissiveness, and Planning"). Hoping for more positive reception of their ideas by the architectural community, she could look to Oldenburg's success as an encouraging precedent.

Oldenburg's art appeared in later projects in which Scott Brown and Venturi applied lessons from the Studios, in proposals for two Bicentennial exhibitions: *Signs of Life: Symbols in the American* City at the Renwick Gallery, Smithsonian Institution, Washington, DC (1976) and *200 Years of American Sculpture* at the Whitney Museum of American Art, New York (1976). Notes by Venturi suggest a "Pop art room" for *Signs of Life*; the proposal lists Oldenburg among the "Photographs and People"—artists, critics, and scholars—who could contribute to their show.[27] In *200 Years,* his work was envisioned as a possible subject for a film or as part of a "Sketch box": "… artist's ideas which have not yet been executed (Oldenburg's city monuments, etc.)."[28] The description of these works as "city" rather than "colossal" monuments, as they were ultimately titled, reinforces urban context rather than relative scale.[29]

Scott Brown was interested in how Oldenburg's art had drawn attention to individual objects and general hierarchies. She articulated his methods (size, surface, location) and proposed poignant implications of his sensorial and contextual perspectives in language that underscores inclusiveness (how he "has made us look"). Her acknowledgment of the "shift in vision and understanding" highlighted Oldenburg's contributions to postwar art and signaled the existence of a common ground upon which artist and architects alike could consider perceptual experiences at the core of their creative strategies, just as it also recalled her goal of finding "new, more receptive ways of seeing the environment" in "On Pop Art, Permissiveness, and Planning." This essay explained the significance of pop art and established terms and concepts that would come to guide her approach to planning and her and Venturi's collaborations on architecture. She introduced the term "strange," which she attributed to Gertrude Stein ("something unexpected"), Francis Bacon ("strangeness in proportion"), and Le Corbusier (references to grain elevators and ships), moving from generalized construct and formal principle to specific example. As she concluded, "it rocks the artist from his aesthetic grooves and resensitizes him to the sources of his inspiration. It may be achieved by breaking rules as did the Mannerists. Here the jolt comes from the unexpected use of a conventional element in an unconventional way ..."[30] This final statement, about sixteenth-century mannerism, anticipates ideas attached to pop art in *Learning from Las Vegas*—"Pop artists used unusual juxtapositions of everyday objects in tense and vivid plays between old and new associations to flout the everyday interdependence of context and meaning, giving us a new interpretation of twentieth-century cultural artifacts. The familiar that is a little off has a *strange* and revealing power"—and is essentially specified, in Studio notes, to Oldenburg's "re-interpretation and re-classification of our cultural artifacts" among many multidimensional, creative and critical sources, inspirations for Scott Brown and Venturi.[31]

Notes

1 Venturi, Scott Brown, and Izenour, *Learning from Las Vegas*, 2.

2 This essay is based on previous publications, including *The Accidental Possibilities of the City* and "Mobilizing Visions: Representing the American Landscape."

3 Venturi, *"Complexity and Contradiction* Twenty-five Years Later," 151.

4 Interview with the author, Manayunk, PA, February 2003. As Venturi acknowledged, "We loved him and learned from him." Colomina, "Learning from Levittown," 65.

5 Scott Brown, "On Pop Art, Permissiveness and Planning," 185.

6 Martino Stierli has written extensively on this topic. See, for instance, Stierli, "Las Vegas and the Mobilized Gaze," 139–147.

7 Rauschenberg's cover of *Time* magazine, "Bonnie and Clyde," December 8, 1967; Lichtenstein's cover, "The Gun in America," June 21, 1968. While Rauschenberg was not a pop artist, his found objects and media images anticipated this style.

8 Scott Brown, "Learning from Pop," 26.

9 Rublowsky, *Pop Art*, 71.

10 Venturi, Scott Brown, and Izenour, *Learning from Las Vegas*, 40–41.

11 See Smith, *Accidental Possibilities*, 26–27, 83.

12 Oldenburg and Williams, *Store Days*, 14

13 van Bruggen, *Claes Oldenburg*, 15; Rottner, "Object Lessons," 182.

14 Venturi, Scott Brown, and Izenour, *Learning from Las Vegas*, 56.

15 Venturi, Scott Brown, and Izenour, *Learning from Las Vegas*, 51.

16 Venturi, Scott Brown, and Izenour, *Learning from Las Vegas*, 78.

17 McCoubrey, "Art on the Road," 22.

18 Oldenburg, interview with Barbara Rose, 18 January 1968, C83. The Barbara Rose Papers, Getty Research Institute, Los Angeles (930100); my transcript.

19 Marcuse, "Commenting on Claes Oldenburg's Proposed Monuments for New York City," 75–76. Williams, "Lipstick Ascending," 116–144.

20 Wrede, "Revisiting 1968–69," 129. See also Blau, "This Work is Going Somewhere," 131–149; "Pedagogy and Politics," 33–66.

21 Rose, *Claes Oldenburg* appears in the bibliography as no. 262, 51; Oldenburg, *Proposals for Monuments and Buildings, 1965–1969* as no. 322, 46. "Studio RHA: Bibliography," 26 January 1970, 225. XIII.A.1, in the Venturi Scott Brown Collection, by the gift of Robert Venturi and Denise Scott Brown, at the Architectural Archives of the University of Pennsylvania, Philadelphia (hereafter cited as VSBC, AAUP).

22 Carroll, "The Poetry of Scale: Interview with Claes Oldenburg," 25.

23 Venturi, Scott Brown, and Izenour, *Learning from Las Vegas*, 78.

24 Oldenburg, quoted in Rose, *Claes Oldenburg*, 103.

25 Scott Brown, "Remedial Housing for Architects Studio," 54.

26 Scott Brown, "Remedial Housing for Architects Studio," 57. Scott Brown has more recently explained, "I was thinking of Oldenburg's soft sculpture, particularly his soft hamburger. If he had a way of artistically interpreting a hamburger, we as architects should be able to artistically interpret a suburban house." Scott Brown, in Colomina, "Learning from Levittown," 65. Critic John Canaday, in his review of the retrospective exhibition, likewise led with hamburgers: "Mr. Oldenburg's gigantic hamburgers ... his collapsed electric fans ... his wall switches and maps and calendars and drum sets ... are entertaining concoctions individually, but en masse, even though they have no schematic formal relationship, they present us with something like a panorama of the 20th-century urban landscape in which most Americans spend most of their time." John Canaday, "Oldenburg as The Picasso of Pop," D33.

27 See notes by Venturi, 31 July 1974; draft of the exhibition proposal, July 1974, which specifies Oldenburg's monuments as the intended works, n.p.; and "Feasibility Study for a City Exhibition in the Renwick Gallery for the Bicentennial Celebration," 31 August 1974, 19, Folders 225.XVI.A.1, 225. XVI.A.219, and 225.VI.7406.14, VSBC, AAUP.

28 "Two Hundred Years of American Sculpture Preliminary Proposal for the Design of an Exhibition at the Whitney Museum," 22 November 1974, 6–7, Folder 225.II.A.7501.06, VSBC, AAUP.

29 Oldenburg first exhibited these works at the Sidney Janis Gallery as "Projects for Colossal City Monuments," a title that emphasized their gigantic size and urban location. The similarity to the architects' term suggests they may have been familiar with this early installation, as the term "city" was subsequently removed from their titles. Oldenburg, *New Work by Claes Oldenburg*, n.p.

30 Scott Brown, "Pop Art, Permissiveness, and Planning," 185.

31 Venturi, Scott Brown, and Izenour, *Learning from Las Vegas*, 86; my emphasis.

"Ultimately, then, it was not about jumping from architecture to planning, but about rethinking what it was to be an architect, and that choosing amelioration over revolution would itself be revolutionary in architecture."

—Denise Scott Brown, *From Soane to the Strip: Soane Medal Lecture 2018*

Part III
1970s –2020s:
Designing

Recollections IV: Denise and Bob on My Mind

Inès Lamunière

Building and Thinking

I met them one January evening, at their apartment on Society Hill—was it on the twelfth floor? It was snowing outside. I was just sixteen, Bob was about to turn forty-five and Denise was thirty-nine.[1] The pale snowflakes and the lights of Philadelphia were framed in the vast floor-to-ceiling bay windows; I.M. Pei's concrete window frames encircled this cityscape like paintings. My brain still foggy from jetlag, I listened to them talking, in that particular accent of theirs: they spoke of South Street, the ghettos, rebellion, and pop culture and about the difficulty of being an architect. Philadelphia was a social, economic, and political battleground. The next day, I embarked on my studies at the Shipley School in Bryn Mawr, then a girls' school, where Denise had enrolled me (incidentally, this would be one of the "campus planning" sites, a project spearheaded by Denise for several years until 1997). It was four months of intensive studies alongside my discovery of a form of American realism: visits to huge derelict factories in north Philadelphia; to suburbia and the Vanna Venturi and Margaret Esherick houses; to deserted, deprived, depressing neighborhoods, and the Guild House; to the Penn campus and the Fisher Fine Arts Library designed by Frank Furness, the Richards laboratories, and Eero Saarinen's girls' dorm (which I liked very much). A gritty, fragmented city. This period that was so prolific for Denise and Bob's "beginnings," to quote Louis Kahn, was sandwiched between their writing, teaching at Penn and Yale, projects (including the competition for the Mathematics Building, 1969) and construction—buildings that I discovered later, when they were published in Bob's "gentle" manifesto of 1966 and his and Denise's of 1972. At my young age, this complexity felt bewildering.

Denise and Bob were from that American elsewhere that I love, which has always attracted me because of my bilingual background. Being a young architect in the 1970s rooted me in the European debate on architecture at the time, one which saw critical regionalism break away from America's internationalist culture, that of the conquering power, from its great historical architects (Mies van der Rohe, Eero Saarinen, Skidmore, Owings & Merrill/ SOM, etc.), through the apostles of a post-modernity that was probably necessary (Philip Johnson, Charles Moore, the New York Five). But where were the Kahns, the Venturis, and the Gehrys in academia and in the European debate on architecture? Where was the dialogue about the metropolises of the new world? Where was art? Where was the making? Kenneth Frampton, my supervisor at the Ecole polytechnique fédérale de Lausanne (EPFL), had no wish at that time, in 1978, to express an opinion on Kahn, and probably even less on the Venturis. The American way, to quote Serge Rezvani, was sullied, putrefaction, most likely also politically tainted, and Europe should keep out of it.

I subscribed to the journal *Progressive Architecture*, and that alternative way of reflecting on the meaning of architecture felt important. In the March 1976 issue, on the occasion of the American bicentenary, the historian and publisher Robert Coombs wrote about the simultaneity of American and European research in these words: "Kahn, Venturi, Denise Scott Brown and Charles W. Moore (at Yale) gradually opened up a Pandora's box of analytical-historicist architecture at approximately the same time that architectural semiology was getting up steam in Europe." But this Pandora's box did not have the same content. Neither the cultural and social environment, and even less the history or the language, were the same. Kahn and Scott Brown/Venturi were as far removed from Europe as Aldo Rossi or Álvaro Siza from America. Even if there were differences over the meaning of architecture between Kahn's covert symbolizing and the Venturis' overt sign making, both were profoundly imbued with the idea that architecture is part of the context of its civilization, producing its self-representations, its images, illusions, and

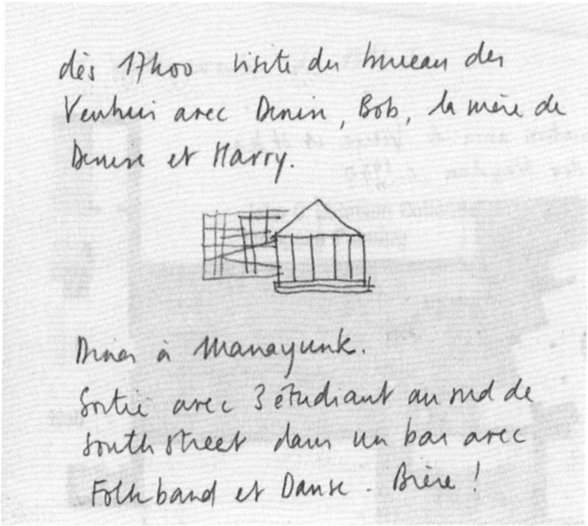

Figure 1: Sketch from my
notebook (September 29,
1990).

*des 17h00 visite du bureau des
Venturi avec Denise, Bob, la mère de
Denise et Harry.*

*Dîner à Manayunk.
Sortie avec 3 étudiant au md de
south street dans un bar avec
Folk band et Dance - Bière!*

memories. One year later, Stanislaus von Moos echoed this idea in a special issue of *werk-archithese*, devoted to Venturi & Rauch.[2]

Paying Homage

It was a Saturday afternoon—September 29, 1990, to be precise. I know because I have the habit of recording everything in little notebooks of sketches and commentaries. That day, after I'd spent a morning at Denise and Bob's Franklin Court (I'd written "Just perfect!"), and a good while with Marcel Duchamp's *The Bride Stripped Bare by Her Bachelors, Even*, the train took me to the office in Manayunk. Denise and Bob were expecting Patrick Devanthéry and myself. It was our first big trip to the East Coast, from Cambridge to Charlottesville, with Philadelphia the main stop. At that time in Europe, since the completion of the National Gallery extension in London, Scott Brown/Venturi had quietly been relegated to the role of heritage thinkers rather than being regarded as contemporary architects; in other words, they had become suspect. And yet this trip was so enriching: Denise and Bob discussed, in front of us, on yellow tracing paper with collages of gray, yellow, blue, and maybe brown strips. "Denise, what do you think? Better this way or that way, closer ... ?" With the help of a postage-stamp–sized sketch, I re-transcribed in my notebook the vertical rhythms and vibrant colors of the proposed extension to Bard College library's classical façade with its colonnade and pediment. It was so inspiring, a "beginning," sketched, live. That entire trip brought me even closer to America, still so raw, still so imperfect. I loved Denise and Bob's work more than that of Kahn (except for Kahn's two Yale buildings). The interior and exterior public spaces that they created with such disconcerting ease, between the complex functions, the distribution of circulation, the insertions of building parts and fragments, the facades (the motifs). Franklin Court, as I've already mentioned. The laboratories: the Clinical Research Building at Penn, the Lewis Thomas at Princeton, the George LaVie Schultz laboratory at Princeton (then under construction). The Gordon Wu Hall at Princeton, the Humanities and Social Sciences Buildings at Purchase. The Institute of Scientific Information at Philadelphia, and the entire older oeuvre, especially the building I did not have time to visit: the Oberlin Museum.

Figure 3: Geneva Water-
front Competition, 2015.

It was all this that I found hard to discuss with my colleagues when Stanislaus von Moos kindly asked me to contribute to a conversation in 1995 on the
influence of the Venturis in Switzerland.[3]

In Moderato Cantabile: Three Personal Projects Influenced
by Venturi/Scott Brown

First of all, Student Housing (1989–93), in association with Patrick Devanthéry.
Von Moos describes this building as having a "Venturian" legacy. Martin Steinmann sees in it the turmoil of semantic structural research, the message of
which remains "open." This first project in an urban setting, at the corner of a
boulevard and Geneva's first classic ring road, led us to think about typologies
of communal student residences. We created two different facades: that of the
bedrooms (square 3 × 3-meter windows with extruded aluminum frames), and
that of the living rooms and shared spaces (ribbon windows stretching across

Figure 4: Town House, Brooklyn, design 2017, under construction.

a surface covered in small squares of gray and yellow glass paste). One is flat, the other curved, two masks or screens facing different urban settings.

Next, Geneva Waterfront (2014). The motto for this competition project could have been "Denise and Bob on the Lake." Devising a master plan for the bay of Geneva meant visualizing and revamping its symbols: Eden, refuge, peace. It meant enlarging and amplifying the features of its setting. The *Jet d'eau* fountain, that extraordinary sculpture of water, light and air: raise the jet from 140 meters to 313 meters to echo the scale of the contemporary city that the Geneva metropolis will become. Reflect the fascinating ballet of pleasure boats in a giant boat on Lake Geneva that will host more than 3,000 people to watch the annual firework displays and future large-scale events on the shores of the lake. The old port landing stage: design a world pavilion, an emblematic building, a sort of marquee that would house philharmonic concerts or political events. But also: extend the long garland of light bulbs and emphasize that line of light that would be mirrored in the lake in calm weather. The ensemble like a new spatial "billboard," both night and day.

And lastly, Town House, Brooklyn (2017–under construction). Building a house in an American city was a dream that had been going round and round in my mind. In a small car, in the subway, on foot, I criss-crossed New York and specifically Brooklyn. Seeking a specific place, a corner lot, to construct a town house, solid, private, with two addresses (Classon and Greene), two front doors, one family. One picture window per facade, no more. A cubic form culminating in a triangle, the Classon facade three stories high and the Greene's two. A screen on one side reminiscent of a facade in a western, initially flat, then tapering at the corner, and finally, in *trompe l'œil* on the side. The interior and the ensemble are simple, not too detailed, almost commonplace, and ordinary for 2022.

Denise visits EPFL

Eleven years ago, Denise came back to Geneva and was invited to give a lecture in the Architecture Department at the EPFL. This was on the occasion of an exhibition of her photographs of Las Vegas at the EPFL, with the ongoing relevance of Scott Brown/Venturi's discourse of the time. I took her to see the SANAA-designed Rolex Learning Center, built in 2008. We had lunch there. She was, as always, articulate but, as usual, not especially empathetic; her comments were acerbic. Whereas for my Swiss colleagues, the building was merely bad detailing, for Denise, it was nothing but a form, a formal design. What a pity![4]

Notes

1   I owe my first meeting with Bob and Denise to my father, Jean-Marc Lamunière. He shared a lasting friendship with them. Bob and he were both born in 1925—one in Philadelphia, the other in Rome.

2   Stanislaus von Moos and Diego Peverelli, eds., *Venturi & Rauch: 25 öffentliche Bauten.*

3   Stanislaus von Moos, Martin Steinmann, Roger Diener, and Inès Lamunière, "Affinitäten, Divergenzen und offene Fragen."

4   Translated from the French by Ros Schwartz.

Figure 1: Aerial photograph of La Sarraz (detail).

"Make Little Plans": Scott Brown at the Fiftieth Anniversary of CIAM

Frida Grahn

On the afternoon of July 1, 1978, about a hundred and fifty people gathered at the Château de La Sarraz, perched on a hill overlooking the plains of western Switzerland (fig. 1), to commemorate the fiftieth anniversary of CIAM, the International Congresses of Modern Architecture, founded at the castle in 1928.[1] During a two-day seminar entitled "Meaning and Architectural Expression,"[2] the medieval stronghold became a convergence point for currents of twentieth-century architecture: on the one hand, of the functionalist tradition, represented by original members of CIAM,[3] and on the other, of a new interest in communication in architecture, represented by Denise Scott Brown and Robert Venturi.[4]

The event took place in the midst of a reappraisal of the CIAM doctrine and was characterized by an ambivalent duality of celebration and critique.[5] CIAM had been the voice of the modern movement, promoting rationalization and a vision of the functional city, as described in the Athens Charter of 1933.[6] The ideas were implemented on a large scale after the Second World War, but the results were soon criticized for their lack of communicative power. The discussion on functionalism versus meaning in architecture was at the core of the deliberations at La Sarraz,[7] but the argument was expanded in the contribution by Scott Brown. Her lecture added a social and political dimension to the largely formalist debate, arguing for user participation and preservation of the existing urban fabric—a consequential message, as articulated in the accounts of media representatives and students who attended the seminar.

On February 2, 1978, the organizer Pierre Bechler sent a letter of invitation by air mail to "Mrs. and Mr. Venturi."[8] Bechler referred to their mutual friend Jean-Marc Lamunière,[9] who was aware that Scott Brown's parents lived in Geneva, which increased the likeliness of a positive response.[10] In early June, Scott Brown confirmed their participation at the seminar and their arrival in

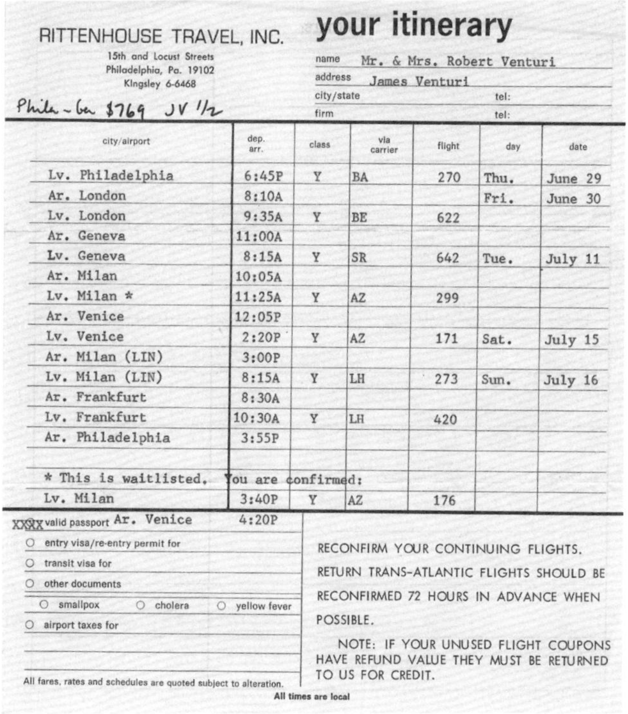

Figure 2: Itinerary, Mr. &
Mrs. Robert Venturi,
June 29 to July 16, 1978,
"La Sarraz Conference
1 & 2 July 1978."

RITTENHOUSE TRAVEL, INC.
15th and Locust Streets
Philadelphia, Pa. 19102
Kingsley 6-6468

Phila - Ln $769 JV 1/2

your itinerary

name Mr. & Mrs. Robert Venturi
address James Venturi
city/state   tel:
firm   tel:

city/airport	dep. arr.	class	via carrier	flight	day	date
Lv. Philadelphia	6:45P	Y	BA	270	Thu.	June 29
Ar. London	8:10A				Fri.	June 30
Lv. London	9:35A	Y	BE	622		
Ar. Geneva	11:00A					
Lv. Geneva	8:15A	Y	SR	642	Tue.	July 11
Ar. Milan	10:05A					
Lv. Milan *	11:25A	Y	AZ	299		
Ar. Venice	12:05P					
Lv. Venice	2:20P	Y	AZ	171	Sat.	July 15
Ar. Milan (LIN)	3:00P					
Lv. Milan (LIN)	8:15A	Y	LH	273	Sun.	July 16
Ar. Frankfurt	8:30A					
Lv. Frankfurt	10:30A	Y	LH	420		
Ar. Philadelphia	3:55P					
* This is waitlisted. You are confirmed:						
Lv. Milan	3:40P	Y	AZ	176		
XXXX valid passport Ar. Venice	4:20P					

O entry visa/re-entry permit for
O transit visa for
O other documents
O smallpox   O cholera   O yellow fever
O airport taxes for

All fares, rates and schedules are quoted subject to alteration.
All times are local

RECONFIRM YOUR CONTINUING FLIGHTS.
RETURN TRANS-ATLANTIC FLIGHTS SHOULD BE
RECONFIRMED 72 HOURS IN ADVANCE WHEN
POSSIBLE.
NOTE: IF YOUR UNUSED FLIGHT COUPONS
HAVE REFUND VALUE THEY MUST BE RETURNED
TO US FOR CREDIT.

Geneva on June 30 (fig. 2).[11] On the morning of the conference, Scott Brown, Venturi, and their young son reached the small town of La Sarraz, checking in at the Hôtel de Ville and joining the welcome lunch for the speakers.[12] Afterward, on their way to the castle, they possibly passed by the Chapelle Saint-Antoine, where the group photo of the first CIAM congress had been taken fifty years earlier, just after the legendary Declaration of La Sarraz had been signed (fig. 3).

Arriving at the castle, Scott Brown and Venturi likely gazed at its two imposing towers from the thirteenth century, embedded in a park with large trees. The seminar was held in a voluminous wooden barn on the premises.[13] The first day included a three-hour session, starting out with a presentation by the Italian architect Alberto Sartoris,[14] followed by one by the Swiss art historian

Figure 3: At the first CIAM congress, Chapelle Saint-Antoine, La Sarraz, June 28, 1928.

Jacques Gubler[15] and another by the Swiss architect Mario Botta.[16] The moderator, René Berger,[17] announced that the presentation by "Venturi" had been moved to Sunday afternoon (probably due to difficulty in finding a projector for the large American slides),[18] after presentations by Vittorio Gregotti, Michel Ragon, and Jean-Marc Lamunière. Berger's handwritten notes leave out Scott Brown, a lapse which seems to have been symptomatic for the event. Jacques Gubler comments in hindsight that "Scott Brown was regarded as an *accompagnatrice*, not as an architect. She was treated and respected as the wife of the speaker," even though she was herself listed as a speaker in the program (fig. 5).[19]

The rescheduling was lamented by the art historian Armand Brulhart, who reported for the newspaper *Journal de Genève*.[20] Their lectures are discussed prominently in his article and in notes by the Swiss architect and writer Lisbeth Sachs, who considered that Venturi's presentation was an "anti-CIAM manifesto," in which he argued for the "decorated shed" and "symbols which speak to the user."[21] Brulhart notes that Venturi's presence "could have been a provocation," pointing out that his message was "the exact opposite" to that of the CIAM "prophet" Le Corbusier.[22]

Scott Brown's lecture, entitled "Political Ideology and Architectural Expression," can be reconstructed using the notes by Sachs, the account by Brulhart, and two pages of handwritten notes by Scott Brown held in the Architectural Archives at the University of Pennsylvania.[23] Her alternative to the Athens Charter was informed by her social planning education and included supporting existing communities, exemplified in the projects for South Street (1968–72) and Fairmont Manor (1972–73) in Philadelphia.[24] In these projects, Scott Brown (and her team) "examines what exists, draws up analyses, suggests proposals inspired by the inhabitants themselves," as Brulhart writes.[25] The strategy involves self-help and "participation of the affected low-income population," but also preservation of the existing building stock. This approach also characterized her work on the projects for the warehouse street The Strand in Galveston, Texas (1974–76) and the old coal mining city of Jim Thorpe, Pennsylvania (1977–79), where the strategy uses rich Victorian architectural heritage to promote the "means of livelihood" of local residents, as Scott Brown notes. In these projects she worked within the establishment to combine economic revitalization, reuse, and building preservation.[26]

Commenting on her lecture in 2021, Scott Brown explains the argument in favor of smaller inventions: "make little plans," she notes, turning Daniel Burnham's dictum into a radically humble statement. Quoting David Crane, she says that planning a city is like "drawing on a river. The river takes the clarity away and eventually it dissolves into nothing."[27] The complexity of cities makes the implementation of universal grand schemes futile and dangerous. She discerns a lack of modesty among her fellow architects, who are often regarded as all-knowing "perfect vision" planners with "20/20-vision at the eye doctor and a long-time-plan for the year 2020. Meanwhile people are starving right at their doorsteps."[28]

Brulhart wrote admiringly of Scott Brown's "conviction," commenting that the "two voices of America proposed no great new idea, no theory, no recipe, but the meaning of their concrete work, not in the service of clients or city officials, but in the service of people and communities." This was in stark contrast to the morning lecture by the architecture critic Michel Ragon who, as Brulhart noted, "presented the utopias of the 1960s and the 'technical'

La maison des artistes
Château de La Sarraz

fondée par Hélène de Mandrot en 1922

ORGANISATION

Dates   ouverture : samedi 1er juillet 78, à 14 h.
       clôture : dimanche 2 juillet 78, à 16 h. 45

Lieu   Château de La Sarraz
       à 20 km. de Lausanne
       route : direction Vallorbe, Lausanne - Cos-
       sonay - La Sarraz
       train : direction Vallorbe

Prix   séminaire selon programme
       y compris apéritif et déjeuner   Fr. 240.—

       suppléments :

       — chambre à 1 lit   avec douche   28.—
                          sans douche   23.—
       — chambre à 2 lits avec douche   48.—
                          sans douche   40.—
       (petit déjeuner compris)

       — souper samedi 1er juillet   32.—
       (vin et café compris)

       séminaire, prix pour étudiants   Fr. 50.—

Délai d'inscription : vendredi 9 juin 1978

vous invite au

séminaire

signification et expression architecturale

samedi 1er et dimanche 2 juillet 1978
au Château de La Sarraz

PROGRAMME

1er juillet	
14.00	allocution de bienvenue
	P. Bechler, architecte, initiateur des manifestations
14.15-17.15	exposé et discussion
17.15	apéritif
2 juillet	
9.30-12.15	exposés et discussion
12.30	déjeuner
14.00-15.30	exposés
15.30-16.45	discussion générale
16.45	clôture du séminaire

INTRODUCTION

L'architecture, l'urbanisme, constitués par un pro-
cessus complexe — nous faisons partie du proces-
sus et en même temps nous le constituons — se
planifient à partir de critères primaires susceptibles
de subir des mutations dans le temps et qui peuvent
prendre des significations particulières dans l'expression même des objets créés.

La signification profonde d'une expression architecturale, constituant en quelque sorte une quatrième
dimension, reste souvent cachée aux utilisateurs,
aux spectateurs, ou même aux spécialistes. Par
contre, à travers des objets physiques, elle peut
acquérir une « image stable » et devenir signaux.

Le séminaire tentera l'analyse et la confrontation
de quelques critères d'approche de la création architecturale réclamant pour elle des significations
propres à sa véritable expression.

Exposés :

M. Robert Venturi, architecte, Etats-Unis
Mme Denise Scott-Brown, architecte, Etats-Unis
« l'environnement social et l'expression architecturale »
« l'idéologie politique et l'expression architecturale »

M. Michel Ragon, professeur, France
« prospective et utopie des années 60 »

M. Vittorio Gregotti, architecte, Italie
« le site et l'expression architecturale — principes
théoriques »

M. Alberto Sartoris, architecte, Suisse
« la signification de l'art dans l'architecture »

M. Jean-Marc Lamunière, architecte, Suisse
« le vécu de l'usager et l'expression architecturale »

M. Mario Botta, architecte, Suisse
« la signification de l'environnement construit et
naturel »

M. Jacques Gubler, historien d'art, Suisse
« la signification de l'histoire, refus et acceptation »

l'animation et la coordination des débats seront as-
surées par M. René Berger, directeur du Musée
cantonal des Beaux-Arts, Lausanne

CARTE D'INSCRIPTION

(prière de remplir en caractères d'imprimerie)

séminaire

signification et expression architecturale

nom   _____

prénom   _____

adresse   _____

pays   _____

tél.   _____

séminaire :		☐ 240.—
suppléments :		
chambre à 1 lit	avec douche	☐ 28.—
	sans douche	☐ 23.—
chambre à 2 lits (2 pers.) avec douche		☐ 48.—
(2 pers.) sans douche		☐ 40.—
souper le 1er juillet 78		☐ 32.—

indiquer le nombre de nuitées

étudiants   ☐ 50.—

nom de l'école   _____

le montant de Fr. _____ sera versé au ccp. 10 - 138 42
après réception de la carte de participation

date   _____

signature   _____

☐ Prière de marquer d'une croix ce qui convient

Figures 4 and 5: Front and back page of the flyer "Signification et expression architecturale."

nightmares of the megalopolises of the future," stating that architects have to be "interested in megastructures, in the cities that we would build under the earth, under the sea, etc. … a prospect which did not leave the students indifferent."[29]

The architecture students present at La Sarraz were not the only ones who objected to Ragon's polemical presentation. Scott Brown and the Zurich architect Alfred Roth, chatting during a break, agreed that visions such as those of Archigram were "frightening."[30] Scott Brown recalls that Roth was "horrified" by Archigram and was likely relieved that she, in spite of being known as a "pop architect," was not agreeing with the British visionaries. Scott Brown recalls comparing CIAM and Archigram, criticizing both for ignoring "the quality of the town as an incremental entity."[31] In the general discussion, Roth had himself become the subject of critique for his large-scale projects, which were, however, according to Scott Brown, "not like the ones by Archigram."[32] Looking back, Scott Brown was delighted at how well she and the CIAM member Roth got along. She was familiar with his Doldertal Houses in Zurich (1935–36, designed with Emil Roth and Marcel Breuer), to which she had been introduced by her longtime friend Robin Middleton when they were students (see his chapter in this volume).[33] Roth, who had previously objected to the presence of the Americans,[34] might have been mollified by their shared aversion. A few years later, Roth would write critically on "Roberto Venturi" [sic] and the "decorated shed," but without mentioning Scott Brown.[35] Roth's skepticism about decoration was discernible in the younger generation listening in the audience at La Sarraz. Marc Angélil, who attended the seminar while he was a student at ETH Zurich, recalls:

> I remember that a small group of students who were studying with Aldo van Eyck at ETH Zurich went to La Sarraz to specifically see and hear what Robert Venturi had to say. We knew of Venturi/Scott Brown from René Furer's [architecture theory] lectures. Venturi showed a lot of flower motifs that he was decoratively applying on facades and furniture. This was somehow disappointing to us. However, the big surprise was Denise Scott Brown who talked about social issues and the role of politics in

architecture, urban design, and planning. In hindsight, her lecture marked my further development, though I did not know at the time how influential she would turn out to be![36]

Scott Brown gave a similar lecture one year later, in November 1979, to a packed auditorium at ETH Zurich. Angélil volunteered as an assistant, handling the slides at the back,[37] not missing out on the opportunity to hear Scott Brown speak a second time, just before completing his Diploma in Architecture in 1979.[38]

The balancing act between critique and celebration at La Sarraz 1978 was received with mixed emotions. The student François de Wolff recalled in 2021 that the event did not live up to its grandiose setting.[39] Two other attendees voiced their confusion in a letter to Berger, asking if the first day of the conference had been about CIAM or about contemporary architecture.[40] In 1978, the ideas of CIAM were seen as too distant to count as contemporary and were too close to be fully historicized.[41]

Scott Brown, however, looks back at the event with fondness, as the first time she and Venturi "went public in Switzerland."[42] Judging from comments and media accounts, her contribution must have been one of the most consequential, even though she was treated as the "wife of the speaker." Scott Brown extended the discussion about meaning in architecture to the scale of the city and its inhabitants, offering a viable alternative to CIAM-inspired *tabula rasa* urban renewal. Presenting her work and ideas at La Sarraz, Scott Brown took part as a practitioner and innovative thinker in her own right. Her opposition to the Athens Charter—a document responsible for almost a "hundred years of wrong-doing"[43]—would be a constant throughout her work. Scott Brown's strategy of "little plans," her advocacy for keeping existing structures, is an early example of dealing with the given, which combined her social, economic, and functional concerns. Her ideas remain relevant today—especially in light of the ongoing climate crisis.

Notes

1 CIAM (*Congrès Internationaux d'Architecture Moderne*) was founded at La Sarraz on June 28, 1928 on the initiative of Hélène de Mandrot (1867–1948), chatelaine and patron of the arts and architecture, by a group of twenty-eight architects who signed the "Declaration of La Sarraz." See Steinmann, *CIAM: Internationale Kongresse für Neues Bauen,* 9–35.

2 French original: "Signification et expression architecturale." This chapter is an excerpt from my ongoing doctoral dissertation entitled "The Swiss Reception of Robert Venturi and Denise Scott Brown, 1970–2000." It is based on unpublished primary sources from Swiss and American archives, including documents held with the Venturi Scott Brown Collection, by the gift of Robert Venturi and Denise Scott Brown, at the Architectural Archives of the University of Pennsylvania, Philadelphia (hereafter cited as VSBC, AAUP). Further documents are held with the Archives cantonales vaudoises, Lausanne (hereafter ACV), in the gta Archives at ETH Zurich and at the Archives de la construction modern at EPF Lausanne (hereafter ACM, EPFL). I wish to thank William Whitaker, Heather Isbell Schumacher, and Allison Rose Olsen for their support during my archival research in Philadelphia. Further thanks go to Rahel Hartmann Schweizer for help in deciphering the handwriting of Lisbeth Sachs, and to François Falconet, ACV, for help with the handwriting of René Berger. I am grateful to Denise Scott Brown, who made me aware of the seminar in La Sarraz in our first telephone conversation in 2017, and to Rosmarie Bechler, Jacques Gubler, Marc Angélil, and François de Wolff for sharing their memories.

3 The guests of honor included Alfred Roth (1903–1998), Henri-Robert Von der Mühll (1898–1980), and Alberto Sartoris (1901–1998). See folders "0172.03.0027" (Bequest of Alberto Sartoris) and "0009.01.004" (Bequest of Henri-Robert Von der Mühll), ACM, EPFL and "131-IL-50" (Bequest of Alfred Roth), gta Archives, ETH Zurich.

4 Robert Venturi and Denise Scott Brown had a considerable reputation in Switzerland, through publications in the journals *Werk* and *Archithese* and dissemination at schools of architecture, such as the Architecture Department at ETH Zurich. The French translation of *Complexity and Contradiction in Architecture* had been released in 1971 as *De l'ambiguïté en architecture.* German translations of *Complexity and Contradiction* and *Learning from Las Vegas* were underway as part of the Bauwelt Fundamente series. For more information, see Grahn, "Beyond Realism." For an in-depth discussion of Scott Brown and Venturi's stance on functionalism, see Denise Costanzo, "Venturi and Scott Brown as Functionalists" and her chapter in this volume.

5 This was preceded by a phase of self-criticism within CIAM, for example during the 1956 Summer School in Venice, which Scott Brown attended. For more information, see the chapters by Denise Costanzo and Stanislaus von Moos in this volume.

6 See Hilpert, *Le Corbusiers "Charta von Athen."*

7 See, for example, Jencks and Baird, *Meaning in Architecture.* The language of the event's description is indebted to discourse on sign theory in architecture: "The deep meaning of an architectural expression ... often remains hidden from users, spectators, or even specialists. On the other hand, through physical objects, it can acquire a 'stable image' and become a sign." Translation from the French original. Flyer "Signification et expression architecturale," "PP 869/134," ACV.

8 A handwritten note by Scott Brown reads "I'd love to go." Pierre Bechler, letter to "Mrs. and Mr. Venturi," February 2, 1978, "General Correspondence (Oct–Dec) 1978," 225.VI.D.219, VSBC, AAUP.

9 Jean-Marc Lamunière (1925–2015) was a Geneva-based architect who taught regularly in Philadelphia. Pierre Bechler (1938–1992) was a well-connected principal of a small architecture office in the town of La Sarraz. Other commemorative activities in 1978 included a series of lectures, film screenings, and an exhibition of furniture design, "Le meuble l'architecture," in collaboration with Alberto Sartoris, on view between June 17 and September 18, 1978. Rosmarie Bechler, interview with the author, La Sarraz, on December 17, 2021. See the exhibition catalogue *Le meuble, l'architecture* for more information.

10 Scott Brown's parents moved to Geneva in the 1960s. She and Venturi visited Switzerland regularly. Scott Brown, interview with the author, Philadelphia, November 30, 2021. Besides Lamunière, other longtime friends included Irène and Stanislaus von Moos. Von Moos was co-founder and editor of the Swiss architecture journal *Archithese,* of which Scott

Brown was on the editorial board and where translations of her writings were published. Scott Brown,

11 Scott Brown, letter to Bechler, June 5, 1978, "General Correspondence (Oct–Dec) 1978," 225. VI.D.219, VSBC, AAUP.

12 Participant register, "PP 869/134," ACV.

13 Venturi, letter to Gubler, July 26, 1978, "General Correspondence (Oct–Dec) 1978," 225.VI.D.219, VSBC, AAUP.

14 Flyer "Signification et expression architecturale," "PP 869/134," ACV and in the unprocessed folder "La Sarraz Conference 1 & 2 July 1978," Denise Scott Brown Home Dead File, Box 34, VSBC, AAUP. Sartoris was one of the signers of the declaration of La Sarraz in 1928.

15 Gubler's doctoral dissertation of 1975 was part of the historicization of CIAM. See Gubler, *Nationalisme et internationalisme dans l'architecture moderne de la Suisse.*

16 A manuscript of Botta's lecture is held with the bequest of Lisbeth Sachs, "114-S-27," gta Archives, ETH Zurich.

17 The Belgian philosopher, art historian and semiologist René Berger (1915–2009) was director of the Cantonal Museum of Fine Arts, Lausanne.

18 Gubler, interview with the author, Basel, October 5, 2020.

19 Gubler, email to the author, November 11, 2020.

20 Brulhart, "La race des prophètes a disparu." ("The race of prophets has disappeared") Translation from the French original.

21 The notes of Lisbeth Sachs (1914–2002) are held in the folder "114-S-27," gta Archives, ETH Zurich.

22 Brulhart, "La race des prophètes a disparu." Translation from the French original.

23 Scott Brown, lecture notes "Signification et expression architecturale. La Sarraz, 20 June '78," folder "La Sarraz Conference 1 & 2 July 1978," Denise Scott Brown Home Dead File, Box 34, VSBC, AAUP.

24 For more on South Street, see the essay by Sarah Moses in this volume. On social planning, see the contributions by Marianna Charitonidou and James Yellin.

25 Brulhart, "La race des prophètes a disparu." Translation from the French original.

26 The projects are described in more detail in Scott Brown's *Urban Concepts.*

27 Scott Brown, interview with the author, Philadelphia, November 30, 2021.

28 The critique is developed in Scott Brown's essay "On Architectural Formalism and Social Concern."

29 Brulhart, "La race des prophètes a disparu." Translation from the French original.

30 Scott Brown, telephone conversation with the author, October 18, 2017.

31 Scott Brown's compares Archigram and CIAM already in 1968, in her essay "Little Magazines in Architecture and Urbanism," 225.

32 Scott Brown, interview with the author, Philadelphia, November 30, 2021. Roth was planning an urban agglomeration for 40,000 inhabitants in Amman at this time. Roth, letter to Gubler, June 2, 1978. "131-IL-50," gta Archives, ETH Zurich.

33 Scott Brown, telephone conversation with the author, March 6, 2022. Middleton knew the project from Roth's *The New Architecture*, published on pages 47–60.

34 "Est-ce que le blabla de Venturi et compagnie arrivera ????" Roth, letter to Gubler, June 2, 1978, "131-IL-50," gta Archives, ETH Zurich.

35 Roth, "Kritische Anmerkungen zur heutigen Situation der Architektur." We can only speculate as to Roth's reasons for leaving out Scott Brown. Sexism might have played a role, although Roth had argued furiously that more attention should be given to Hélène de Mandrot, as the initiator of CIAM at La Sarraz in 1928. Gubler, email to the author, September 4, 2021.

36 Angélil, email to the author, October 26, 2021.

37 Angélil, email to the author, December 13, 2021.

38 In the 1980s, Angélil would teach at the Graduate School of Design at Harvard University and then at the University of Southern California in Los Angeles before returning to ETH Zurich as Professor of Architecture and Design (1994–2019). See also Angélil, "Gewöhnliche und aussergewöhnliche Architektur" and Angélil, "Gewöhnliches thematisieren oder eliminieren?"

39 de Wolff, email to the author, November 19, 2021.

40 Isabelle Martin and Michel Parrat, letter to René Berger, July 1, 1978, "PP 525/1570," ACV.

41 The historicization of CIAM began following the foundation of the CIAM Archive at the gta Archives at ETH Zurich in 1967. See Steinmann, *CIAM: Internationale Kongresse für Neues Bauen.*

42 Scott Brown, telephone conversation with the author, October 18, 2017.

43 Scott Brown, telephone conversation with the author, March 6, 2022.

Exile and Redemption: Denise Scott Brown, Josef Frank, and the Meanings of Postmodernism

Christopher Long

One of the inevitable prices of exile is loss—loss of place, loss of family and community, and, all too often and most irrevocably perhaps, loss of one's culture. For some, such loss is impossible to overcome. Too many exiles drift along in a fixed place of dislocation never to be cast off. Yet, for others, the profound losses of exile can open new possibilities, new vistas—powerful new avenues for living and thinking.

The meanings of exile came home with heightened relief to Denise Scott Brown, as she tells it, when she first learned of the Viennese-born architect Josef Frank and his work and ideas. In her essay "Reclaiming Frank's Seat at the Table," published as an introduction to Frank's complete published writings in 2012, Scott Brown writes that her first encounter with Frank brought a profound sense of self-recognition:

> When Robert Venturi and I "met" Frank in 2005 in Vienna, his life seemed to have paralleled ours; not only in personal history, but through the experiences and ideas we shared as architects. His career held important revelations for us and I would have been happy to dance (waltz?) to his tune while interweaving our three sagas in work and thought.[1]

In describing what she had found in him that was so arresting, Scott Brown observed that she and Frank—far more than her American-born husband—shared a deeper kinship. For one, both came from assimilated Jewish backgrounds. Both also knew the experience of exile—personally and through those they encountered. In the early 1930s, Scott Brown recalls, around the time Frank found safe haven in Stockholm after fleeing the rise of fascism in his native Austria, her "parents made plans to build a modern house in Johannesburg. Some refugees were already arriving in South Africa and my childhood was accompanied by these exiles from fascism. So were my student years on three continents, and many of them were my teachers and mentors."[2]

Even more, the shared feelings of exile that Scott Brown and Frank harbored brought for each an unavoidable intellectual shift. Their worlds quaked, and with that trembling came the toppling of old idols and old certainties. More than anything else, what drew Scott Brown to Frank and his world on that first encounter in 2005 was a recognition that they had traversed much of the same intellectual terrain, and they had found themselves at journey's end at nearly the same place.

Josef Frank was doubly—one might say, even triply—an exile. Born in Vienna in 1885, the son of a well-to-do textile merchant, he studied architecture in the early years of the twentieth century, when the *Wiener Moderne,* Vienna's modern movement, was already in full swing.[3] He began his architectural practice with two of his former classmates from the Technische Hochschule, Oskar Strnad and Oskar Wlach, around 1910. Early on, Frank produced villas and interiors for the city's *haute bourgeoisie,* but after World War I he turned more and more to the cause of social housing. He also became fixated on reframing the way in which people lived. In 1925, with Wlach and another friend, Frank opened a home furnishings shop, Haus & Garten, not far from the Opera and the Secession building. What Frank and Wlach proffered was a new version of modernity, one that contrasted with that being advocated by Josef Hoffmann and his adherents in Vienna and most of the leading modernists in Germany: furnishings and other household objects that were simple and comfortable, yet without the driving impulse toward unified stylistic expression or purity that characterized much of the modernist design of those years. Their idea was not to forge a new modernism, but rather an alternative one, one with fewer strictures that allowed for more possibilities. In his later years, Frank increasingly expressed his belief that modernism and freedom were synonymous, a conviction that flew in the face of much of the architectural discourse of the time. Haus & Garten was about a vibrant eclecticism, where everything could be purchased without theoretical "instruction," to be mixed and matched at will. Frank's avowal of a modernism of freedom rather than one of compulsion, however, left him outside the modern architectural mainstream. He moved even further away in his writings of the late 1920s and early 1930s, especially in his book *Architektur als Symbol: Elemente deutschen neuen Bauens.*[4] Frank's clarion call was for a design ethos liberated from dogma and astringency. He wanted a modernism that was rich, colorful, pleasant, and new—but still aware of, and even making references to, the historical past.

Exiled to Stockholm after Austria's brief civil war in February 1934, Frank began producing furnishings and other objects for Estrid Ericson's interiors shop Svenskt Tenn. Soon, he became the firm's head designer. It was in those years, just before the Second World War, that he helped to lay the basis for "Swedish Modern" and everything that followed in its train. Today, one can witness Frank's hand, the imprint of his personal revolution, in many of the wares found in IKEA stores around the world.

Despite his myriad successes and his now global reach, Frank's own path was far from easy. In late 1941, in the face of the growing Nazi threat, he and his Swedish-born wife Anna sought refuge in New York. Frank remained there until 1946, and he traveled back to the city at least once or twice in the later 1940s. He continued to churn out designs for Svenskt Tenn (his total output for the company would come to hundreds of individual pieces), but more and more he found himself preoccupied with questions of what modernism could and should be.

It was at this time (though, of course, neither of our protagonists was aware of it) that Frank's special orbit began to coincide with that of Scott Brown. Born Denise Lakofski in Northern Rhodesia (now Zambia), she witnessed a world— the sunset days of British colonial occupation and the certainties that had gone with it—that was fast disappearing. Soon, the family moved to South Africa, and Scott Brown, while still a teenager, began working during the summers with various local architects. She studied architecture at the University of the Witwatersrand in Johannesburg and the Architectural Association in London—just at the time Frank was formulating some of his most piercing critiques of modernism. She married Robert Scott Brown in 1955, and the couple spent the next three years traveling in Europe. In 1958, she began graduate studies in the planning department at the University of Pennsylvania, an experience that would be transformative for her.

The year 1958 was also pivotal for Frank. That year, he published his most searing assault on modernism, an essay he titled "Accidentism."[5] Its main theme was a critique of a discursive, "stereotyped" modernism, which Frank was convinced could never reflect the complexity and richness of modern life or fulfill the true desires of modern people. He writes:

> Every human being needs a certain degree of sentimentality to feel free. This will be taken from him if he is forced to make moral demands of every object, including aesthetic ones. What we need is variety and not stereotyped monumentality. No one feels comfortable in an order that has been forced upon him, even if it has been doused in a sauce of beauty. Therefore, what I suggest are not new rules and forms but a radically different attitude toward art. Away with universal styles, away with the idea of equating art and industry, away with the whole system that has become popular under the name functionalism.[6]

Frank thought that what was required instead was a multifarious aesthetic, one that would allow people the greatest possible freedom. The idea of "accidentism," his answer to the problem of modern uniformity, was based on the concept of happenstance, on the possibilities of pure chance. Frank stopped short of calling for a fully aleatoric modernism—a notion that was popular at the time in some artistic circles. (In the late 1950s, the American composer John Cage was experimenting with just such a system, writing music by employing the *I Ching*.) Frank instead proposed an aesthetic that "looked like" it had come about by chance.

It was an unfortunate retreat in some ways, but it was less the result of timidity than a sense of practicality. (Making architectural decisions solely on the basis of the *I Ching* is highly problematic, if not absurd.) Still, there is a true radicality embedded in Frank's late attack on modernism, one born of a deep sense of loss and a belief that the way forward would require a wide-ranging reorientation.

Although it would take her some time to formulate it for herself, Scott Brown, too, knew that sense of loss—what had been taken away by the experiences of exile, of the dislocations of modern life, and the supreme shock of the Shoah.

She came increasingly to believe that the reaction to modernism, the scorching critique that became the foundation of her own "postmodernism," was rooted in that loss. The nascent reappraisal of modernism was both a symptom and a product of that loss. Years later, in an interview with Marta Nowak, she expanded on this idea:

> Postmodernism—our Postmodernism—was derived in part from Africa. It also came from pre- and post-World War II theological thinking about the Holocaust. Considering the millions of deaths, moralists admonished that people were not innocent and that it was sinful to see oneself as innocent given the evil that had prevailed. That notion was called Postmodernism, and it entered the humanities, art, and religion long before architecture heard of it.[7]

These themes resounded often in Scott Brown's writings and pronouncements. She frequently repeated or expanded her conviction that her version of postmodernism—the true reaction to the decline of architectural modernism—was founded on a broader sense of dislocation, as she states in an interview with Frida Grahn in 2019:

> … "postmodernism" is a theological concept and a literary one. The notion of loss of innocence comes out of a critique of fascism and the experiences of Europe. To me, that seems a very important basis if you are also concerned with social questions. The planning education that I had at Penn took me deep into sociology, social planning and social activism. I really believed that we could bring that together with love of beauty and other hopes. So, I think that the earlier more primary origin of postmodernism is what gives it its strength.[8]

But even before that time, Scott Brown had been careful to draw distinctions between her own view of postmodernism's origins and what others were saying (and doing). In 2007, in another conversation, she had stated, "Other levels of Post-Modernism I feel very sympathetic with—with Post-Modern theologists who talk about our post-Holocaust loss of innocence or those who celebrate pluralism and diversity. But not with what the Post-Modernist architects think."[9] This last sentence is perhaps the most revealing. It lays bare what

Scott Brown believes were the profound differences between the postmodernism she and Frank shared and those who came after, those who jumped on the postmodern bandwagon late and without the same baggage—an intense sense of loss and displacement. For them, she implies (more or less correctly, one should add) that postmodernism all too often was a game of appearances, not a true coming to terms with a fraught past. That version of postmodernism was superficial and lacking in real intellectual underpinnings. What Scott Brown so admired in Frank was that he never fell prey to this sort of gamesmanship. His modernist critique (like hers and Venturi's) was always the result of serious probing and acutely felt hurt.

In "Reclaiming Frank's Seat at the Table," Scott Brown presents a lengthy recounting of where her and Venturi's beliefs overlapped with Frank and where they differed. I cannot reproduce all of it, but here is a small sampling:

> Like us, [Frank] refers to history without imitating it. But there is no sign in his architecture of the tension in ours between Modern asymmetry and Palladian centrality, suggested then subverted. And our "allusion" might be too close to imitation for him. But he accepts the existence of symbolism in architecture, including in modern architecture.[10]

> [Frank] quotes Gottfried Semper, "First provide some new ideas; then we architects shall find architectural expression for them." Explaining that Semper is referring to visible symbols of a new social order, he adds, "in recent decades, we have become acquainted with more than enough new societal forms of this sort. For me, this evokes Nazi imagery at Nuremberg, but Frank means us: "Modern architecture, inspired by its close linkages with industry and with standardization, began to come into line with these totalitarian symbols, without understanding what that meant."[11]

If Scott Brown was very much aware of important differences between Frank's ideas and her own (and those, for that matter, she shared with Venturi), between Frank's postmodernism and the one the couple helped to craft, she has less to say about why that was the case. From today's vantage point, it is clear that those differences were the result in part of how they regarded architecture's mission—especially its role in modern life. Scott Brown began her career in a time of social protest, urban renewal, and with a conviction that social science held the answers to our cities' pressing problems. She was firm in her belief that the path to urban renewal had to be complex and variegated, that the "one-sided response" of the modernist urban planners (and, for that matter, Jane Jacobs) would ultimately fail and cause great damage in the process.[12] She found physical planning often wanting (because "'physical' planners, for good or ill, love pattern"), but she thought that real progress in the way in which we construct our cities was possible.[13]

Frank, too, was a social thinker: he joined the Austrian Socialist party while still a teenager, and he believed that the role of the architect was to improve how people live. But Frank mostly thought of individuals—how one's personal experiences could be enhanced—not of collective solutions. Even while he was designing some of the great *Gemeindebauten* for the Vienna municipality in the 1920s and early 1930s, he remained focused on the domestic life of the individual occupant.

Scott Brown saw this. At one critical point in her essay about Frank, she charges him with a kind of reverse formalism: "I think [Frank] was fleshing out Accidentism by itemizing the components of Modernism and considering what the opposite of each might be. They give him a romantic, symbolic architecture of chance; of impure curves, sloping roofs, handcraft, rough and natural materials, adobe shapes, strong patterns, and pretty flowers."[14] To some degree, Scott Brown is correct. Yet I think she may have missed some of the satirical edge of Frank's critique (which he often cloaked with a tinge of his own special Viennese humor). Frank loved his pretty flowers (and, in one of his late drawings, quite succulent cabbages), but he always saw these as devices to relieve some of the tedium of modern existence (which, of course, was something he shared with Scott Brown and Venturi: his own love of ornament and pattern closely paralleled theirs). But he certainly had no desire to replace one formalism—especially a romanticized one—with another.

What separated Frank and Scott Brown far more was a generational disparity. Frank began his career more than two decades before Scott Brown was born, and he experienced the modern movement almost from its outset. Scott

Brown's career commenced much later, when the discussions about modernism's shortcomings were becoming fully apparent and a discourse of discontent was widely shared. Frank was one of the tiny handful of early modernists (Adolf Loos and Hans Scharoun were among the others) who developed a critique of modernism even while it was still in its ascendancy. By the later 1920s, if not before, Frank saw, with uncanny clarity, how mainstream modernism's adherents had adopted a set of beliefs that were both shallow and potentially damaging. The headlong drive toward stylistic uniformity and the acceptance of functionalism or any other form of dogma (at the expense of all other architectural values) he regarded as tragically misguided.

Frank accomplished all this long before his exile, before World War II, the Holocaust, and the shift of mood that followed. If his experiences of the 1940s and 1950s left him embittered and uncertain about how to proceed, they were not the wellspring of his critique, as they were—far more—for Scott Brown. Frank's sense of loss, like that of Adolf Loos before him (from whom Frank derived many of his core beliefs), came from the changes they witnessed taking place around them, the dislocations of modernization, rapid urbanization, and social shifts that had already become a fact of life for many since the latter part of the nineteenth century and that were becoming acute already in the 1920s and 1930s. Frank's assault on modernism, like that of Loos, had to do precisely with what they considered a failed response by those who should have known better: modern architects themselves. The difference was that Frank's targets were the leading modernists of the 1920s and 1930s (and beyond), whereas Loos's were mostly those that preceded them, during the Viennese *fin de siècle.*

Scott Brown, who came of age later, during and after the Second World War, found another crisis, and she adopted a different (if closely related) set of positions. What she and Frank shared, though, was a conviction that the crisis of modernism was the crisis of modern life itself. It was never simply a matter of style or the choice of theory over pragmatism, never a matter of easy corrections. Neither sought to replace one system with another. They saw the problems of modern life with a coruscating clarity. Their world quaked, and they sought to pick up the pieces and make meaning out of them.

Notes

1   Scott Brown, "Reclaiming Frank's Seat at the Table," 21.

2   Scott Brown, "Reclaiming Frank's Seat at the Table," 43. Scott Brown mentions, among others, her teachers Manfred Marcus and Arthur Korn, both German refugees.

3   On Frank's early years, see Long, *Josef Frank: Life and Work,* esp. chapters 1 and 2.

4   Frank, *Architektur als Symbol.*

5   The essay first appeared in the Swedish journal *Form.* See Frank, "Accidentism," and was later reprinted in German in *Baukunst und Werkform* as "Akzidentismus." It appears in its entirety in his *Schriften / Writings,* vol. 2, 372–387.

6   Josef Frank, "Accidentism," in *Schriften / Writings,* 385.

7   Denise Scott Brown, interviewed by Marta Nowak, 2013.

8   Denise Scott Brown, interviewed by Frida Grahn, 2019. Greenberg's essay "Theology after the Shoah" provides some of the background for Scott Brown's ideas about postmodernism. I am deeply grateful to Frida Grahn for her insights and suggestions, particularly with regard to Denise Scott Brown's ideas about a theologically derived postmodernism. See also Eaglestone, *The Holocaust and the Postmodern.*

9   Rattenbury and Hardingham (eds.), *Learning from Las Vegas: SuperCrit #2,* 137.

10   Scott Brown, "Reclaiming Frank's Seat at the Table," 27.

11   Scott Brown, "Reclaiming Frank's Seat at the Table," 27.

12   Scott Brown, "Reclaiming Frank's Seat at the Table," 39.

13   Scott Brown, "Reclaiming Frank's Seat at the Table," 39.

14   Scott Brown, "Reclaiming Frank's Seat at the Table," 39.

Context I: Looking at the Real World. Interview with Jacques Herzog

Jacques Herzog and Frida Grahn

Frida Grahn: Between 1999 and 2018, you led the urban research institute ETH Studio Basel, together with Pierre de Meuron, Roger Diener, and Marcel Meili. *Learning from Las Vegas* has often been understood as a model for contemporary research studios on cities, such as Studio Basel. They all analyze urban conditions by doing field studies, use interdisciplinary methods and graphics as analytical tools, and are built on teamwork and produce publications coauthored with students ... I was a student at Studio Basel in 2008, and somewhat surprisingly the book was not required reading. I've been wondering to what extent the studio concept was influenced by *Learning from Las Vegas*?

Jacques Herzog: We studied under Lucius Burckhardt and later under Aldo Rossi, both of whom placed a very strong emphasis on the city. Burckhardt's preferred method was to discover and describe a city's sociological patterns by strolling around various urban areas, which was perhaps not so different from Scott Brown's ideas. On the other hand, Rossi insisted on the permanence of urban typologies. We enjoyed and were influenced by these totally contrasting methods—by both ways of looking at and trying to understand what "city" means. Soon after graduation, we started to analyze our hometown of Basel with its historical, social, and political evolution in very specific conditions, as well as its strategic position at the intersection of three countries: Switzerland, France, and Germany ... Everything we did with our students was based on the perception and description of the urban conditions of cities around the globe. We discussed the theories of Lucius Burckhardt and French philosopher Henri Lefebvre—but not explicitly *Learning from Las Vegas*. In earlier years, though, Pierre and I had been rather inspired by Venturi's *Complexity and Contradiction*.

FG: I see, but was *Learning from Las Vegas* significant for you for other reasons? In an interview with Hubertus Adam and Christoph Bürkle (2011), you state that *Learning from Las Vegas* was important due to its introduction of pop art into architecture. Its authors refer to Ed Ruscha, Roy Lichtenstein, Andy Warhol, and Claes Oldenburg. When did you first read the book? When did you first come into contact with the work of Scott Brown/Venturi?

JH: In the early 1970s, while studying with Lucius Burckhardt and Aldo Rossi. I don't remember when I first read *Learning from Las Vegas*. I liked that it introduced pop art to architects, who would otherwise not have been in touch with popular culture as a source of inspiration. My own affinity and interest in pop, however, is strongly linked to artists rather than architects. I was fascinated by Ruscha's gas stations, Hamilton's collages of "today's homes," Oldenburg's blown-up objects. Clearly our Ricola Storage in Mulhouse, where silkscreen-printed polycarbonate panels with a Blossfeldt motif in serial repetition cover and define the entire building, would have been impossible without my admiration for Andy Warhol's work. As a side remark: though the inspiration came from pop art, the result is not pop, but rather an "earnest" effect of the spiritual in an otherwise totally banal industrial urban context outside Mulhouse.

FG: In other words, you knew of pop art before you read *Learning from Las Vegas*?

JH: Oh yes, long before—I was interested in art rather than architecture before I began to study at the ETH. But Venturi/Scott Brown were key in introducing pop into the mind of many architects, most of whom hadn't been aware of that powerful movement in art before. Burckhardt is not about pop. He could rather be seen as an avant-gardist of the ecological movement. Burckhardt liked to walk—or rather stroll around—with us students discovering and examining so-called unimportant places in, around, and between cities. This is certainly something that both Pierre and I took with us from that time. Even to this day, we keep being fascinated by ordinary things, ordinary architecture, ordinary aesthetics, ordinary life. The good thing with ordinary objects is that they are rather invisible. Lucius Burckhardt liked that, just as we still do now. That may sound like a paradox, since we sometimes do buildings that are so visible and iconic …

FG: Could you expand a bit more on the similarities between Burckhardt and Scott Brown?

JH: Both Scott Brown and Burckhardt wanted to reorient the gaze of architects away from some academic idealism towards the real world built around them at that time. The normal world—with the difference that the normal architectural aesthetic in the US looked very different, more spectacular and appealing than in Switzerland or Germany.

FG: The title of the second edition of *Learning from Las Vegas* has the addition *The Forgotten Symbolism of Architectural Form*. Scott Brown/Venturi see the discovery of "communication as a function of architecture" as one of the book's main achievements. The idea that architecture is a language was widespread in the 1970s and 1980s. In *Archithese* (1982) and elsewhere, you take a critical stance towards symbolism and semiotics. How did you arrive at that conclusion?

JH: A commercial sign and a symbol are different things. As an architect, you cannot build a "symbol," but you can make a work which is or features a commercial sign. Any architecture, however, has the potential to eventually become a symbol, for peace or for revolution, for hope or for disaster. Time will tell. This is very rarely in the hands of those who commission or design something.

FG: Both commercial signs and symbols carry meaning, based on conventions more or less accepted by society. So, you are saying that a building can't introduce itself as a new symbol, but that it can carry signs with a predefined meaning? In other words, it's possible to decorate a shed, but not to design a building recognizable as a "duck" … ?

JH: Don't make it more complicated than it is! Buildings can become symbols of power, oppression, and other negative connotations, like for instance the former Nazi temple that later became the "Haus der Kunst" in Munich. Today's generation of visitors hardly remember its dark origins. Often such origins fade away over time and buildings have to live on their own without the "symbolic" or the "sign" aspect that was originally infused when they were created. Think of the Pan Am Building in New York City, which survives pretty well with a totally different brand name. Why? Because of its architectural and urbanistic qualities: its specific position in the city, its enigmatic shape, its modernistic optimism ...

FG: You mentioned *Complexity and Contradiction*—what has the book meant to you?

JH: I loved *Complexity and Contradiction in Architecture* and read it with great interest parallel to Rossi's *Architettura della città*. Both came out in the same year. They are the last serious and influential theoretical texts, even to this day. All young students in those post-1968 years were inspired by them. But today, the eroticism and newness of these two books has faded away. They have turned into ordinary books recalling a specific historic moment in architecture.

The Rule of Flux.
Notes on Denise Scott Brown and Venice

Stanislaus von Moos

"Blur"—the absence of clear contours in a phenomenon—is first of all a condition of visibility. In architecture, it can also be an aesthetic program, perhaps even a style (the style of following no "style"), and in that sense it is certainly also a business model. In urbanism and planning, however, the absence of clear contours, the permeability of boundaries, and beyond that the "unpredictability" of almost anything that affects the shape of the built environment are facts that have to be reckoned with from the start. Due to their "dynamic" nature, processes like the growth, differentiation, and contraction of cities and villages simply do not seem predestined to crystallize once and for all into any fixed form. As Denise Scott Brown has put it: Planning a city is like "drawing on a river. The river takes the clarity away and eventually dissolves into nothing."[1]

Interest in the potential of "blur" is relatively new among architects, at least in Europe—and thus also in Switzerland, where I am based. The year 1987 may be no more than a randomly picked date. In that year—in the midst of heated debates over the remodeling of Zurich's main railway station—Luigi Snozzi gave a series of lectures on urban planning. Alarmed by the tendency for existing railway stations to be transformed into shopping malls, he showed how railroad tracks, which connect city centers to the rest of the country and beyond, could be turned into a tool for rethinking the city and urban planning at large. Architects should take up the challenge of developing concepts aimed at preventing vacated areas from falling prey to the vagaries of speculation, Snozzi argued.[2] Three years later, Herzog & de Meuron, together with Rémy Zaugg, published a series of planning studies under the title "Basel, eine Stadt im Werden?" ("Basel, a City in the Making?") (fig. 1). As had been the case with Snozzi, the starting point for planning was not the morphology of the historic city or any traditional form of conurbation, but rather the wide strips of

Figure 1: Proposal for a linear quarter structure in which high-rise buildings confront the existing buildings on the other side of the Rhine. Herzog & de Meuron, Rémy Zaugg, "Eine Stadt im Werden?" Urban Study, Basel, Switzerland (1991–1992).

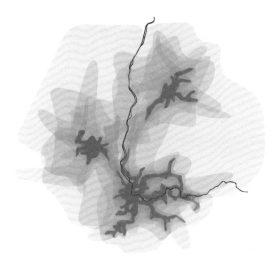

Figure 2: Herzog & de Meuron, "Metropolitan region Basel – Mulhouse – Freiburg," Synthesis: Topography, Settlement, Economy.

railway tracks and existing river courses—in this case the bend of the Rhine along which the old city center of Basel has developed. In images developed in this way (to be regarded as working hypotheses, not construction plans), the riverine landscape appears like a broad boulevard connecting the corners of Switzerland, Germany, and France (fig. 2).[3]

To illustrate the logic of this kind of urban development, Herzog & de Meuron naturally refer to Venice and Manhattan, cities that, as they describe it, have "coagulated into natural space." Whereas it is only at the actual bend

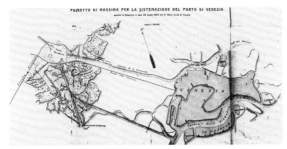

Figure 3: Project for the re-organization of Venice's harbor area showing Venice in its maritime setting, Venice and Porto Marghera, Banda Civile di Venezia, 1904.

of the Rhine that Basel's process of becoming a city can be traced as a three-dimensional operation—i.e., where the inner city becomes an agglomerate—in Venice or in Manhattan, this operation, like a chemical substance caught in its very process of crystallization, has involved the entire surface of those cities. "The city imitates the forms of nature. The mass of buildings—*palazzi* in Venice and skyscrapers in Manhattan—appear to condense the tendentially flat topographical facts into three-dimensional volumes."[4] On the other hand, the very shape of Venice, as it has been handed down in hundreds of plans and vedutas, is the footprint of the geological and hydrographic forces that produced it. Like a liver or a heart displayed on the surgeon's operating table, supplied by its blood vessels, the city appears on sixteenth-century maps (such as those of Jacopo de Barbari, dated 1500 and of Benedetto Bordone, dated 1528), as well as in early twentieth-century hydrographic schemes: powerful prefigurations of what Fumihiko Maki may have had in mind when he coined the term "fluid city" in 1964 (fig. 3).[5] Although Basel, as "an agglomeration of largely independent, heterogeneous parts, both in terms of politics and of culture," is far from coming even close to such conditions, the trend was nevertheless recognizable: "The new settlement form no longer opposes or contrasts with the landscape, but merges with it." One day, the result was bound to emerge: "Nature and urban space have become mutually dependent and interpenetrating parts of a common entity—the city."[6]

Understanding urbanization not in formal terms, but rather in terms of systems theory—as resulting from processes and sequences of movements within changing parameters and growth factors—already had a long tradition by

1990, certainly in the United States.[7] By then, Denise Scott Brown's writings had already been part of this tradition for decades—quite apart from *Learning from Las Vegas* (it is no secret that the book nominally coauthored by her, Robert Venturi, and Steven Izenour was essentially undertaken at her initiative). That said, there is no evidence that Venice was much on their minds when, together with her husband and partner Robert Venturi, Denise prepared the "Learning from Las Vegas" studio scheduled at Yale, in 1968, nor is that city ever invoked in the two versions of the book that resulted from it (1972 and 1977). Hence, when I was invited some forty years later to organize a conference about "Architecture After Las Vegas," it was neither documentary evidence nor a desire to revive the classical trope of Venice as "Rome's counter-image" that led me to choose "A View from the Gondola" as the title for my introduction (2010). Nevertheless, besides randomly parodying Bob's and Denise's lofty "View from the Campidoglio," that paper proposed nothing short of substituting Venice for Rome as the "magic wand" capable of illuminating the saga of Venturi, Scott Brown and Associates (VSBA) and Las Vegas.[8] If I am now returning to the argument, despite lingering doubts as to the plausibility of such a retroactive "city contest,"[9] it is in the light of some writings by Denise that I could not have known at the time of that conference.

•

A View from the Campidoglio leaves no room for doubt about the benchmark for the authors' outlook as architects and researchers: the Caput Mundi is the reference. It had already been implied in Venturi's first book, *Complexity and Contradiction in Architecture*, both by way of the buildings shown and the arguments discussed. But then, as learned architects and latter-day Grand Tourists, both Venturi and Scott Brown couldn't help sharing the lure of Venice as the enlightened Anglo-Saxon's imaginary city par excellence. As I have pointed out elsewhere, they probably seldom visited Italy without stopping in Venice, and not only because of the Biennale.[10] In fact, the first important film footage ever devoted to them was not only partly shot in Venice, it even involves a rather hilarious passage showing the couple in a gondola.[11] Similar to the experience of the city through the windshield of your car—relevant to the discovery of Las Vegas—the gondola offers but an unstable perspective, especially if compared to the certitudes of "Roma Aeterna." Not by coincidence, Martin Filler's 1983 documentary actually sets in with a view of traffic flow on an American freeway. And on the other hand: doesn't the rendering of VSBA's well-known Ponte dell'Accademia project of 1988 include a paper cutout of a gondola that might almost have been taken from one of Le Corbusier's sketches drawn during a lecture on Venice given at the Istituto Universitario di Architettura di Venezia (IUAV) in 1952?[12]

The "fluid" city as a concept did not originate in Venice, but the Venetian Lagoon that cut its contours into the city's shape may have facilitated or even encouraged an early interest in city dynamics among architects. The CIAM Summer School held there in 1956 appears to have been a turning point in this respect. It is a matter of interest here, as Denise Scott Brown took part in the course. Her recollections of the experience are scattered and somewhat summary, however. In an essay entitled "Towards an Active Socioplastics," she writes about her discovery of Italy in 1956:

> After a period of work in England, Robert Scott Brown and I left for a study tour in Europe (...). Here too, given the enormity of the rebuilding task, it was hardly surprising to find architects deeply focused on urbanism and social housing. Summer School in Venice and some weeks in the architecture office of Giuseppe Vaccaro in Rome reinforced our intention, first articulated at the AA, to continue our training in architecture via the study of city planning.[13]

And she continues, passing over whatever the Venice school might have been able to offer in terms of her professional interests: "We knew this should be done in America, where the education covered a wider scope and was more intellectually based than in England."[14]

Was the Summer School no more than an accidental interruption of the young couple's Grand Tour, as this summary report suggests, not much more than an occasion to visit Piazza San Marco with Gardella, Albini, and others, and to take snapshots of the pigeons and of the laundry waving above the canals (fig. 4)? "We just lived, that is, we walked around Venice all day

Figure 4: St. Mark's Square with pigeons. Photograph by Robert Scott Brown.
Venice canal with laundry. Photograph by Denise Scott Brown. Both photos were taken
during the CIAM Summer School at the IUAV (Istituto Universitario di Architettura di
Venezia), 1956.

photographing," she added in her more recent recollections. Some money that had arrived from home served as "a great fillip for our photography."[15]

> We were all in love with the pigeons and we have a postcard that says Coca Cola in pigeons ... We used to go to Piazza San Marco with the elder architects from the conference, people like Franco Albini and Ignazio Gardella. Gardella could stand there, suddenly swoop down, pick up a pigeon and launch it. That's a real Venetian skill.[16]

A Venetian friend who owned a "*sandolo*, a flat-bottomed, working boat, good for photography and hauling things in Venice," as she writes, further ignited her passion for picture-taking: "... one night we all went out in it on the Grand Canal in the midst of convoys of tourist gondolas and despite the gondoliers' invective."[17] But the day-to-day vehicle was the traghetto. "CIAM hired them to take us around so we went on them often. You would stand and wobble. So here we're photographing as we're going somewhere the school was taking us."

There was more than mere picture-hunting. "Summer school in Venice brought heartfelt confrontations between Modernists, old, new, and very new (us students). Robert's and my passionate Brutalism drew indulgent smiles from our elders as they remembered their youth, and there was a handover of sorts between generations as they described how Modernism had been a symbol of freedom for them during Fascism (...)."[18] And she continues:

> Venice was the beginning of so much for us: it was our introduction to the world camaraderie among architects that I still rely on, and perhaps the beginning of my seeing in rectangles for some years, the professional deformation of photographers. Even now I use my Venetian photographs for lecturing, and I think it was this summer, 1956, that brought us our first glimpse of American Pop Art—at the Venice Biennale in an international show of young artists in an Italian pavilion."[19]

In retrospect, the 1956 CIAM Summer School marked both the beginning of CIAM's terminal agony and the emergence of Team 10.[20] As Gabriele Scimemi reported in *Casabella*, the Athens Charter was already considered totally obsolete by the younger generation of CIAM architects who ran the school (in particular Ignazio Gardella and Franco Albini).[21] Instead of understanding the city in terms of static functions, these architects had begun to study socioeconomic and circulatory forces as key factors of city dynamics. Scimemi specifically refers to a group of the summer school participants, Denise and Robert Scott Brown among them, who used the transportation lines connecting Venice, Mestre, and Marghera as generators of settlement form, while others explicitly visualized "flows" as models of urban form in their plans.[22] As Denise specifically remembers: "The school project that year was a plan for Mestre, Venice's industrial mainland across the lagoon. Of course we designed a linear city."[23] She then writes about the diagonal shortcuts for pedestrians envisioned in the plan ("we had seen them in use in English cathedral closes and Venetian *campos*") before continuing: "Also on our plan were attempts to show buildup of density and activity as I saw it at stops on the London underground. I think we drew circles representing a gradience of these factors towards stops long before we studied social ecology at the University of Pennsylvania."[24]

The program was a familiar one at IUAV in those years. It would resurface in Ludovico Quaroni's later studies on the urbanization of the area around Porto Marghera, Mestre, and Venice Airport. Quaroni, a determined advocate of the unity of architecture and city planning, is widely known for his reconstruction of Matera in southern Italy, yet more poignant in this context are his vigorous drawings of cityscapes on tracing paper, "which found their inspiration in Venice's primary and natural element, water" (fig. 5).[25]

•

In the early stages of Denise and Bob's process of "learning from Las Vegas," Caesars Palace was the Casino that surpassed all the others in terms of imperial allure and iconography. Thus it naturally slipped into a key position within the couple's Capitoline outlook.[26] In the meantime, since Caesars Palace has been eclipsed by the Venetian Convention and Expo Center (inaugurated in 1999, thirty years after the start of the Las Vegas study), the "View from the Gondola" may have acquired additional legitimacy. Together

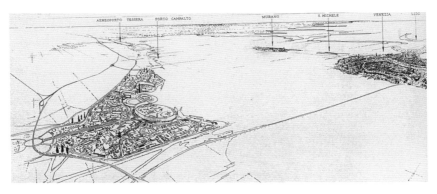

Figure 5: Ludovico Quaroni. Urbanization project for the Quartiere CEP di S. Giuliano, Mestre (Venice), 1959.

with the pastiche of Venetian palaces at its base, "the world's largest hotel complex," whose 8,108 rooms and suites are stacked into a colossal piece of quasi-Corbusian Ville Radieuse, is a veritable empire within the entertainment industry. As a marketing idea and trademark, The Venetian has since been exported to Asia—so that the Venetian Macao in China, inaugurated in 2007, not only houses the largest casino ever built since this type was invented (in Venice, by the way), but is actually the world's largest inhabitable building altogether. After all, if Venice was the exemplary fun city of the eighteenth and nineteenth centuries, today it literally works like a branch of Las Vegas— at least in terms of the souvenir industry.[27] That alone makes it a topical location for ethnographers as they "learn from Las Vegas."

However, the "Stones of Venice" also involve more specifically architectural challenges. Due to its age-old and continually evolving role in the global tourist economy, the city has had and continues to have no choice but to work hand in hand with the fields of preservation, restoration, and inevitably also reconstruction, in order to prepare for its next life cycle. It is no coincidence that endeavors of this type, more akin to Viollet-le-Duc than to Ruskin, became important in the work of Venturi, Scott Brown and Associates—as they now also are, by the way, in the current work of architects such as Herzog & de Meuron. Rem Koolhaas not only designed an elegant gallery space within the

"Venetian" complex in Las Vegas—in his powerful restoration of the Fondaco dei Tedeschi he transformed what had become a shabby post office into a high-end tabernacle of "the Venetian syndrome" right along the Grand Canal.[28]

•

"Flow" had been a popular metaphor in the social sciences ever since the 1950s—David Crane had already referred to the "navigational analogy" in city planning in 1953[29]—and by now the "fluid city" is a widely shared way of thinking about urban processes. As to the visualization of that trope in terms of architecture, it has arguably never become a shared practice since the times of Erich Mendelsohn, except perhaps for Quaroni's "Brutalist/Expressionist" Piazza della Vasca in Grosseto (completed in 1971) and some aspects of 1990s blob mania.[30] Its neo-historicizing version, in any case, has remained a specialty of VSBA, if not actually a measure of the firm's eccentricity in terms of design. If it is true that VSBA's quasi-biomorphological aesthetic reflects an understanding of the city as the result of a process and curvilinear movement within ever-changing contextual parameters of growth—in short, an understanding of the city as "fluid," indeterminate, and systems-driven rather than form-driven—then the unbuilt Yale Mathematics Building addition (1969) can be seen as an early illustration of this (fig. 6). For Colin Rowe, the artfully clumsy juxtaposition of old and new in this project was a sign of Venturi's failure to deal successfully with the problem of bulk imposed by the brief. I have argued that this "failure" should rather be seen as part of a design strategy concerned with the nature of the city as the physical result of growth processes.[31] Seen in this context, is not the "oversized" mass of Ignazio Gardella's House on the Zattere in Venice (1953–58) a precedent of sorts for the Mathematics Building, at least in relation to its awkward dialogue with its much smaller neighbor (a church)?[32] The house was under construction when Denise attended Gardella's summer school.

As with most cities of the past, the growth inscribed in these footprints has occurred incrementally, by movements of expansion and contraction responding to the changing parameters of topography and circulation pattern. Flux, by definition, follows the law of gravity—valleys and canyons are shaped in

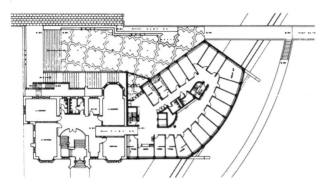

Figure 6: Venturi and Rauch (the firm that would become Venturi, Scott Brown and Associates). Yale Mathematics Building Competition. First Floor plan, 1969–70.

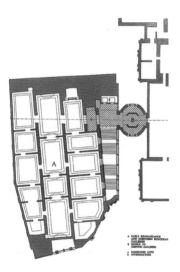

A EARLY RENAISSANCE
  AND NORTHERN EUROPEAN
  GALLERIES
B BRIDGE TO
  EXISTING GALLERIES

1 PASSENGER LIFTS
2 INTRODUCTION

Figure 7: Venturi, Scott Brown and Associates. Sainsbury Wing, National Gallery extension, London, United Kingdom. Gallery floor, 1986–91.

this way, loops of rivers, deltas built up by the ongoing deposit of sediment, etc.—but in the universe of civilization, there is indeed no better example for an aquatic determinism of urban form than Venice. Perhaps the best view of the city's origins from "the primordial fluid that slowly coagulates and allows vegetation to grow on the mud that is the origin of life," as Marcel Brion and René Huyghe put it, is to be gained from a one-hour vaporetto ride from Venice to Torcello (see fig. 3).[33] As to the basic rectangles of palaces, shipyards, churches, etc. that constitute Venice's urban fabric as built, they can't help being stretched and squeezed in order to fit into the curvilinear city form. Even the Basilica di San Marco, the Doge's Palace, and the Piazza San Marco have to painstakingly negotiate their orthogonal layout with the organoid form of the city as a whole. It is hard not to be struck by the way the plan of Venturi and Scott Brown's National Gallery extension in London resonates with the site plan of Piazza San Marco and even with San Marco itself (fig. 7).

On site, however, arguably the most "Venetian" among the Italianate features of the National Gallery extension is the access stairwell to the Gallery Floor. While its manipulation of perspective is sort of Roman baroque in reverse, its length and its nature as an urban observation deck makes one think of the pedestrian walkway across the Rialto Bridge. The fascination with Venice as a system of stairs is almost a trope among architects of the generation that is of interest here. In a lecture given at the 1952 CIAM Summer School (not the one Scott Brown attended), Le Corbusier made a point of singling out the "stairwells to the sky" as they appear in Venice's essential locations.[34] Some twenty years later, what he had in mind became a recurring theme in Luchino Visconti's *Death in Venice,* in which stairs interrupting the flow of people pushing through the streets function like unexpectedly appearing beams of light, instantly transforming the crowd onto which they are projected into a group of individuals. In her *Suite Vénitienne* (fig. 8), Sophie Calle has made this cinematographic experience into an artist's book (1988).[35] As if to multiply this experience (and challenge the very invention of the elevator), Paul Rudolph organized movement into and within his Art & Architecture Building at Yale—one of the birthplaces of Las Vegas learning (completed in 1963)—as a mesmerizing succession of wide and narrow, large and very small stairs.

Figure 8: Sophie Calle.
Photograph from *Suite
vénitienne/Please Follow
Me,* 1988.

Figure 9: The Doge's Pal-
ace with view across the
Porta della Carta towards
the courtyard and the Scala
dei Giganti, Venice, Italy.
Photograph, late nine-
teenth century.

241

Figure 10: Venturi and Rauch (the firm that would become Venturi, Scott Brown and Associates). Humanities Building, State University of New York, Purchase, NY. View of "interior street" ending in stairs, 1968–73.

Not surprisingly, with VSBA the theme is handled in a comparatively laconic way. The stair that concludes the long hall of the Humanities Building at the New York State University at Purchase (1973)—a "modest" project, but in some ways a precedent for the Sainsbury Wing stairwell—is but one example (fig. 10). In one of our conversations (probably dating back to the late 1970s), Denise referred to the Scala dei Giganti in the context of this project.[36] Her unexpected reference to Venice made me then stumble over a strange succession of further art-historical references. Indeed, Venetian painting systematically exploited the scenic potential of stairs, as seen in many works by Veronese, Tintoretto, and Titian, among others. As did Venetian statecraft: with its freestanding position in the courtyard of the Doge's Palace and its combination with the elevated tribuna at its top, the Scala dei Giganti is an archetype of the very principle of a ceremonial stairway. Its location directly opposite the Campanile of San Marco, but separated from it by a tunnel created by a long arcade ("key-hole," as Gordon Cullen would have called it), makes whatever act is performed on it into a public spectacle. Not to mention the Scala's physical remoteness from the public arena of the Piazzetta, which made the effect all the more magical (fig. 9). No wonder that with his *The Execution of the Doge Marino Faliero* (1825–26), the painter Delacroix initiated a tradition of bloodthirsty nineteenth-century history painting featuring the Scala as a backdrop.[37] Buried beneath the surface, such resonances with art, history, and the everyday may not be of great help as one tries to find one's way from the Museum Lobby to the Gallery Floor in the Sainsbury Wing. But they are what makes architecture stick in one's mind.

What else can be said of Venice as an implied touchstone of Denise's and her partners' work? Some of VSBA's projects openly reflect conventions of facade composition that are standard in Venice and in the Veneto from the sixteenth to the nineteenth centuries, be it in their "vernacular" or "modest" materiality (brick), be it in the way they are organized in terms of base, shaft, and attic, or in the way they celebrate symmetry or by displaying quasi-Palladian lunette windows (Guild House, Philadelphia; Gordon Wu Hall, Princeton, etc.; the minuscule reproduction of Palladio's Villa Zeno in Cessalto in Bob's *Complexity and Contradiction* would hardly be necessary as a clue).[38] But that is yet another story.

Notes

1 Denise Scott Brown quoted after Frida Grahn, "'Make Little Plans': Scott Brown at the Fiftieth Anniversary of CIAM," in this volume.

2 Snozzi, *Das Unding über den Geleisen*, 38, 45, and passim, Snozzi linked his discussion to the competition project that he had submitted for Zurich in 1978 (together with Mario Botta). On the context, see Huber, *Hauptbahnhof Zürich*, 181–182. The following essay is part of an ongoing exploration of transatlantic "histoires croisées" in architecture and urban design since the 1950s. Parts of the sections on Denise Scott Brown and on Herzog & de Meuron have been (or will be) published in greater detail elsewhere. The first part is a draft version of my introduction to Stanislaus von Moos and Arthur Rüegg, *Twentifive x Herzog & de Meuron* (Göttingen: Steidl), forthcoming. The section on Denise Scott Brown and Venice is developing arguments developed at greater length in "A View from the Gondola," in von Moos and Stierli, *Eyes That Saw,* 325–371; but see also note 8 below.

3 Herzog, de Meuron, and Zaugg, "Eine Stadt im Werden?" The Swiss Federal Department of Regional Development distinguishes between five metropolitan regions for the territory of Switzerland and its immediate vicinity: Basel, Bern, Zurich, Geneva–Lausanne, and Ticino.

4 Herzog, de Meuron, and Zaugg, "Eine Stadt in Werden?" 30.

5 Maki, *Investigations in Collective Form.* On the history of mapping the Laguna and its impact on the conceptualizations of Venice's "forma urbis" see Plant, *Venice, Fragile City*, 392–93

6 Herzog, de Meuron, and Zaugg, "Eine Stadt im Werden?" 29, 43.

7 The urban planner Konstantinos Doxiadis pioneered this approach already in the 1950s; see Wigley, "Network Fever." On the role of "systems theory" for architecture and urban design in general, see Scott Brown, "Between Three Stools" and also her "Architecture as Patterns and Systems." To the best of my knowledge, Scott Brown does not refer to Doxiadis in her writings. Jacques Herzog himself traces "Die Stadt im Werden" back to the methodological ideas of his teachers Aldo Rossi and Lucius Burckhardt, and in particular to Burckhardt's method of "strolling research," which was "perhaps not so different from Scott Brown's ideas," as he adds in Frida Grahn's interview with him in this volume. In this connection, see my own essay on the "theory" of Herzog & de Meuron, "Präzision der Unschärfe."

8 Venturi and Scott Brown, *A View from the Campidoglio*. See also above, note 1.

9 On the classical trope of Venice as "Rome's counter-image," see Hüttinger, "Il Mito Di Venezia," 187–226 and in particular 198–201.

10 See "A View from the Gondola," 327; 339–343 and passim.

11 Bletter, Filler and Blackwood, *Beyond Utopia*.

12 For illustrations see von Moos, *Venturi, Rauch & Scott Brown*, 141–143 and below, note 34.

13 Scott Brown, "Towards an Active Socioplastics," 27. For more recollections on her Italian experiences in 1955/56, see also her "Working for Giuseppe Vaccaro."

14 Scott Brown, "Towards an Active Socioplastics," 27.

15 Scott Brown, "Wayward Eye," draft, dated 2013. Sections from that manuscript were later integrated in Scott Brown, *From Soane to the Strip*, with several photographs from Venice.

16 Figure caption from Scott Brown, *From Soane to the Strip*.

17 Scott Brown, "Wayward Eye" (no pagination).

18 Scott Brown, "Wayward Eye."

19 Scott Brown, "Wayward Eye."

20 Mumford, *The CIAM Discourse on Urbanism*, 247–265.

21 Gabriele Scimemi, "La quarta scuola estiva del CIAM a Venezia." On the CIAM Summer Schools in Venice in general, see Maddalena Scimemi, "Venezia Internazionale." See also the essay by Denise Costanzo in this book for a more detailed analysis.

22 Gabriele Scimemi, "La quarta scuola estiva del CIAM a Venezia."

23 Scott Brown, "Wayward Eye."

24 Scott Brown, "Wayward Eye."

25 As Maristella Casciato puts it, in "Learning from Italy (1954–1966): Transatlantic Exchanges and Encounters," unpublished manuscript (2010). On Quaroni's well-known projects for the satellite city between Mestre and Venice Airport, which owe much to Le Corbusier's Plan Obus for Algiers (1959 and 1931, respectively), see Ciorra, *Ludovico*

Quaroni 1911–1987, Figs. 38–43; 152–153. Scott Brown remembers Quaroni as having helped her and Robert to find work in the office of Giuseppe Vaccaro in Rome but does not refer to his work in "Wayward Eye."

26   Venturi, Scott Brown, and Izenour, *Learning from Las Vegas*, 48–51.

27   For an illustrated overview of "The Venetian" empire, see Scheppe and the IUAV Class on Politics and Representation, *Migropolis.*

28   Dal Co, "Dove Danzano Grilli Mirabili." See Scheppe, *Migropolis*, 38–49 for the project itself.

29   Crane, "Chandigarh Reconsidered." It speaks for itself that, when referring to Louis Kahn's proverbial categorization of urban traffic lines into "Go" Streets, "Stop" Streets, "Docks," etc., Denise Scott Brown would later rename them "rivers," "canals," "harbors," etc., in "A Worm's-Eye View of Recent Architectural History," 104. For Kahn's terminology, see "Toward a Plan for Midtown Philadelphia."

30   Ciorra, *Ludovico Quaroni.*

31   Rowe, "Robert Venturi and the Yale Mathematics Building" and von Moos, "Secret Physiology," in *Venturi, Scott Brown & Associates,* 34–36. My observations on the "footprints" of architecture and city growth owe much to conversations with Denise Scott Brown. Among her recent writings on these subjects, see "Activities as Patterns," 120–141 and "Las Vegas Learning, Las Vegas Teaching."

32   "An uneasy dweller" despite its precious detailing, as Margaret Plant notes in *Venice, Fragile City*, 344.

33   Brion and Huyghe, *Se Perdre Dans Venise*, 19.

34   Le Corbusier, "A propos di Venezia," quoted from the Italian version of a transcript published in *Giornale economico di Venezia* (Paris: Fondation Le Corbusier, n.d.). Translation by the author. See also *Gazzetta di Venezia* no. 27 (September 1952).

35   See von Moos, "A View from the Gondola," 365–371.

36   von Moos, *Venturi, Rauch & Scott Brown*, 37; 163–165.

37   Francesco Hayez's variation on the theme of Delacroix's *The Execution of the Doge Marino Falieri* probably being the best known example. For a classic introduction to the political symbolism of architecture and public space in Renaissance Italy, see Lotz, "Sixteenth-Century Italian Squares," 74–116 (for Piazza San Marco, see in particular 83–84).

38   Venturi, *Complexity and Contradiction in Architecture*, 94. Cf. my "A View from the Gondola," 361–365.

Context II: On Homelessness, Housing, and Hospices

Hilary Sample

The intersection of public health, institutions of care, and cities dominates our thinking and actions after two years of the Covid-19 pandemic. Health's convergence with architecture has never been more topical. Yet, ahead of her time, in the fall of 1989, Denise Scott Brown offered a design studio at Harvard Graduate School of Design titled "The Architecture of Well-Being." Intersecting public health, architecture, and the city, she structured the syllabus around questions of designing for a variety of health conditions and the institutions associated with them: the public health crisis of homelessness and shelters, as well as hospices for the dying.[1] Across the 38-page brief, she sought out social programs for students to explore, all with the impetus to develop a closer understanding of how to better comfort society through design and learn how architects can "contribute to the process of institutional definition and redefinition."[2]

I discovered Scott Brown's seminar syllabus in the course of developing my research project "Sick City" while I was a visiting scholar at the Canadian Centre for Architecture. From the brief I gathered that the studio was divided into phases such as "Physiognomy" and "Facilities in a Cultural Context," and accompanied a public lecture by Scott Brown entitled "Emerging Institutions and their Architecture" on October 11, 1989. At the time, she had three teaching assistants to support the studio: Frederic Schwartz, Maryann Thompson, and Charlie Rose, all of whom became well-regarded architects (Schwartz sadly passed away in 2014). Students rotated weekly to organize the studio needs, sharing tasks and ordering supplies. The studio itself ran under the concern of looking out for one another and creating support within the studio itself. Tasks were broken down and assigned. Similarly, the studio brief followed the same pattern and called for a division of labor: The topic "Equipment of Well-Being" would be undertaken by two people; "Well-Being

Facilities in the Home" by one person, "Facilities for the Homeless," the "Wandering," and the "Dying" by two people each. Types of forms that were explored included pools, spas, yoga spaces, Finnish saunas, psychiatric services, homeless shelters, Japanese baths, Mogul gardens, and cure cottages,[3] all referenced in an extensive bibliography on pages 2–18. The research was followed by a one-month project designing a sauna, emerging institutions of well-being and their architecture, followed by research into the following topics: "Well-Being Institutions for the 21st Century" (two people) and "The Public Institutions of Cambridge" (five people), "Do-Good, Well-being Institutions Historically and Today" (one person), and "Your Choice." It was an exhaustive list of tasks and subjects to engage in, accompanied by an equally exhaustive list of books and articles to read, including one full page with a selection of Scott Brown's own writings and those coauthored with Robert Venturi and their office.[4]

Taking stock of our moment of the pandemic, I think back on my generation that grew up with the AIDS epidemic. The subsequent devastation on the gay community affected associated institutions and buildings in the city that were offering life-sustaining activities, such as bathhouses, which were shuttered and closed as a result of the epidemic. The fabric of the city changed, but in many ways it did not change fast enough. Hospitals and clinics were not equipped to handle such an outbreak, and I distinctly remember the Philadelphia ACT UP group staging theatrical "die-ins." Information was shared through the distribution of flyers across neighborhoods, and it wasn't until 1985 that the San Francisco AIDS Foundation produced the first brochure in the nation about women and AIDS. Reflecting on the times leading up to Denise Scott Brown's syllabus, it occurs to me that she never explicitly acknowledges the AIDS epidemic in the text, despite the particularly striking effects it had in her hometown of Philadelphia. It is important, however, to read the syllabus through this lens. Scott Brown takes her students through lessons to further a distinction between individual and institutional care, reimagining how institutions house people and groups, and how these institutions are named. One example is the hospice, an institution that had only recently been formed in the United States. Scott Brown wrote: "The concept of well-being has also been separated from health and applied, through the hospice movement, to death. A hospice—a place of comfort for the dying, away from a hospital—is an example of a new institution recently defined in our society; one where the physical housing has named the institution."

To me, Scott Brown's writings reflect an empathy for how society works collectively. The urban tissue is seen as a body with a nervous system and interconnected synapses. In my view, her writings, her buildings, and her photography are all forms of activism, calling for a collective reaction and action. At this moment, as the pandemic has yet to subside, there is concern about still unknown long-term health consequences. What we do know is that the pandemic has compounding effects, and that shelters, housing, and hospices, along with large-scale institutions such as laboratories and hospitals or small clinics—all of these types are not enough during vulnerable times. A considered syllabus may enable students to understand scenarios from the past and may provide an opportunity for them to speculate on future ones. In her brief, Denise Scott Brown focuses on a limited number of types of spaces and the distinction between institution-making and informal organizations, which helps us see what exists and why. Her selected curation, in review, I believe, illuminates the spaces for what is yet to come.

Notes

1   The brief begins, "To our credit we have a growing concern, although not to the degree needed, for the well-being and shelter of the homeless, including those [who are] permanently on the move and require salving way-stations to ease their journey through city streets." Denise Scott Brown, "The Architecture of Well-Being," Harvard Graduate School of Design, 1989, in the Venturi Scott Brown Collection, by the gift of Robert Venturi and Denise Scott Brown, at the Architectural Archives of the University of Pennsylvania, Philadelphia.

2   Scott Brown notes in the brief that "sometimes the role of the architects is to see a new institution emerging from trends in the society and to help define what that institution can be, how architects can contribute to the process of institutional definition and redefinition."

3   A "cure cottage" is a building type developed in upstate New York for the treatment of tuberculosis, 1870s–1945.

4   Interestingly, in connection with health-care institutions, Venturi designed and built the North Penn Visiting Nurses' Association Headquarters 1960–63—although this building was more concerned with complexity and contraction of form than with the function of the institution.

Evidently—On "Learning from Everything"

Aron Vinegar

In this essay, I want to explore the relationship of evidence to speculation in Denise Scott Brown's writings. I will focus on the strange arrhythmia between the plethora of evidence summoned forth in her approach to "learning from everything" and the implications of the word speculation—including one of the most basic, which is a going beyond the given and actual.[1] My claim is that speculation is *immanent* to a certain sense of evidence; it is literally *generated out of it*, but not in terms of evidence serving as the foundation or grounds for a progressively speculative movement forward, beyond, or towards a higher and more complete gathering, unity, or synthesis. Perhaps the paronymic resonances between the French adverb *évidemment*, which means "evidently/obviously," and noun *évidement*, "emptying/spilling out," is a close approximation to the relationship between evidence and speculation that I am trying to face up to. *Evidently* suggests a condition of filling up, saturation, excessive presence, overflowing, and an emptying out. Although Scott Brown's *Having Words*—the aptly titled collection of her essays—implies the possession and implementation of choice words and their performance in acts of situated debate, argumentation, or polemic, "having words" is also voiced as a truncated present participial phrase, which suggests an ongoing and *infinite* act of wording that is of a piece with being dispossessed, exposed and, at times, engulfed by those very words.[2]

Facing the Unfaceable

I was struck by the persistent use of the words "facing," "faced," and "face" as verb, noun, and adjective in Scott Brown's *Having Words* (I counted at least ten occurrences in the book).[3] One of the most striking instances is the phrase "facing the unfaceable," a formulation that resonates with similar phrasings in her writing, such as "thinking the unthinkable" or "measuring the unmeasurable."[4] To my mind, this terminology resonates with the desire of psychoanalysis to formulate an as yet nonexistent science that could account for the odd kind of evidence that the unconscious raises. The techniques of psychoanalysis are of a piece with dealing with this kind of evidence (more on this in the section on "Everything" below), and thus the kinds of "facing" involved are not primarily or straightforwardly communicative, readable, or figurative. In the traditional encounter between analyst and analysand the latter does not face the analyst, such that any exigency in this encounter is always predicated on indirection, evenly distributed/suspended attention, and delay, that would allow the evidence to move, vibrate, and proliferate as it is continually exposed. Thus, "facing" here is not an exterior, readable surface that registers signs of an interior depth, nor is it necessarily the stance of being positioned opposite to someone or something. In fact, it is more akin to a with-holding and a holding-back that runs counter to our immediate assumptions about what these two terms suggest. The "facing" we are talking about in Scott Brown's work is a tenacious maintaining right at the surface of the world that is a mode of active passivity that allows one to be "faced with unmeasurables."[5] Simultaneously, this facing is also a preposterous turning toward—a "walking behind" and a "rear elevation"—that, of course, does not entail literally walking behind the facade in order to expose what is hidden in what we might call an act of *shedding*.[6] Perhaps the condition and technique of the deadpan that is raised by Scott Brown registers a sense of facing that is both a tenacity and an openness.[7] I still think that Heidegger's phrase "resolute raptness" captures this kind of facing, although I would like to insist that this openness is not a tragic abyss, but rather manifests itself in the everyday as a blinking, flashing, short-circuiting, cutting off, cutting out, or simply as a blankness.

Thus, "facing" is not simply about a mode of evidencing that implies a way of showing that is clearly understood and seen, or that gives primacy to legibility and communication. All the "learning *froms*" that Scott Brown articulates are not only an indebtedness *to* something, but also forms of leave-taking, departure, displacement, and turning away that resist precipitous acts of foreseeing, knowing, and figuring things out, thus allowing grounds to exist on the surface in such a way that the ground faces itself (Scott Brown's Duck is precisely that hyperbolic mode of cutting and figuring out, that is simultaneously a cutting off and suffocating that *ducks* that "learning from").[8] Although Denise Scott Brown seems to use Le Corbusier's phrase "eyes that do not see" to criticize those who refuse to "face the unfaceable," it seems to me that her mode of seeing and facing precisely tarries with the occlusions, opacities, and blind spots that ensure that the abyss of the face, gaze, and unthought are always at play in her writing, representing, thinking, and building. As Emerson puts it in one of his journal entries: "Everything in the universe goes by indirection."[9]

Everything

Everything is potentially in evidence for Denise Scott Brown. But this "learning from everything" does not mean that everything and anything goes. Hers is not a postmodern ironic stance, often characterized (caricatured?) as a playful indifference, in which antagonism, conflict, and tension are flattened out into a plurality of styles and positions, thus echoing capitalism's general equivalence and fungibility. Like the play between "evenly suspended attention" on the part of the analyst and "free association" on the part of the analysand, the purpose is not to precipitously foreground, isolate, and cut out specific words, but rather to distribute the same weight and attention to everything that is happening. This is a form of active passivity—the word *passibility* strikes the right tone—that is potentially attuned to everything ... in the right mood. It is an approach that would delay judgment, not in order to eschew judgment, as Scott Brown notes in her essays "Pop Art, Permissiveness and Planning" and "Learning from Pop"—but rather to acknowledge that it is precisely "... the act of postponing, of carrying to infinity, that makes judgment possible."[10] (Some might characterize that opening as a time for research and data gathering, others might find those terms woefully inadequate. Count me among the latter.) In any case, it would force us to come up with new criteria, approaches, and stances—whether they be representational, verbal, or built—that would help us to think about everything that is happening: "fundamental, terrible, wonderful, insignificant, and crucial at the same time."[11] Evidently, these infinite "signs of life" are, at times, screeching with a day-glow intensity and at other moments they register as a barely detectable whisper … but we are accountable for all of them.

If Denise Scott Brown is a reluctant but persevering modernist, it is perhaps because she recognizes that "[t]he time of modernity," as Jean-Luc Nancy has noted, "is followed by the time of things."[12] Doing justice to "everything in evidence" is a condition that might entail a positive embrace of indifference that would run counter to our dominant privative sense of the term that indicates a lack of difference or affective engagement, as a way to account for minute differences and singularities, without precipitously hierarchizing them or prematurely gathering and subsuming them into a given form of community, meaning, or signification. It would be an "evidence of a different order."[13]

The Sigh and the Heap

There is a certain drive towards exhaustion at the heart of Scott Brown's writing, thinking, and making that is not merely a sign of world-weariness, whether that be characterized by pessimism, cynicism, or irony. I am talking about an exhaustion that is absolutely necessary for any experience and experiment of and at the limit of a given practice, form, or era, up to and including its saturation point. Exhaustion would be simultaneously an imperative and technique necessary for the in-finite task of "measuring the unmeasurable," "facing the unfaceable," and "thinking the unthinkable." Exhaustion is inseparable from Scott Brown's imperative that we "must judge, albeit, one hopes, with a sigh."[14] There are many instances of this exhaustion at play in her work and they are some of the most compelling forays into new experiments and experiences in architecture in the very literal sense of pushing to, at, and beyond limits.[15] It might involve testing the saturation point of late modernism itself in the form of the overly-expressive Duck that chokes on its own inability to express and communicate; or it might entail the "intolerable wrestle with words and meanings" (T.S. Eliot) that can manifest as a map of the Las Vegas Strip in *Learning from Las Vegas*, showing "every written word seen from the road," as if all signs had fallen to the ground in an unruly heap; or even a testing of our limits with regard to being spoken at and for through Scott Brown and Venturi's (at times) hectoring and hyperbolic repetition of clichés and claims (again, a doubling down on doubling down); or it might manifest itself as an obsession with how "analysis terminable and interminable" (Freud) delays and reconfigures what synthesis might mean in terms of new forms of writing and representing; or it might entail exploring the very limits of our ways of gathering a world, like the format of the book, which is thoroughly tested and surpassed in *Learning from Las Vegas* (1972), resulting in its repetition as another book with the same title, and whose chaste form is voided out from its saturated pages (or is it the reverse?). For me at least, Denise Scott Brown's "having words" attests to the fact that she is not interested in establishing a firm ground or foundation for a practice of writing, thinking, and building, but rather is driven by incessant, necessary, and contingent acts of grounding that are unsettling, insoluble … and foundering. That is evident to me in reading her words.

Notes

1   My notion of "evidence" is, in part, informed by Jean-Luc Nancy's exhaustive rethinking of that term in significant stretches of his writing. For example, see Nancy, *L'Évidence du film/The Evidence of Film: Abbas Kiarostami*. More directly, Rem Koolhaas has been the architect most attuned to the relationship between evidence and speculation, and is clearly inspired by the work of Denise Scott Brown and Robert Venturi in this regard. But my primary inspiration in writing this piece, at every turn, has been the words and writings of Denise Scott Brown.

2   Scott Brown, *Having Words*.

3   Scott Brown, *Having Words*, 15, 17, 25, 39, 55, 66, 69, 83.

4   Scott Brown, *Having Words*, 66, 83, 153.

5   Scott Brown, *Having Words*, 83.

6   Scott Brown, "Denise Scott Brown in Conversation with Enrique Walker," 54.

7   The deadpan was a technique that Denise Scott Brown was clearly aware of and that she, along with Robert Venturi and Steven Izenour, employed to great effect in *Learning from Las Vegas*—both the studio and the book—and in her essays "Pop Art, Permissiveness and Planning" and "Learning from Pop," often in reference to Ed Ruscha's photographic books. I have addressed the issue of the deadpan in *I am a monument: on Learning from Las Vegas*, and in "Ed Ruscha, Heidegger, and Deadpan Photography," 28–49.

8   On "the ground becoming face, facing itself" see Nancy, "The Look of the Portrait," 243.

9   Emerson, *The Journals and Miscellaneous Notebooks of Ralph Waldo Emerson*, 104. The complete quote is: "Everything in the Universe goes by indirection. There are no straight lines."

10   Scott Brown, "Pop Art, Permissiveness, and Planning," and Deleuze, "To Have Done with Judgment." The issues of delays in judgment—or as Scott Brown calls it judgment "with a sigh"—have been important to my rethinking of the concept of indifference, which is related to a course that I have been teaching on that topic for a few years now, and which I continue to draw upon in my writing.

11   Foucault, "The Masked Philosopher," 323–324: "What we are suffering from is not a void but inadequate means for thinking about everything that is happening. There is an overabundance of things to be known: fundamental, terrible, wonderful, insignificant, and crucial at the same time."

12   Nancy, "*Res ipsa et ultima*," 318.

13   Nancy, "Corpus" and "The Extension of the Soul," 49 and 140.

14   Scott Brown, "Learning from Pop," 23.

15   Jean-Luc Nancy emphasizes the "*ex-periri*"—the pirating of all foundations and the exhaustive spreading out to and pushing at the very limit—that is at the heart of all experience and experiment worthy of the name.

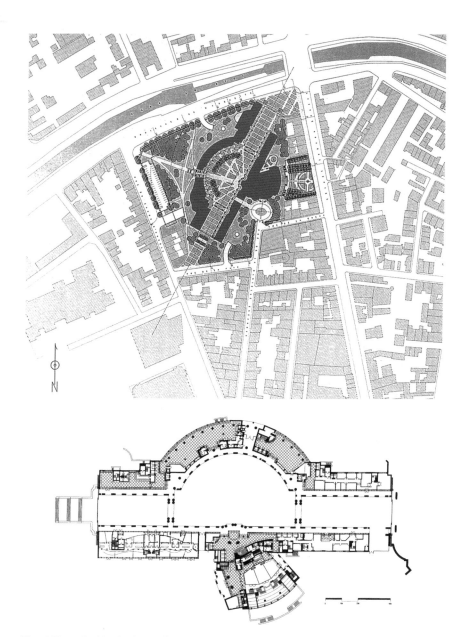

Figure 1: Master plan (above) and ground floor plan (below).

Recollections V: Exploring Denise Scott Brown's Methods

Françoise Blanc

> Architecture is the window through which I view my world, personal and professional. The span between architecture and planning—and then some—is the range of concerns that I bring to my work. Urban design is a type of design I do or am involved in. This is not a question of scale but of approach.[1]
>
> —Denise Scott Brown, *Urban Concepts*

As Denise Scott Brown's partner in the process of designing and implementing a large civic building in France, namely the Provincial Capitol in Toulouse, I can testify to the highly valued role she played and the crucial steps that her path took. Learning from—and with—Denise was a wonderful and decisive experience that shaped my architectural career and, most of all, my teaching of architectural history and design. I have followed in her footsteps with a sense of admiration for her critical method, and I enjoy sharing it with my own students. The following is an attempt to enter into Denise's splendid, dialectical way of thinking, which never loses track either of the vivid and unexpected forces of reality or of a poetic view of architectural creation, always maintaining a strong rational understanding of contemporary phenomena in our societies.

From Urban Concepts to Architecture, "Learning from Planning"

To explore Denise's methods of architectural design is to enter into her "world," as she writes in her book *Urban Concepts* (1990). It is a large universe, sensitive and rational, spontaneous and cultivated, vivid and complex, including a wide "range of concerns." Talking about the "span between architecture and planning," she opened up for us the indefinite intermediate field between these two sides that were opposites in the modern tradition. Going back to her thinking, tracing back the path that she took in her pedagogical research and her professional practice ("to watch a good architect learn to be an urban designer," as she writes in *Urban Concepts*), we can look at how architecture can learn from urban design. This means pulling the wires of a brilliant and seductive mechanism: it makes it possible to overcome the difficulty of matching scales, understanding socioeconomic skills as well as aesthetic and formal moves, to combine "both/and" in a "difficult whole," in the words of Robert Venturi.[2] It shows us how to design architecture without "paralipomena"—that is, as Denise writes, "things that have been left out."[3]

Denise's training in urban design, with the legacy of social concepts, nourished a broad understanding of architectural phenomena. Through her design methods (with their sources in her multicultural origins and the hybrid character of her education), Denise developed a singular style of teaching and practicing, a "nexus between architecture and planning."[4] This rich heritage, described in the chapters of this volume, which she celebrates as an "elixir," produced a critical character in her that is sometimes in surprising contrast to customary expectations, encouraging a poetic way of apprehending contexts, nourished by a taste for equivocation and ambiguity. Expressed with an aesthetic in which pluralism guided her work, her sensibility is accompanied by a singular approach to contemporary reality, facing the rapid changes of a heterogeneous society. Her attentive view, sometimes ironic, of the banality and ordinariness of the city surrounding us goes along with a deep knowledge of the European architectural and urban heritage, of contemporary American culture, of social sciences and planning disciplines, and of the artistic practices of the twentieth century, particularly pop art. The need to understand and respond to the urban context and the role of history is the very material of her architectural projects.[5]

The mannerist approach is a driving force for her: it generates concepts and patterns with the dynamic of rule-breaking.[6] It releases a significance that, in its complexity, makes it possible to act on both the urban and the architectural scale, designing in a multilayered way, combining "all the layers at once."[7]

With an "urban designer's way,"[8] managing interdisciplinary knowledge, articulations, and even contradictions, Denise approaches the architectural design process by looking at the way in which social arrangements influence physical forms. She bases her research on multiple relations, focusing "more on relations between objects, more on linkages, contexts and in between places, than on the objects themselves."[9] The analysis of contexts, existing buildings, and complexes is closely connected with design as "illustration, prediction, or statement of intention,"[10] interpreting and reading the materials and relating them to their design problems. This thinking and this system of values arises from a decision to start from the surrounding landscape and from a desire to design architecture that is inscribed into daily life. The "FFFs"—form, forces, and function—as Denise writes in *Urban Concepts*, interact in a dialectical synergy that allows architectural design to play in various registers and to articulate the necessary different points of view. Here we may recall Denise's conclusions in the book *Architecture as Signs and Systems*, written with Robert Venturi, which are particularly useful in the case of the building in Toulouse:

- Multi-scaled rather than "human"-scaled
- Accommodating rather than constricting
- Revelatory rather than reductive

for buildings that:

- Accommodate multiple options over generations rather than meet functional mandates for the first generation only
- Face hard problems, rather than ignore them to fit into a desired form
- Enter into a discernable and ongoing discussion with context
- Allow many interpretations rather than one truth
- Reveal rather than demonstrate.[11]

These statements elaborate the idea of an appropriate architecture, starting from the construction of a multileveled reading. The difficulty is to create a

unique architecture that includes more levels of reality and is based on an approach of continual adaptation: the architecture expresses multiple qualities, through which relationships with the context, history, tradition, and particular circumstances of the project are established. In the following, we will take a closer look at how these ideas were implemented in practice.

A Civic Building as a Laboratory

The Toulouse Provincial Capitol Building, the Hôtel du Département de la Haute-Garonne, is an illustration of Denise's approach. Most of Denise's design strategies were implemented in this project, which was completed with Robert Venturi and their partners. Their team of young architects (of which I was part) was fascinated by the intensity of the exchanges and discussions, the topics ranging from the analysis of Toulouse's architecture, history, and social aspects—for all of which we had to prepare materials for the design meetings. Denise contributed a very convincing, vivid, and intelligent understanding of the difficult context: her urban design method, described in the second part of *Architecture as Signs and Systems,* "Learning from Planning," determined the design. The *parti*[12] for the large building complex originated from Denise. The mannerist reference is permanently present, from the urban to the architectural scale; it is used as a way of resolving substantial contradictions in

Figure 2: Alternation and breaking up: the curtain wall of the Hall d'honneur (opposite page, left); the central semi-circular space and a bridge (opposite page, right); Bob, Denise, and the linkage of a bridge with the curved central space (this page).

the context and the program. It was full of contrast, abundant, and ambitious, with more than 40,000 square meters of surface area in a single megastructure that was to be sited on three hectares of industrial wasteland, a changing urban context between the Canal du Midi and the northern entrance of the historic center of Toulouse. The scale was large compared to the surrounding neighborhood and the historic city fabric.

The international competition, launched by the French departmental administration in 1990, was won by the office of Venturi, Scott Brown and Associates (VSBA) and their partners.[13] Their proposal was inscribed into the architectural and urban character of the city, related to its history and to French institutional and local architecture.[14] The project responded to the program's high demands with a rigorous functional unit complex, based on the double identity of administrative offices and political headquarters, housing the elected assembly for the region. It was a delicate task: the building had to combine the repetitive character of office units for an extensive administration with the official functions of political life and its discerning representatives. Most of all, it had to symbolically express the decentralization of political power in France.[15]

The project, fully completed in 1999, is a perfect illustration of Denise's convictions, examining multiple links with the surrounding context and its numerous sociocultural practices and uses. It became a true design laboratory, in which the components and formal choices for the building were elaborated, in continuity with the issues that Denise has explored throughout her career. It is an illustration of her critical thinking on "form, forces, and function" as well as "patterns and systems."[16] The project corresponded deeply with her concerns and with concepts shared with Robert Venturi, categories such as "form, symbol, context, ornament."[17]

A Parti Starting from a Reading of the Context—from Urban Design to Architecture

The *parti* divided the building in two wings of five floors. A central axis crosses the entire site diagonally from southwest to northeast, connecting two parts of the city through a "shortcut"[18]—the old northern entrance on the Canal du Midi and the new neighborhood in the contemporary city with its sports, commercial, and congress complexes. The *parti* was dictated by Denise's conviction that the complex would be a meaningful part of the city, and that it must combine a range of contradictory urban aspects, such as the historical axis, the presence of the canal, the contemporary social uses, and the traditional practices of institutional buildings in the region. A multilevel dynamic was implemented that made it possible to find layout solutions at the scale of the building itself as well as of the surrounding neighborhood, designing interior and outdoor spaces simultaneously (fig. 1).

The complex was organized around its own public space, a semicircular square and a pedestrian street, being "both–and" in the words of Robert Venturi[19]—*both* a long link *and* a central focused place. The two wings[20] are connected by glazed bridges, at two places on each floor, allowing for continuous horizontal circulation around the central outdoor space, linking the services and functions on both parts. The bridges thus reinforce the concept of a "whole"—"the difficult whole."[21] The vertical circulation gathers at four strategic points connected by horizontal walkways, creating spatial events that promote social exchanges in everyday administrative life.

"The Street Through the Building"[22]

The urban setting inspired both the *parti* and the architectural devices. These devices structure the distribution of spaces and become meaningful as symbolic elements. The long regular corridors on the floors, like streets sharing the perspective with the outdoor urban spaces seen behind the glass, are reminders of *both* everyday administrative life *and* its relationships with the social life of the city. Denise writes, "Learning from Kahn, Crane and transportation planning we have taken this internal street, tied it to external pathways that lead to the building, and made it the spine of the public sector of our buildings."[23]

The light, the materials, and the framing participate in creating unexpected events: the corridors meet a large open hall or a bridge over the central public space. They are the expression of a rich, "multiscaled," "accommodated," and "revealed"[24] style of design. The consistency and rhythm that order the entire composition are based on the adaptation of exceptions that regulate the details within the general order. The organization and implementation of the program elements are thus designed with interacting formal, symbolic, contextual, and ornamental devices (fig. 2).

Interpretations "Rather than One Truth"

The composition of the open outdoor spaces allows an articulated dialogue with the context: on the west side of the building, along the Canal du Midi, there is a landscaped park of one and a half hectares. Along the historical axis of the northern entrance of the city, the *Avenue Honoré Serres,* lies a garden *à la française.* The heart of the building accommodates the principal and secondary entrances, from which a hierarchy of pedestrian and vehicle access routes to various streets is organized. There are two main entrances facing each other, known as *Hall d'honneur* on the east side and *Hall d'accueil* on the west, both opening into the semicircular central public space. Their symbolic function is expressed through their monumental forms. A strong

Figure 3: The entrances at the urban scale: north (left) and south (center and right).

new order of porticos is created by the contrasting materials: stone and brick columns and a glazed "Miesian" steel-frame interior facade, rendered Palladian through their shape and alternating with wooden doors. They are also an interpretation of an important traditional device in urban public spaces in France, particularly in Toulouse and the southwest region.[25] On the north side wall, a forecourt and two freestanding columns mark and embellish the main entrance of the complex, reinterpreting the nineteenth-century columns by Toulouse architect Urbain Vitry (fig. 3).[26]

Composing the "Difficult Whole"—a Shared Concept with Venturi

As mentioned above, the complex "whole" is a central question that is expressed in numerous forms of alternation and "breaking up," in Denise's words. These are resolved in the detailed implementation of architectural elements such as banal windows and monumental curtain walls. Each function can be understood through the unitary composition of its various elements, such as the diverse ground floor services that are unified by a repetitive order and the scale of the continued portico.

The collaboration with Robert Venturi is visible through the implementation of several shared principles: *contradiction, both/and*, changes of scale, and de-contextualization (fig. 4). Thinking in contradictions is developed in numerous ways: in the relationship between the interior and the exterior, with a

Figure 4: Plurality of the facades: the portico on the "interior" central space (left), the "exterior" west facade (center), and the Assembly wing facade (right).

reversed composition of the facade materials: a majority of red bricks with alternating white limestone layers composes the facades of the interior spaces, while the exterior façades are composed with a majority of white limestone; in the formal expression and uses of the interior axis as public urban spaces (streets and squares are by definition exterior open spaces); in the juxtaposition of ordinary, repetitive windows versus monumental curtain walls, as exceptional elements. It is also seen in the apparent simplicity of the repetitive and regular offices, in contradiction with the monumentality and sophistication of highly significant architectural elements, such as the large atrium above the *Hall d'honneur* (fig. 5).

The singularity and scale of the Assembly Hall illustrate contradiction as well: its volume and implementation make complex articulations of particular forms possible, linked with regular elements, allowing surprises and tension effects (such as the large stairs leading to the hall). Changes of scale are introduced frequently into the entire composition of the building: in the size and the repetition of the windows, and in the pattern of the curtain wall of the Assembly wing. The stone columns at the main entrance also illustrate this design process: they signify the passages under the bridges from the central space to the interior street and access to the entrances in the main halls.

Denise Scott Brown and Robert Venturi wanted to create a complex that can be *both* a building *and* a piece of city, since its functions and scale include *both* public *and* private uses. It thereby symbolizes *both* daily life *and* official political and governmental events.

Figure 5: Interiors: The great atrium above the *Hall d'honneur* (left), monumental stairs to the Assembly Hall (center), view of the Assembly Hall (right).

A Meaningful Influence

In the light of these questions, the completed building for the *Hôtel du départ-tement* in Toulouse thus represents a historical and educational model, an eloquent illustration, rich with meanings that go beyond the specific context: its scope of reference extends to Denise's entire work. It also refers to longtime sharing of ideas with Robert Venturi, implying a fundamental questioning of sign and substance. A view that dares to continue to desacralize certainties and play with conventions in order to reach the heart of real life.

Denise's influence illuminated the entire design process for the building in Toulouse; it applied visionary and experienced thinking, relating architecture and urban design, expressed by her in the following words: "Urban design is the subtle organisation of complexity, the orchestration of sometimes inharmonious instruments, the awareness that discord at a certain level can be resolved as harmony at another."[27]

Notes

1 Scott Brown, *Urban Concepts,* 19.

2 Venturi, *Complexity and Contradiction,* 88.

3 Scott Brown, *Urban Concepts,* 6.

4 Scott Brown, *Urban Concepts,* 12.

5 See the monograph by Stanislaus von Moos, *Venturi, Rauch & Scott Brown, Buildings and Projects.*

6 Denise enthusiastically evokes the lectures on classicism given by John Summerson, particularly on John Soane, and the education of the "eyes." Scott Brown, *Urban Concepts,* 9.

7 This recalls the design of the building in Toulouse, which was elaborated with different registers, explained by Venturi and Scott Brown in *Architecture as Signs and Systems.*

8 Scott Brown, *Urban Concepts,* 13.

9 Scott Brown, *Urban Concepts,* 19.

10 Scott Brown, *Urban Concepts,* 13.

11 Venturi and Scott Brown, *Architecture as Signs and Systems,* 220.

12 "The *parti* is the assumption made that informs the design as well as the choice of approach when realizing the scheme." Curl, *Oxford Dictionary of Architecture,* 484.

13 The New York architectural firm Anderson Schwartz Architects and the Toulouse architectural group Hermet (A4), Blanc, de Lagausie, Mommens (HBLM), directed by Daniel Hermet, who died in 2007.

14 The Hôtel du Département de la Haute-Garonne in Toulouse is the only building constructed in France by VSBA.

15 A series of decentralization laws in France between 1983 and 1986 modified the division of powers between municipalities, departments, regions, and the French state. New administrative headquarters were therefore built in various departments during the 1990s, with new programs. International architecture competitions were organized for the buildings, for example in Marseille.

16 Scott Brown, "Architecture as Patterns and Systems, Learning from Planning."

17 These are the terms used in a lecture by Venturi and Scott Brown given in Tokyo in 1990, published in the catalogue of the exhibition *Venturi Scott Brown and Associates, May 21–31,* and in Venturi, *Iconography and Electronics upon a Generic Architecture.*

I have had long conversations with Venturi about these categories.

18 Venturi and Scott Brown, *Architecture as Signs and Systems,* 172.

19 Venturi, *Complexity and Contradiction,* 30.

20 The two wings are 25.0 meters high and 14.4 meters wide, with lengths of 179 meters (west wing) and 166 meters (east wing).

21 Venturi, *Complexity and Contradiction,* 89.

22 Another example of "The Street Through the Building" is found in the First Campus Center at Princeton University (1996–2000), described in Venturi and Scott Brown, *Architecture as Signs and Systems,* 133.

23 Scott Brown, "The Redefinition of Functionalism," in Venturi and Scott Brown, *Architecture as Signs and Systems,* 160.

24 Terms used by Scott Brown in *Architecture as Signs and Systems,* 220. See also note 18.

25 As in squares such as the Place du Capitole in Toulouse or the Place des Vosges in Paris, or the numerous squares of the Bastides in the southwest region.

26 They were erected in 1832 at the entrance of the Pont des Minimes bridge and demolished in 1940.

27 Scott Brown, *Urban Concepts.*

"And last, you will notice during this loosely chronological description I have used more and more the first person plural, that is, 'we'—meaning Denise and I. All my experience representing appreciation, support, and learning from, would have been less than half as rich without my partnership with my fellow artist, Denise Scott Brown. There would be significantly less dimension within the scope and quality of the work this award is acknowledging today—including dimensions theoretical, philosophical, and perceptive, especially social and urban, pertaining to the vernacular, to mass culture, from decorative to regional design— and in the quality of our design where Denise's input, creative and critical, is crucial."

—Robert Venturi, Acceptance Speech, Pritzker Prize

Epilogue

Figure 1: Robert Venturi and Denise Scott Brown on the terrace of Vanna Venturi House. They lived there for six months after their marriage in 1967. Photograph by George Pohl, 1964 (detail).

1 + 1 > 2: Letter to Biljana, Notes to Frida

Denise Scott Brown

From: Denise Scott Brown
Sent: Sun, Feb 13, 2022 at 6:21 PM
To: Biljana Arandelovic
Cc: Jeremy Tenenbaum, Frida Grahn
Subject: Reply to Biljana, Information on Denise

Dear Biljana,

I very much enjoyed our telephone conversation and I do apologize that this reply has taken me so long. But as we talked it became clear to me that what you and various other writers, mainly women, want to know about me has not been written. In fact, the appearance of *Learning from Las Vegas* taught architects about our lives up to its date of publication. Thereafter, although much was written, it was largely about Bob. So I wrote this account of what I have done from 1967, when we married, till today. I describe projects, methods we used, how we worked together, and the scope of my work.

My collaboration with Bob started at the University of Pennsylvania in 1960, but moved to his office in 1967 when we married. Arrangements were at first informal. Times were bad and my help was needed. Without discussing contracts or salary I started work on office projects, and our teaching was included as part of the broad weave of our practice.

Then, in 1968, my social planner colleagues asked me to join in stopping an expressway on Philadelphia's South Street. Four years of volunteering as advocates and planners for the low-income communities there brought approval of our plans, avoidance of the Expressway, and experience and some notoriety for me. But others were selected to develop our plans.

However, urban work soon followed and augmented the outlook and income of the firm. In 1969 I was made a partner. Bob and I continued our peripatetic studios, lectures, and writing, raised our child and, as we grew, I helped on our firm's Westway project and ran neighborhood and Main Street planning projects in Philadelphia, Santa Monica, Memphis, Miami Beach, Princeton, Austin, Galveston, Boonton, Jim Thorpe, and others. And members of our office staff—Steve Izenour and Mary Yee, for example—had learned to offer the finely-grained detail of social planning, regional and Main Street economics, mapping, and graphics that these plans required.

When 1970s governments removed funding for urban planning, our firm could not subsidize the hours needed for responsible social planning. We reassessed, looked outward, and found architectural commissions in London (Sainsbury Wing of the National Gallery, 1991), Toulouse (Provincial Capitol Building, Département de la Haute-Garônne, 1999), and Kirifuri, Japan (Mielparque Nikko Kirifuri Resort, Nikko National Park, 1997), plus a programming project for the Smithsonian's Museum of the American Indian (1992).

Three of these large and exciting civic commissions filled our lives from the mid-1980s to the mid-1990s but, though we and they knew we could never be their architects, programming for the American Indian Museum was, for me, deeply fulfilling, owing to the amazing information we learned about the purposes, uses, and correct display of their treasures, and the fun of joining members of different Indian nations, as in-jokes, ribbing, and laughter, incomprehensible to us, rippled across the boardroom table.

Campus Planning

At Penn, the campus and West Philadelphia served as areas for studio projects and research. When I changed from student to teacher in 1960, I added photography around Penn for use in teaching. Planning faculty meetings were arenas for debate on pedagogy of all kinds, but particularly on relationships between interdisciplinary coursework and studio, and I learned more about teaching studio from planning school than I did from architecture at Penn. Then for a while, I was Penn's campus planner.

So when, in 1988, a request came to plan for the Dartmouth College campus, I knew campus planning issues and town–gown relationships. More followed

Figure 2: John Rauch, Steven Izenour, Denise Scott Brown, and Robert Venturi at the office on 333 South 16th Street, Philadelphia, 1970s.

and, as our experience grew, we discovered that a "learning from" walkabout to share first reactions and early thoughts was a good way to meet and greet our clients, even though their approach was often, "I've lived and worked here for 30 years but never noticed that!" But we were, all of us, "innocents"—they of planning procedures, we of the campus—and we stored our early impressions to revisit during the process.

Our examination of building types suggested that the origins of college halls, labs, and studio buildings could lie in mills and warehouses of the industrial revolution. But West Philadelphia housing, beside the University and beyond it to the west, revealed multiple creative departures from Philadelphia's colonial Center City, signaling that in the world's then biggest heavy-industry region, good numbers of the working population were rich enough to own homes. In designing academic buildings, we studied these environments and settings, physical and intellectual, plus the requirements of different disciplines, and their linkages—with each other, the campus, and the city. And in campus planning we pulled them together.

Here the interdisciplinary connections I had made while teaching served me well, as I debated with faculty members on what they loved most. When asked "Where should the math building go?" I answered, "It depends what you think of math. Is it the handmaiden of the sciences, the muse of the arts, the grounding of all structure, the shock troops of IT, or, at its best, inspired puzzle solving?" All eyes turned to the head of the math department. He lay low, eyes peeking out, the grin of his jaw just visible. He was a crocodile in the Limpopo River, aping a log. Then, widening from grin to beam, he said, "All of the above."

Math disciplines must be near everything. And Main Street should be near enough. In the 1990s, life scientists called for buildings that encouraged exchanges among scientists in various disciplines, for the discoveries these could bring. And formula-filled whiteboards in lab floor coffee lounges raised the question, "Where will the next Nobel prize be hatched, at the lab bench or over coffee?"

My plans had, since the 1950s, tied campus activities together using the linkage diagrams of land use planning, desire lines of transportation, central place theories of regional economics, plus land and water programs of natural scientists. And although modern architecture held that functionalism is how the bedroom relates to the bathroom, and this is what to show on the outside, for me the tools of urban planning teach "functionalism for the outside." And, put together, this can respond to the faults of Le Corbusier's Radiant City—the vision behind the Athens Charter and the cause of urban problems for 100 years.

Our campus planning helped locate new buildings, and some of these became commissions for us. Given a choice, we picked the project that would best help implement our plan and guide future planning. At Penn, I produced the *parti* for the campus center I had recommended as campus planner. It converted historic spaces indoors and out, including basement and service spaces at the heart of the campus, to a campus center precinct. At the University of Michigan, it was a life sciences complex bridging a state highway and connecting the main campus to the medical center.

Figure 3: Denise Scott Brown and Robert Venturi at the office on 333 South 16th Street, Philadelphia. Photograph by George Pohl, 1968.

Working with Bob

I turned to Bob for advice on these projects, as he did to me on his. But most of our projects were shared between us and there were often two design *partis*.

"When you have Bob and Denise you have double your problem," said one client, and an intern in our office wrote simply, "1 + 1 > 2." These views, wry or happy, apply to many of our ideas—but function, especially the notion of functions of the outside, always lay behind Bob's "planning from the outside in" and my "outside functionalism."

We paralleled each other but at different scales. Bob worked from the piazza, street, or parking lot to building entries, and on to the activities, space sequences, and circulation of inner functions. My work spanned and sought guidance from urban surroundings, and the tools, social and physical, planners use for harnessing the forces that shape form. And in evolving basics for our project, urban contexts, a million memories, and loves led our linking of gossamer patterns of the space economy to mannerist complexities that interrupted their systems.

In the process, we noted that uneven and sloping sites endowed universities with buildings whose first floors are at ground level, while the basements protrude above ground at the back and have windows there. Into these large, evocative spaces, we introduced campus centers, an architecture archive and exhibition space, a small conference center, and a student-run art gallery—leading to the sighs of visiting students saying, "I wish our school had this!"

Toulouse

Bob and I had each seen Toulouse as students and been moved by it. But when a design competition was announced for the Haute-Garonne administration building in 1990, our further learning began from the air. We noted how the red-brick city center stood out from the red and white, brick, stone, and stucco of the outskirts, and that the site cleared showed how big the "Conseil Général" would be. Abutted on two sides by medieval streets rebuilt with modest twentieth-century buildings, edged on a third by a canal lined by a high wall and trees and on the other side by the Avenue Honoré Serres.

This busy highway fronted the site, bridged the canal, then continued past a small shopping center. On its way, it gave pedestrian access to the site at the bridge, making this a candidate for the main entrance to the complex. And at a corner diagonally opposite on the medieval side, connections with a smaller road and a second shopping center suggested a second entry.

From the air, and without yet understanding it, I began to think that this complex would have one or more routes through it, and that walls along them should be of red brick like the inner city, with outer walls of brick and limestone like those at the perimeter. Once home, and with a supply of maps, documents and programs, Bob and I met in our office with two friends of long standing, Fred Schwartz, an architect in our firm, and Françoise Blanc, from Toulouse and the French Academy at Rome, and one of our four French project members.

Fred began, "We have room here for five slab buildings, and down here for four more." But I suggested placing an axis diagonally across the site—providing a shortcut across it and modeling the "chicken bone" plan of a shopping center with stores along it and at its two ends. A five-story slab on either side could serve the needs of the Department and, surrounded by a large landscaped space, only their narrow ends would confront the small-town streets and buildings at the entrances.

In one wing the public would do its business with the Department. The other would hold the Assembly Hall, the *Hall d'honneur,* and spaces leading to and serving them. Two "passerelles," glass-lined bridges, took people between the wings at every floor, ending at corridor coffee corners on either side. At ground level, arcades and a few trees would create shade, and give entry to various activities, including dining, a daycare center, and its playground. Below was basement parking, reached via its own side-street entry.

Figure 4: Aerial photo of Toulouse Provincial Capitol Building, France, in association
with Anderson / Schwartz Architects and Hermet-Blanc-Lagausie-Mommens /
Atelier A4. Photograph by Matt Wargo, 1999.

These ideas started in our re-meet with Toulouse by air, with an overview of
the patterns and relationships that city and site offered each other. But they
derived too from walking donkey paths in the Transvaal, pedestrian shortcuts
across English cathedral closes, reading London street studies by Alison and
Peter Smithson, backpacking in medieval Europe, and a multidisciplinary
planning education in the US. These begot, *inter alia,* my belief that diagonal
shortcuts were a kind offer to urban pedestrians.

Figure 5: Toulouse Provincial Capitol Building. Photograph by Matt Wargo, 1999.

At that first meeting, a quick survey of movement and activity patterns at about a quarter-mile (400-meter) radius around the site—with wider glances at the old city—produced the first *parti*, or rather, the first hypothesis. There was a lot to be tested as we placed programmed facilities, densities and activities, old and new, in relation to the city and each other. But this first *parti* sketched out the directions of the building itself, its access points and, through these and major routes, its high- and low-density activity points and open spaces, plus the connection and cognition between its parts.

Figure 6: Courtyard
bridges at Toulouse
Provincial Capitol Building.
Photograph by Matt
Wargo, 1999.

Bob strongly supported these ideas. As heir to his father's business, he had owned a fleet of delivery trucks, and he and I had supervised the company while building our practice as architects. So, while unconnected to his education in architecture, Bob knew delivery routes in greater Philadelphia, as well as pilgrim routes in Rome. I too had studied Nolli maps, and the relation of piazzas and church entrances. But added to mine were courses in land use, transportation, and urban and regional economics.

From that we moved to *parti* two and studied sequences of major spaces leading indoors and out, asking what would determine their activities and shape their forms. Bob's first idea was to ennoble the central portion of our diagonal by introducing a crescent on its Department side between the two passerelles. This alludes to the Royal Crescent in Bath that he and I shared our love for in the first week of our friendship. On the other side, a steel and glass Palladian entry for pedestrians to the Assembly Hall is Bob's odyssey in loosening and enlivening Mies van der Rohe.

Then he applied the warehouse themes of our lab buildings to offices on both sides, skillfully joining that order of architecture to the one suggested in *parti* one. I liked the way he jammed the warehouse window pattern into the steel and glass of the Palladian entrance, and we planned the photographs to re-semble *beaux arts analytiques.*

At the back I took on the problem of joining curved and straight walls. But the major entry, scaled to receive pedestrians from the bridge, was classic Bob. He discovered two monumental columns that had marked the early Avenue Honoré Serres, and recast them as flattened silhouettes that mediated scales between tall building fronts, bulky columned doorways, and people entering.

Then we made a discovery. We had collected, we thought, all historical maps of the site, but found another while in construction. It showed a small street exactly where we had designed our shortcut across the site. So, by returning a street to its original location between two small shopping centers, we main-tained an activity pattern perhaps a thousand years old.

The passerelles gave access from and to all floors. They were an expensive solution, but people soon announced that they were finding their way around well and no longer confusing private and public space. Their glass walls helped orient users and so did the sunsets, sunrises, blue sky, and fluffy Med-iterranean clouds that they reflected. The vista from the main entrance under the passerelles ended in one small house at the far end across the road. And in the afternoon, a sun blast from its window caught your eye at the bridge entrance.

We had hoped that our public way and shortcut could serve as other streets in Toulouse do, for food, book, and antique markets, but it was made avail-able for ceremonial uses only. Then to my joy, a market appeared, at my sec-ond choice—the main route through the parking lot from cars to elevators. So, people got their market but without a blue sky above.

The next task was to develop the relationships from the inside out as sketched in the first *parti.* Here our collaborators assumed major roles, first in design development, then in production, and we and they visited the site and Phila-delphia to check samples, details, and drawings. But the Assembly Hall was still a major odyssey for us and especially Bob. Its clerestory windows ad-mitted the floating Mediterranean sky, and below them were glassed spaces, adapted from Baroque churches, but lined with slotted insulation panels over-painted with clouds.

Before that, smaller acoustic panels provided further insulation for seats on a podium facing seats in the hall. All were lovingly detailed and constructed from a forest of beech trees saved for 300 years for this occasion. And along the sides and back were glass-fronted cubicles for translators and the press. I helped choose a geometrically patterned carpet in black and white to give scale in that large room. And Bob and I, lacking light in the hall still under construction, were faced with a need to choose, right then, the pattern of black, grey and white bands, substitutes for column capitals, in the Hall. So, when Bob's eyes could not, I chose.

But I did not expect to be involved in the acoustic panel mix-up. We had used the panels before with success. They came from Germany and had been off-white when we received them in England. Here, they were bright pink. Everyone was shouting, and they expected me to handle it. I got on the phone to Germany. No, they said, there was no pink when they sent them. But, looking around, we saw pink sawdust everywhere from the chairs that their makers had constructed in situ. "Get a vacuum cleaner," I advised—and it worked.

Later, I was sitting in an apartment in Geneva when on the TV came our Hall. The city of Toulouse was using it to announce the production of a new Airbus. Overseas projects were a way to see the world in depth rather than as tourists, and an opportunity to visit family, as we did in stopping in Switzerland to be with my parents on our way to Toulouse.

In 1972, we bought a house large enough to hold our nieces and nephews, siblings and parents. And to maintain and restore this art nouveau house and its English Romantic landscape we had the help of about sixty architecture students who spent summers living with us and working on the house and yard. And this huge extended family come back to show proudly their families and we have had years of reference-writing for promising people. And all the while, we wrote articles and books, adding to and commenting on the theory we had established in earlier books. *Architecture as Signs and Systems: For a Mannerist Time* (2004) updated and furthered *Learning from Las Vegas* (1972) based on ideas from later projects.

Figure 7: Denise Scott Brown explaining the campus plan of Tsinghua University in Beijing, China. Photograph by Ke Feng, 2004.

In 2012, our firm passed to younger principals, and we slowly retired. Bob died in 2018 but, with a small support staff, I talk, write, photograph, exhibit, and advise. I am working now on a further update on what I now see at the far end of three long, low career curves starting in Africa, continuing in Europe, and ending in the US. I now have more understanding than I thought I would ever find when I told Arthur Korn at the age of twenty: "I have a need for structure." Perhaps so, but soon thereafter, I think I found that enthusiasm gives better support than structure.

Biljana, I applaud your diligence in taking time to work through this on your own. You are doing a great thing. Bob and I worked on our publications without funding. Yale paid for our Las Vegas studio and, if I remember, the only outside contribution to it was $1200. For the rest we used our free hours. The results were worth the effort, and yours will be too.

With all good wishes, Denise.

Figure 8: Denise Scott Brown, Venturi/Scott Brown House by Milton B. Medary, designed 1907. Wissahickon Avenue, Philadelphia. Photograph by Carl C. Paatz, 2019.

From: Denise Scott Brown
Sent: Friday, February 18, 2022 4:07 pm
To: Frida Grahn
Subject: Fwd: Reply to Biljana, Information on Denise

Dear Frida,

Biljana is very happy, and so am I. Would you like to take the next step with her by asking if you can use my letter to her in your book? Reassure her that I would love this, and love seeing her first name at the head of the letter, with, if you agree, no second name. I love that the name Biljana is used as a generic, where in England or America it would be Mary. For me a generic Biljana welcomes the world. And her second name, if she wants, can be used elsewhere.

Please tell her that we are working now on a few additions to the text, explaining that my joy in architecture and in my practice with Bob has been described elsewhere but that to explore our joint creativity requires dates, description of the changing scope of our work from 1960 on, and of our methods of working together, as academics and practitioners.

I have chosen our Conseil Général building in Toulouse to illustrate our ways of working on a project together. This is a late project, but its methods evolved from our early work together and applied to most of our projects. The exception is our houses. Bob designed most of them without me and with a project manager from the office. They were personal odysseys for him, but strangely, his greatest learning journeys, the Vanna Venturi house and the Lieb house, I was deeply involved in.

I led our teams for urban and campus planning and design, and for project programming, and was lead designer for architecture complexes at Penn, Michigan, and Dartmouth. But Toulouse illustrates our joint collaboration with members of our firm and other firms in a large project; it shows how, as our staff grew more diverse, we were able to make richer offerings to clients, and how our whole firm seemed to become happier as a result.

Young architects in big firms often feel mistreated (the Pritzker Prize petition was full of the complaints of architectural interns), but ours seemed to feel that though the going was tough it owed more to the construction industry than to our practice, and that when I talked about joint creativity it engaged their talents too and offered them opportunities for growth. Then one of our interns described Bob's and my joint creativity as: "1 + 1 > 2."

So I hope Biljana will answer with an energetic yes!

Please let me know what happens and how you will continue. And thank you so much for all the work you are doing. This gets to be a brighter and brighter story. D

From: Denise Scott Brown
Sent: Wednesday, April 27 2022 at 6:02 am
To: Frida Grahn
Subject: "A bag of tools"

Dear Frida,

This is an attempt to cover briefly in my paper the profound effect of the social planning movements on architecture schools in the 1960s. You could summarize it as a bag of tools that disciplines in and out of the school provided for the forms of thinking needed to replace the Athens Charter. Through them, I learned to run studios in architecture very different from the ones at the time. I need you to help me decide on the spot for this, and condense it to a couple of sentences. Read it on the plane and perhaps we can talk about it when you get back.

See you soon, D

In his article in this book, James Yellin, one of my first students in my first year of teaching and a planner, not an architect, has given a succinct description of an ongoing and creative battle between two very young planning teachers: Paul Davidoff and me.

In addition to us, there were other people concerned in the planning school, also young. Herbert Gans, who later became a famous professor of social urbanism and planning and also my friend, was one such person. Robert [Scott

Brown] and I met him while he was a participant observer in Levittown. We also learned from the ideas produced through his professor, Robert Merton, from which he took his sociology, from his Stuyvesant bricks and rich people in New York to the slums of Boston, where immigrants were settling, and later from Philadelphia and New Jersey, where those immigrants were moving to the suburbs and getting affordable housing from builders like Levitt. As much as Paul Davidoff, Gans helped to change the face of urban planning through this research, but at the same time, and particularly at the University of Pennsylvania, systems planning had started with the computer ENIAC (Electronic Numerical Integrator and Computer), which was invented and used there by groups of people in economics and transportation. This created equivalent passions, and some of them were able to fire the imagination of architects.

These were my colleagues in the years that I was on the faculty—I learned from them as a student and a colleague, and they from me. And the economic tools I learned I put together with the passions of Davidoff and the broad knowledge of all of them to create what I call my "bag of tools," with which I sought to replace the now almost 100-year-old Athens Charter, which was never a good formula for urban planning. As an African who has trekked more donkey paths than Le Corbusier, I am taking him with me on the donkey—using this traditional transportation system as a key to more complex ones, to what I call "outside functionalism" and to better tools for architects.

Glossary

Beaux arts analytiques: A way of composing architectural drawings developed in the Ecole des Beaux Arts to show relationships among building elements.
Desire lines of transportation: A way of mapping the movement of people between their workplaces and their homes.
Town–gown relationships: Expression to describe the relationships between cities and their universities, in which the "gown" colloquially refers to the academic world (the "academic robe").

Figure 1: Denise: "Pre-Raphaelite selfie in a Las Vegas motel. The camera flash off the ice bucket gave me a halo." Photo by Denise Scott Brown, Las Vegas, 1965.

"So You'd Like To See The World?"

Jeremy Eric Tenenbaum with captions by Denise Scott Brown

How does Denise Scott Brown—architect, urbanist, teacher, and writer—see the world?

As a white Jewish woman born and raised in 1930s and '40s Southern Africa, Denise has always observed from a liminal perspective. In London for her continued education, she saw as a traveler, student, and practitioner; in Europe and America with her first husband Robert Scott Brown, she saw as a student, young practitioner, and tourist; later she became a teacher, architect, and urban planner.

What were her reasons for photographing through each of these stations of her life?

In Africa, Denise photographed in the way we all do: to capture her home, her world. What was this place, South Africa—between wars, in the time of apartheid? An art teacher insisted "depict what's around you"—meaning the picturesque—but Denise also saw wealth, poverty, modes of living both familiar and strange.

In Europe, Denise photographed to document, learn, fall in love. She studied urbanism, functionalism, natural and artificial systems, and very different approaches to housing. In Venice, Denise and Robert Scott Brown photographed both vast and intimate spaces: Piazza San Marco glamour (albeit through a veil of pigeons), courtyards spanned by clotheslines, and the yawning lagoon.

In America, Denise photographed to study the wild vernacular, beauty of industrial romance, and forces subtending urban form. She discovered Las Vegas, an object lesson in signage and form, and introduced it to her second husband and partner Robert Venturi. Driving together, Denise and Bob played "I Can Name Something Uglier Than You Can ... And Love It." *Learning from Las Vegas* is *least* about Las Vegas: it's an ethical and practical parable for learning from the world.

Denise explored symbolism and communication—those functional necessities early modernism overlooked. She learned from the ugly and ordinary as well as the heroic and original, embracing the validity of both high and low art, solemnity and irony, mess as well as monument.

Look at this Los Angeles car and highway and houses and industrial systems and natural landscapes: how can they all abide? In this sea of systems, you can't obey all the rules all the time. You must see a way through the conflict. One way is to steer by *mannerism*, the navigation of contradictory systems not by eliminating rich complexity but by drawing conflicts together into a difficult whole.

Figure 2: African children looking at the camera. Denise: "Apartheid made South African cities places of white people and black adults serving them. You didn't see black children in cities, but you saw them in the townships. These children might be wondering, 'What are these white people doing out here?'" Photo by Denise Scott Brown, Johannesburg, 1956.

Figure 3: African housing. Denise: "My first reaction to Soweto housing, as to Levittown which it resembles, was horror. But learning led me to understand its urbanism and social value. It gave people permanence on the land, so important to developing roots, tools, and the beginning of generational wealth." Photo by Denise Scott Brown, Johannesburg, 1956.

Figure 4: The Venice Lagoon. Denise: "The most open space in any city is likely to be its river or lake. When I studied in London and felt its buildings falling over my head, I found respite along the Thames. In Venice for the CIAM Summer School, Robert Scott Brown and I discovered vast space in its lagoon." Photo by Denise Scott Brown, Venice, 1956.

Figure 5: Red car on a Los Angeles highway. Denise: "Pure industrial romanticism. As part of a studio course, I asked the LA Department of Transportation to organize a tour for my students. We spent the day riding the highways. As I wrote, 'Put a group of architects, urban designers and social planners in a sightseeing bus and their actions will define the limits of their concerns. The architects will take photographs of buildings or highways or bridges. The urban designers will wait for that moment when the three are juxtaposed. The social planners will be too busy talking to look out of the window.'" Photo by Denise Scott Brown, Los Angeles, 1966.

Figure 6: Las Vegas signage. Denise: "*Architettura minore* along the Las Vegas Strip."
Photo by Denise Scott Brown, Las Vegas, 1966.

Figure 7: Las Vegas gas station giant. Denise: "I took a different photo of 150 of
these giant sign spectaculars stacked together. There's nothing so grand that if you
put 150 of them together they don't look ridiculous. Alone, though, this fellow looks
very impressive." Photo by Denise Scott Brown, Las Vegas, 1966.

Figure 8: Two girls walking past "I love you" graffiti. Denise: "Len Freed taught me Cartier-Bresson: how he would stand and wait for a miracle to pass by his camera. So I did the same. I watched this yellow wall with its dark lettering until two girls ran past. If you wait and watch, you'll eventually spot a miracle." Photo by Denise Scott Brown, Philadelphia, 1961.

Denise sees in wayward ways. Even when unglamorous, her photos are exuberant with these intersecting systems and vertiginous juxtapositions. A beautiful photo can be ugly; the answer to a problem might be painful but still the right solution.

Denise's photos are ethical lanterns. For photographers and architects and everyone learning to see their way through the world, Denise's life and hard-fought observations offer inspiration.

Denise (she swears) is not a photographer. But after a lifetime of images, she continues to see and shape her world through photography: now using her iPhone to capture her home, her evolving intimate world. Denise's eyesight pales; focus weakens and colors shift. So now more than ever her maxim remains: "Don't think why—shoot quick—before it gets away!"

1966 Las Vegas: Denise style, spoofing Robert Moses, looking with Corbu at the backs of the buildings

Figure 9: Denise Scott Brown and Robert Venturi in the Las Vegas desert, off the Strip.
Denise: "I am monarch of all I survey." Photos by Denise Scott Brown and Robert Venturi, Las Vegas, 1966.

Bob style, Magritte style, tower of Pisa, with mannerist plays of scale

Bibliography

Angélil, Marc M. "Gewöhnliches thematisieren oder eliminieren? Die neue Studie über Venturi, Scott Brown & Associates." *Werk, Bauen + Wohnen*, no. 4 (2001): 56–58.

Angélil, Marc M. "Gewöhnliche und aussergewöhnliche Architektur." *Werk, Bauen + Wohnen*, no. 7–8 (1990): 24–27.

Anon. "South Africa." *Architectural Review* 96, no. 574 (October 1944): 93–128.

Architectural Design 60, nos. 1/2: see Scott Brown, Denise, [and Andreas C. Papadakis, ed.] *Urban Concepts.*

Banerjee, Tridib, and Anastasia Loukaitou-Sideris, eds. *Companion to Urban Design.* London: Routledge, 2011.

Banham, Reyner. "The New Brutalism." *Architectural Review 118*, no. 708 (1955): 355, 358–361.

Barriere, Phillipe et al. "Interview with Denise Scott Brown and Robert Venturi." *Perspecta*, 28 (1997): 127–145.

Baudin, Antoine. *Hélène de Mandrot et la "Maison des Artistes" de La Sarraz.* Lausanne: Payot, 1998.

Belogolovsky, Vladimir. "Learning from Robert Venturi and Denise Scott Brown." In *Artistic Bedfellows: Histories, Theories, and Conversations in Collaborative Art Practices*, edited by Holly Crawford, 116–126. Lanham: University Press of America, 2008.

Berson, Lenora E. "The South Street Insurrection." *Philadelphia Magazine* 60, no. 11 (November 1969), 87–92, 174–182.

Birch, Eugénie L. "From CIAM to CNU: the Roots and Thinkers of Modern Urban Design." In *Companion to Urban Design*, edited by Tridib Banerjee and Anastasia Loukaitou-Sideris, 9–29. London: Routledge, 2011.

Blake, Peter. "Co-op City: The High Cost of Hideousness." *New York Magazine* (August 19, 1968): 28.

Blake, Peter. *God's Own Junkyard: The Planned Deterioration of America's Landscape.* New York: Holt, Rinehart and Winston, 1963.

Blanc, Françoise. "L'Hôtel du Département à Toulouse, Une architecture américaine?" *Midi-Pyrénées Patrimoine* [Université de Toulouse II–Le Mirail], no. 14 (April–June 2008), 70–76. [Special issue on *Modernités du XXe Siècle.*]

Blau, Eve. "Pedagogy and Politics: Making Place and Learning from Las Vegas." In *Eyes That Saw: Architecture after Las Vegas*, edited by Stanislaus von Moos and Martino Stierli, 33–66. Zurich: Scheidegger & Spiess; New Haven, CT: Yale School of Architecture, 2020.

Blau, Eve. "This Work is Going Somewhere: Pedagogy and Politics at Yale in the Late 1960s." *Anyone Corporation Log* 38 (Fall 2016): 131–149.

Bletter, Rosemarie, Martin Filler (writers) and Michael Blackwood (director). *Beyond Utopia: Changing Attitudes in American Architecture* [documentary film]. New York: Blackwood Productions, 1983. Available at: https://www.michaelblackwoodproductions.com/project/beyond-utopia-changing-attitudes-in-american-architecture/ (accessed May 9, 2022).

Blunt, Anthony. *Artistic Theory in Italy 1400–1650.* Oxford: Clarendon Press, 1940.

Blunt, Anthony. "Mannerism in Architecture." *RIBA Journal* 56, no. 5 (1949): 195–201.

Boonin, Harry D. *The Jewish Quarter of Philadelphia: A History and Guide, 1881–1930.* Philadelphia: Jewish Walking Tours of Philadelphia, 1999.

Brion, Marcel, and René Huyghe. *Se perdre dans Venise.* Paris: Arthaud, 1986; reprinted Grandvilliers: La Tour Verte, 2012.

Brownlee, David B., David G. De Long, and Kathryn B. Hiesinger. *Out of the Ordinary: Robert Venturi, Denise Scott Brown and Associates; Architecture, Urbanism, Design.* Philadelphia: Philadelphia Museum of Art in association with Yale University Press, 2001.

Bruggen, Coosje van. *Claes Oldenburg: Mouse Museum/Ray Gun Wing.* Cologne: Museum Ludwig, 1979.

Brulhart, Armand. "Séminaire international à La Sarraz. Architecture: la race des prophètes a disparu." *Journal de Genève* (July 8–9, 1978) [no page numbers].

Buckley, Craig. *Graphic Assembly: Montage, Media, and Experimental Architecture in the 1960s.* Minneapolis: University of Minnesota Press, 2019.

Butler, Judith. *Gender Trouble: Feminism and the Subversion of Identity.* New York: Routledge, 1990.

Canady, John. "Oldenburg as The Picasso of Pop." *New York Times*, September 28, 1969, D33.

Calle, Sophie. *Suite vénitienne.* Paris: Editions de l'Etoile, 1983.

Caplan, Andrew. *South African Jews in London.* London: Royal Holloway University of London, 2011. Available at: https://www.academia.edu/73520662/South_African_Jews_in_London (accessed April 28, 2022).

Carroll, Paul. "The Poetry of Scale: Interview with Claes Oldenburg." In *Claes Oldenburg: Proposals for Monuments and Buildings, 1965–1969*, 11–37. Chicago: Big Table, 1969.

Charitonidou, Marianna. "The 1968 Effects and Civic Responsibility in Architecture and Urban Planning in the USA and Italy: Challenging 'Nuova Dimensione' and 'Urban Renewal.'" *Urban, Planning, and Transport Research* 9, no. 1 (2021): 550–580. Available at: https://doi.org/10.1080/21650020.2021.2001365 (accessed May 7, 2022).

Charitonidou, Marianna. "Denise Scott Brown's active socioplastics and urban sociology: from Learning from West End to Learning from Levittown." *Urban, Planning, and Transport Research* 10, no. 1 (2022): 131–158. Available at: https://doi.org/10.1080/21650 020.2022.2063939 .

Charitonidou, Marianna. "Ugliness in architecture in the Australian, American, British and Italian milieus: Subtopia, between the 1950s and the 1970s." *City, Territory and Architecture* 9 (2022): 1–19. Available at: https://doi.org/10.1186/s40410-022-00152-7 .

Cheng, Irene, Charles L. Davis, and Mabel O Wilson. *Race and Modern Architecture: A Critical History from the Enlightenment to the Present*. Pittsburgh: University of Pittsburgh, 2020.

Chipkin, Clive. *Johannesburg Style: Architecture and Society, 1880s–1960s*. Cape Town: David Philip Publishers, 1993.

Choi, Rebecca. "Black Architectures: Race, Pedagogy and Practice, 1957–1966." PhD diss., University of California at Los Angeles, 2020. Available at: https://escholarship.org/uc/item/1hf2k57z (accessed April 28, 2022).

Ciorra, Pippo. *Ludovico Quaroni 1911–1987. Opere e Progetti*. Milan: Electa, 1989.

Colomina, Beatriz. "Learning from Levittown: A Conversation with Robert Venturi and Denise Scott Brown." In *Worlds Away: New Suburban Landscapes*, edited by Andrew Blauvelt, 49–69. Minneapolis: Walker Art Center, 2008.

Colomina, Beatriz, Craig Buckley, and Urtzi Grau. *Clip, Stamp, Fold: The Radical Architecture of Little Magazines, 196x to 197x*. Barcelona: Actar, 2010.

Cook, John W., and Heinrich Klotz. *Conversations with Architects*. London: Lund Humphries, 1973.

Costanzo, Denise. "Text, Lies and Architecture: Colin Rowe, Robert Venturi and Mannerism." *Journal of Architecture* 18, no. 4 (2013): 455–473.

Costanzo, Denise. "'A Truly Liberal Orientation': Laurance Roberts, Modern Architecture, and the Postwar American Academy in Rome." *Journal of the Society of Architectural Historians* 74, no. 2 (June 2015): 223–247.

Costanzo, Denise. "'I Will Try My Best to Make It Worth It': Robert Venturi's Road to Rome." *Journal of Architectural Education* 70, no. 2 (October 2016): 269–283.

Costanzo, Denise. "Venturi and Scott Brown as Functionalists: Venustas and the Decorated Shed." *Wolkenkuckucksheim—Cloud-Cuckoo-Land: International Journal of Architectural Theory* 17, no. 1 (2012): 9–25. Available at: https://www.cloud-cuckoo.net/journal1996-2013/inhalt/de/heft/ausgaben/112/Beitraege/2.1%20%20%20Costanzo.pdf (accessed April 28, 2022).

Countryman, Matthew J. *Up South: Civil Rights and Black Power in Philadelphia*. Philadelphia: University of Pennsylvania Press, 2006.

Crane, David. "Chandigarh Reconsidered: The Dynamic City." *Journal of the American Institute of Architects* (1953): 32–39.

Crenshaw, Kimberlé Williams. "Mapping the Margins: Intersectionality, Identity Politics, and Violence Against Women of Color." *Stanford Law Review* 43, no. 6 (July 1991): 1241–1299.

Critchley, Matthew. "Mannerism and Method: Class and Artistic Agency in the Writing of Anthony Blunt, 1934 to 1949." *Architectural Theory Review* 24, no. 2 (2020): 164–181.

Curl, James Stevens. *Oxford Dictionary of Architecture*. Oxford: Oxford University Press, 1999.

Custer, Lee Ann. "Teaching Complexity and Contradiction at the University of Pennsylvania, 1961–65." In *Complexity and Contradiction at Fifty*, edited by David B. Brownlee and Martino Stierli, 30–47. New York: The Museum of Modern Art, 2019.

Dainese, Elisa. "Histories of Exchange: Indigenous South Africa in the *South African Architectural Record* and the *Architectural Review*." *Journal of the Society of Architectural Historians* 74, no. 4 (December 2015), 443–463.

Dal Co, Francesco. "Dove Danzano Grilli Mirabili. Venezia, il Fondaco dei Tedeschi, OMA: Paradossi e Reinvenzioni." *Casabella* 863–864 (2016): 26–37, 38–49.

Davidoff, Paul. "Advocacy and Pluralism in Planning," *Journal of the American Institute of Planners* 31, no. 4 (1965): 331–338. Reprinted in *A Reader in Planning Theory,* edited by Andreas Faludi, 277–296. Oxford: Pergamon Press, 1973.

Davidoff, Paul, and Thomas A. Reiner. "A Choice Theory of Planning," *Journal of the American Institute of Planners* 28, no. 2 (1962) 103–115. Reprinted in *A Reader in Planning Theory,* edited by Andreas Faludi, 12–39. Oxford: Pergamon Press, 1973.

Davis, Charles L. *Building Character: The Racial Politics of Modern Architectural Style.* Pittsburgh, PA: University of Pittsburgh Press, 2019.

Deleuze, Gilles. "To Have Done with Judgment." In *Essays Critical and Clinical,* translated by Daniel W. Smith and Michael A. Greco, 126–135. Minneapolis: University of Minnesota Press, 1997.

De Long, David G., Helen Searing, and Robert A.M. Stern, eds. *American Architecture: Innovation and Tradition.* New York: Rizzoli, 1986.

de Monchaux, Nicholas. *Spacesuit: Fashioning Apollo.* Cambridge, MA: MIT Press, 2011.

Didelon, Valéry. *La controverse Learning from Las Vegas.* Wavre, Belgium: Mardaga, 2011.

Dillon, Clay. "Royal Theatre Closed After 50 Yrs.; Now 'Gravestone' in a Dying Era." *Philadelphia Tribune,* 1968, 2.

Donohoe, Victoria. "Advocacy Planners Put Hope in Ghetto." *Philadelphia Inquirer,* July 6, 1969, 6.

Du Bois, W.E.B. *The Philadelphia Negro: A Social Study,* with an introduction by Elijah Anderson. Philadelphia: University of Pennsylvania Press, 1996.

Dubow, Saul. *A Commonwealth of Knowledge: Science, Sensibility, and White South Africa, 1820–2000.* Oxford: Oxford University Press, 2006.

Eaglestone, Robert. *The Holocaust and the Postmodern.* Oxford: Oxford University Press, 2004.

Emerson, Ralph Waldo. *The Journals and Miscellaneous Notebooks of Ralph Waldo Emerson,* vol. XV (1860–66), edited by Linda Allardt and David W. Hill. Cambridge, MA: Belknap Press of Harvard University Press, 1982.

Farrell, William E. "Vast Co-op City Is Dedicated in Bronx." *New York Times* (November 25, 1968): 1, 43.

Fausch, Deborah. *The Context of Meaning in Everyday Life: Venturi and Scott Brown's Theories of Architecture and Urbanism.* PhD dissertation, Princeton University, 1999.

Fausch, Deborah. "The Knowledge of the Body and the Presence of History: Toward a Feminist Architecture." In *Architecture and Feminism,* edited by Debra Coleman, Elizabeth Danze, and Carol Henderson. New York: Princeton Architectural Press, 1996.

Fausch, Deborah. "She Said, He Said: Denise Scott Brown and Kenneth Frampton on Popular Taste." *Footprint* 8, no. 1 (2011): 77–89.

Fausch, Deborah. "Ugly and Ordinary: The Representation of the Everyday." In *Architecture of the Everyday,* edited by Steven Harris and Deborah Berke, 94–95. New York: Princeton Architectural Press, 1997.

Fausch, Deborah. "'Ugly': The architecture of Robert Venturi and Denise Scott Brown." In *Architecture and Ugliness: Anti-Aesthetics and the Ugly in Postmodern Architecture,* edited by Wouter Van Acker and Thomas Mical, 153–174. London: Bloomsbury Visual Arts, 2020.

Fontenot, Anthony. *Non-Design: Architecture, Liberalism, and the Market.* Chicago: University of Chicago Press, 2021.

Foucault, Michel. "The Masked Philosopher." In *Ethics: Subjectivity and Truth,* edited by Paul Rabinow, translated by Robert Hurley and others, 323–324. New York: New Press, 1997 (Essential Works of Foucault, 1954–1984, vol. 1).

Frampton, Kenneth. "Place, Production and Architecture: Towards a Critical Theory of Building." *Architectural Design* 52 (July–August 1982): 28–45.

Francia, Evelina. "Learning from Africa: Denise Scott Brown Talks About Her Early Experiences to Evelina Francia." *The Zimbabwean Review* (1995): 26–29.

Frank, Josef. "Accidentism." *Form* 54 (1958): 160–165. Reprinted as "Akzidentismus," *Baukunst und Werkform* 14 (1961): 216–218 and in Josef Frank, *Schriften / Writings,* 372–387.

Frank, Josef. *Architektur als Symbol. Elemente deutschen neuen Bauens.* Vienna: Schroll, 1931 [1930].

Frank, Josef. *Schriften / Writings,* edited by Tano Bojankin, Christopher Long, and Iris Meder. 2 vols. Vienna: Metroverlag, 2012.

Franzen, Ulrich. [Letter to the editor.] "Co-op City Controversy: Letters to the Editor." *Progressive Architecture* (April 1970): 8.

Friedlaender, Walter. *Mannerism and Anti-Mannerism in Italian Painting.* New York: Columbia University Press, 1957.

Gabor, Andrea. *Einstein's Wife: Work and Marriage in the Lives of Five Great Twentieth-Century Women.* New York: Viking, 1995.

Gans, Herbert J. "City Planning and Urban Realities." *Commentary* (February 1, 1962): 172.

Gans, Herbert J. *The Levittowners: Ways of Life and Politics in a New Suburban Community.* New York: Pantheon Books, 1967.

Gans, Herbert J. "Racialization and Racialization Research." *Ethnic and Racial Studies* 40, no. 3 (2017): 341–352.

Gans, Herbert J. *The Urban Villagers: Group and Class in the Life of Italian-Americans.* New York: Free Press of Glencoe, 1962.

Gilbert, Lynn, and Gaylen Moore. *Particular Passions: Women Who Have Shaped Our Times.* New York: Potter, 1981.

Golec, Michael. "Format and Layout in *Learning from Las Vegas.*" In *Relearning from Las Vegas,* edited by Aron Vinegar and Michael Golec, 31–47. Minneapolis: University of Minnesota Press, 2009.

Grahn, Frida. "Beyond Realism: The Swiss Reception of Venturi and Scott Brown." *Wolkenkuckucksheim— Cloud-Cuckoo-Land: International Journal of Architectural Theory,* no. 42, 2022 : 23–46.

Greenberg, Irving. "Theology after the Shoah: The Transformation of the Core Paradigm." *Modern Judaism* 26, no. 3 (October 2006): 213–239.

Greenspan, Elizabeth. "Star System." *Believer Magazine* 137 (October 21, 2021): 1–24.

Gregotti, Vittorio, Jean Marc Lamunière, René Furer, Alan Gowans, Michael Müller, Alan Colquhoun, and Colin Rowe. "Einige Echos." *Werk-Architese* 64, no. 7/8 (1977): 63. [Special issue: *Venturi & Rauch: 25 öffentliche Bauten. Bâtiments publics*]. Available at: https://www.e-periodica.ch/digbib/view?pid=w-bw-003%3A1977%3A64%3A%3A469#471 (accessed May 8, 2022).

Gubler, Jacques. *Nationalisme et internationalisme dans l'architecture moderne de la Suisse.* Lausanne: L'Age d'Homme, 1975.

Hein, Carola. *The Routledge Handbook of Planning History.* New York: Routledge, 2018.

Herbert, Gilbert. *Martienssen and the International Style.* Cape Town: Balkema, 1975.

Herzog, Jacques, Pierre de Meuron, and Rémy Zaugg. "Eine Stadt im Werden?" *archithese* 22, no. 6 (1992): 28–43.

Higgins, Dennis M., and William Weisenbach. "Crosstown Expressway is Denounced as One of the Worst Civic Disasters." *Philadelphia Inquirer,* April 12, 1967, 45.

Hilburg, Jonathan. "Well Lived: Denise Scott Brown Memorializes Robert Venturi," *The Architects' Newspaper,* November 6, 2019. Available at: https://www.archpaper.com/2019/11/denise-scott-brown-memorializes-robert-venturi/ (accessed April 28, 2022).

Hilpert, Thilo, ed. *Le Corbusiers "Charta von Athen." Texte und Dokumente. Kritische Neuausgabe.* Braunschweig: Vieweg, 1984.

Huber, Werner. *Hauptbahnhof* Zürich. Zurich: Scheidegger & Spiess, 2015.

Hüttinger, Eduard. "Il Mito Di Venezia." In *Venezia Vienna. Il mito della cultura veneziana nella cultura asburgica,* edited by Carlo Pirovano, 187–226. Milan: Electa, 1983.

Hunter, Marcus Anthony. *Black Citymakers: How the Philadelphia Negro Changed Urban America.* Oxford: Oxford University Press, 2013.

Huxtable, Ada Louise. "A Singularly New York Product." *New York Times* (November 25, 1968): 43.

Jacobs, Jane. "The City's Threat to Open Land." *Architectural Forum* 108, no. 1 (January 1958): 87–90, 166. Available at: https://www.usmodernist.org/AF/AF-1958-01.pdf (accessed April 28, 2022).

Jacobs, Jane. *The Death and Life of Great American Cities.* New York: Random House, 1961.

Jacobs, Jane. "Redevelopment Today." *Architectural Forum* 108, no. 4 (April 1958): 109–113. Available at: https://www.usmodernist.org/AF/AF-1958-04.pdf (accessed April 28, 2022).

Jacobs, Jane. "What is a City?" *Architectural Forum* 109, no. 1 (July 1958): 63–65. Available at: https://www.usmodernist.org/AF/AF-1958-07.pdf (accessed April 28, 2022).

Jaynes, Gerald D., David E. Apter, Herbert J. Gans, William Kornblum, Ruth Horowitz, James F. Short, Jr, Gerald D. Suttles, and Robert E. Washington. "The Chicago School and the Roots of Urban Ethnography: An Intergenerational Conversation with Gerald D. Jaynes, David E. Apter, Herbert J. Gans, William Kornblum, Ruth Horowitz, James F. Short, Jr, Gerald D. Suttles and Robert E. Washington." *Ethnography* 10, no. 4 (2009): 375–396.

Jencks, Charles. *Modern Movements in Architecture.* Harmondsworth: Penguin, 1973.

Jencks, Charles, and George Baird, eds. *Meaning in Architecture*. London: Barrie & Rockliff, Cresset Press, 1969.

Jessor, Herman J. "Herman J. Jessor, Co-op City Architect, Comments upon the Authors' Text." *Progressive Architecture* (February 1970): 73.

Kahn, Louis. "Toward a Plan for Midtown Philadelphia." *Perspecta* 2 (1953): 11–27.

Kamnitzer, Peter. "Computer Aid to Design," *Architectural Design* 9 (1969) 507–508.

Klemek, Christopher. "Jane Jacobs and the Transatlantic Collapse of Urban Renewal." In *Contemporary Perspectives on Jane Jacobs: Reassessing the Impacts of an Urban Visionary*, edited by Dirk Schubert, 171–184. London: Routledge, 2014.

Klemek, Christopher. *The Transatlantic Collapse of Urban Renewal: Postwar Urbanism from New York to Berlin*. Chicago: University of Chicago Press, 2011.

Kulić, Vladimir, and Mira Stanić, "Form, Forces and Functions/Forma, sile i funkcije," *Oris* 18, 100 (2016): 52–79.

La Maison des Artistes, Château de La Sarraz, ed. *Le meuble, l'architecture*. 1978. [exhibition catalogue]

Lavin, Sylvia. *Architecture Itself and Other Postmodernization Effects*. Montréal: Canadian Centre for Architecture; Leipzig: Spector Books, 2020.

Lavin, Sylvia. *Everything Loose Will Land: 1970s Art and Architecture in Los Angeles*. New York: Distributed Art Publishers; Nuremberg: Verlag für moderne Kunst Nürnberg, 2013.

Lavin, Sylvia. "Oh My Aching Antenna: The Fall and Rise of Postmodern Creativity." *Log* 37 (Spring/Summer 2016): 214–227.

Leach, Andrew. "Dilemmas without Solutions." In *Complexity and Contradiction at Fifty: On Robert Venturi's "Gentle Manifesto,"* edited by Martino Stierli and David B. Brownlee, 98–113. New York: Museum of Modern Art, 2019.

Leslie, Stuart W. *The Cold War and American Science: The Military-Industrial-Academic Complex at MIT and Stanford*. New York: Columbia University Press, 1993.

Levin, Ayala. "Learning from Johannesburg: Unpacking Denise Scott Brown's South African View of Las Vegas." In *Writing Architectural History: Evidence and Narrative in the Twenty-First Century*, edited by Aggregate Architectural History Collaborative, 235–246. Pittsburgh, PA: University of Pittsburgh Press, 2021.

Levy, Evonne. *Baroque and the Political Language of Formalism (1845–1945): Burckhardt, Wölfflin, Gurlitt, Brinckmann, Sedlmayr*. Basel: Schwabe, 2015.

Levy, Paul. "How Philly Neighborhoods Killed the Crosstown Expressway" [video]. October 19, 2017. Gloria Dei (Old Swedes') Church's Sanctuary, Philadelphia, Pennsylvania. 1:14:26. Available at: https://www.youtube.com/watch?v=dmoL9XPOsms.

Long, Christopher. *Josef Frank: Life and Work*. Chicago: University of Chicago Press, 2002.

Lotz, Wolfgang. "Sixteenth-Century Italian Squares." In Wolfgang Lotz, *Studies in Italian Renaissance Architecture*, 74–116. Cambridge, MA: MIT Press, 1977.

Magris, Claudio. *Utopie et désenchantement*. Paris: Gallimard, 2001.

Maki, Fumihiko. *Investigations in Collective Form*. St. Louis, MO: Washington University, 1964.

Maki, Fumihiko. "Thoughts about Plazas; Recollections. From the Nagoya University Toyoda Memorial Hall to the Consolidated Offices of Kanazawa Ward, Yokohama." *Japan Architect*, no. 12 (1971): 39–50.

Marchi, Leonardo Zuccaro. *The Heart of the City: Legacy and Complexity of a Modern Design Idea*. London: Routledge, 2018.

Marcuse, Herbert. "Commenting on Claes Oldenburg's Proposed Monuments for New York City." *Perspecta* 12 (1969): 75–76.

Massey, Jonathan. "Review: Power and Privilege." *Journal of the Society of Architectural Historians* 75, no. 4 (216): 497–498.

McCoubrey, John W. "Art on the Road." In Denise Scott Brown, Robert Venturi, and John W. McCoubrey, *The Highway*, 19–26. Houston: Menil Foundation, 1970. [Catalogue of the exhibition "The Highway," January 15–February 25, 1970, Institute of Contemporary Art, University of Pennsylvania.]

McLeod, Mary. "Venturi's Acknowledgments: The Complexities of Influence." In *Complexity and Contradiction at Fifty: On Robert Venturi's "Gentle Manifesto,"* edited by Martino Stierli and David Brownlee, 50–75. New York: Museum of Modern Art, 2019.

McLeod, Mary. "Wrestling with Meaning in Architecture: Learning from Las Vegas." In *Eyes That Saw: Architecture After Las Vegas*, edited by Stanislaus von Moos and Martino Stierli, 67–92. Zurich: Scheidegger & Spiess; New Haven, CT: Yale School of Architecture, 2020.

McQuade, Walter. "The High-Rising Monotony of World Housing." *Fortune* (July 1968): 80.

Meyer, Kimberli, and Susan Morgan, eds. *Sympathetic Seeing: Esther McCoy and The Heart of American Modernist Architecture and Design*. West Hollywood, CA: MAK Center for Art and Architecture; Nuremberg: Verlag für Moderne Kunst; New York, NY: Distributed Art Publishers. 2011.

Mingardi, Lorenzo. "Reweaving the City: The CIAM Summer Schools from London to Venice (1949–57)." In *Post-war Architecture Between Italy and the UK: Exchanges and Transcultural Influences*, edited by Lorenzo Ciccarelli and Clare Melhuish, 107–126. London: University College London Press, 2021.

Minnite, Diane L. "Chronology." In *Out of the Ordinary: Robert Venturi, Denise Scott Brown and Associates; Architecture, Urbanism, Design*, edited by David Brownlee, David G. De Long, and Kathryn B. Hiesinger, 244–252. Philadelphia: Philadelphia Museum of Art in association with Yale University Press, 2001.

Miranda, Carolina A. "Architect Interview with Denise Scott Brown." *Architect Magazine*, April 5, 2013. Available at: http://www.architectmagazine.com/design/architect-interview-with-denise-scott-brown_o (accessed May 7, 2022).

Moholy-Nagy, Sibyl. [Letter to the editor.] "Co-op City Controversy: Letters to the Editor." *Progressive Architecture* (April 1970): 8.

Moos, Stanislaus von. "Präzision der Unschärfe." In *Fünfundzwanzig x Herzog & de Meuron*, edited by Stanislaus von Moos and Arthur Rüegg. Göttingen: Steidl, 2022 [forthcoming].

Moos, Stanislaus von. "A View from the Gondola: Notes on History, Spectacle and Modern Architecture." In *Eyes That Saw: Architecture After Las Vegas*, edited by Stanislaus von Moos and Martino Stierli, 325–371. Zurich: Scheidegger & Spiess; New Haven: Yale School of Architecture, 2020.

Moos, Stanislaus von. "Lachen, um nicht zu weinen. Interview mit Robert Venturi und Denise Scott Brown." *Archithese*, no. 13 (1975): 17–32.

Moos, Stanislaus von. *Venturi, Rauch, & Scott Brown: Buildings and Projects*. New York: Rizzoli, 1987.

Moos, Stanislaus von. *Venturi, Scott Brown & Associates. Buildings and Projects, 1986–1998. With Project Descriptions by Denise Scott Brown and Robert Venturi and an Interview by Mary McLeod*. New York: Monacelli Press, 1999.

Moos, Stanislaus von, and Diego Peverelli, eds. *Venturi & Rauch: 25 öffentliche Bauten. Bâtiments publics*. Niederteufen, Switzerland: Niggli, 1977. [Special issue of *Werk-Archithese* 64, nos. 7/8]. Available at: https://www.e-periodica.ch/digbib/view?pid=w-bw-003%3A1977%3A64%3A%3A469#471 (accessed May 8, 2022).

Moos, Stanislaus von, and Martino Stierli. *Eyes That Saw: Architecture after Las Vegas*. Zurich: Scheidegger & Spiess; New Haven, CT: Yale School of Architecture, 2020.

Moos, Stanislaus von, Martin Steinmann, Roger Diener, and Inès Lamunière. "Affinitäten, Divergenzen und offene Fragen." *Archithese*, no. 6 (1995): 59–63.

Mumford, Eric. *The CIAM Discourse on Urbanism, 1928–1960*. Cambridge, MA: MIT Press, 2000.

Mumford, Eric. *Defining Urban Design. CIAM Architects and the Formation of a Discipline, 1937–69*. New Haven: Yale University Press, 2009.

Murray, Bruce K. *Wits, the "Open" Years: a History of the University of Witwatersrand, 1939–1959*. Johannesburg: Witwatersrand Press, 1997.

Naish, Paul D. "Fantasia Bronxiana: Freedomland and Co-op City." *New York History* 82, no. 3 (Summer 2001): 259–285.

Nancy, Jean-Luc. "Corpus." In *Corpus*, translated by Richard Rand, 2–121. New York: Fordham University Press, 2008.

Nancy, Jean-Luc. *L'Évidence du film/The Evidence of Film: Abbas Kiarostami*. Paris: Éditions Klincksieck, 2007.

Nancy, Jean-Luc. "The Extension of the Soul." In *Corpus*, translated by Richard Rand, 136–144. New York: Fordham University Press, 2008.

Nancy, Jean-Luc. "The Look of the Portrait." In *Multiple Arts: The Muses II*, edited by Simon Sparks, 220–247. Stanford: Stanford University Press, 2006.

Nancy, Jean-Luc. "Res ipsa et ultima." In *A Finite Thinking*, edited by Simon Sparks, 311–318. Stanford: Stanford University Press, 2003.

Nowicki, Matthew. "Composition in Modern Architecture." *Magazine of Art* 42 (March 1949): 108–11.

Nowicki, Matthew. *Writings and Sketches of Matthew Nowicki*, edited by Bruce Harold Schafer. Charlottesville: University Press of Virginia, 1973.

Ockman, Joan, and Rebecca Williamson, eds. *Architecture School: Three Centuries of Educating Architects in North America*. Cambridge, MA; MIT Press, 2012.

Oldenburg, Claes. *New Work by Claes Oldenburg*. New York: Sidney Janis Gallery, 1966.

Oldenburg, Claes. *Proposals for Monuments and Buildings, 1965–1969*. Chicago: Big Table, 1969.

Oldenburg, Claes, and Emmett Williams. *Store Days: Documents from "The Store" (1961) and "Ray Gun Theater" (1962)*. New York: Something Else Press, 1967.

Orazi, Manuel. "Building Arguments: Interview with Denise Scott Brown." *Abitare* 506, October 2010, 155–157.

Orleans, Peter, and William Russell Ellis, eds. *Race, Change, and Urban Society*. Beverly Hills, CA: Sage Publications, 1971.

Osborn, Michelle. "The Crosstown is Dead, Long Live the Crosstown?" *Architectural Forum* 135, no. 3 (October 1971): 38–41.

Osborn, Michelle. "Saving Picturesque South Street." *Philadelphia Evening Bulletin*, September 1968.

Pacchi, Carolina. "Epistemological Critiques to the Technocratic Planning Model: the Role of Jane Jacobs, Paul Davidoff, Reyner Banham and Giancarlo De Carlo in the 1960s." *City, Territory and Architecture* 5, no. 17 (2018). Available at: https://doi.org/10.1186/s40410-018-0095-3 (accessed May 7, 2022).

Pevsner, Nikolaus. "The Architecture of Mannerism." In *The Mint: A Miscellany of Literature, Art and Criticism*, edited by Geoffrey Grigson, 116–38. London: Routledge, 1946.

Pevsner, Nikolaus. "The Development of a Contemporary Vernacular in the Transvaal." *Architectural Review* 113, no. 678, June 1953, 360–382.

Pevsner, Nikolaus. "Gegenreformation und Manierismus." *Repertorium für Kunstwissenschaft* 46 (1925): 243–262.

Pinder, Wilhelm. "Zur Physiognomik des Manierismus." In *Die Wissenschaft am Scheidewege von Leben und Geist*, edited by Hans Prinzhorn, 148–156. Leipzig: Verlag von Johann Ambrosius Barth, 1932.

Plant, Margaret. *Venice, Fragile City: 1797–1997*. New Haven Yale University Press, 2002.

Poerschke, Ute. *Architectural Theory of Modernism: Relating Functions and Form*. New York: Routledge, 2016.

Puckett, John L., and Mark Frazier Lloyd. *Becoming Penn: The Pragmatic American University, 1950–2000*. Philadelphia: University of Pennsylvania Press, 2015.

Quaroni, Ludovico. *Immagine di Roma. Fotografie di Ludovico e Livio Quaroni*. Bari: Laterza, 1969.

Rattenbury, Kester, and Samantha Hardingham, eds. *Robert Venturi and Denise Scott Brown: Learning from Las Vegas: SuperCrit #2*. Abingdon: Routledge, 2007.

Reiner, Thomas A., Robert J. Sugarman, and Janet Scheff Reiner. *The Crosstown Controversy: A Case Study*. Philadelphia: University of Pennsylvania Transportation Studies Center, Center for Urban Research and Experiment, 1970.

Rockwell, David, and Bruce Mau. *Spectacle*. New York: Phaidon Press, 2005.

Rodwin, Lloyd, and Bishwapriya Sanyal, eds. *The Profession of City Planning: Changes, Images, and Challenges, 1950–2000*. New Brunswick: Center for Urban Policy Research / Rutgers University Press, 2000.

Roediger, David R. *Working Toward Whiteness: How America's Immigrants Became White: The Strange Journey from Ellis Island to the Suburbs*. New York: Basic Books, 2006.

Rose, Barbara. *Claes Oldenburg*. New York: Museum of Modern Art, 1970.

Ross, Andrew. *No Respect: Intellectuals & Popular Culture*. New York: Routledge, 1989.

Roth, Alfred. "Für eine realitätsbezogene, konstruktive Architekturkritik." *Werk-Archithese* 64, no. 5 (1977): 44–47.

Roth, Alfred. "Kritische Anmerkungen zur heutigen Situation der Architektur." *Schweizer Ingenieur und Architekt* 10, no. 47 (1983): 1107–1110.

Roth, Alfred. *La nouvelle architecture, présentée en 20 exemples / Die neue Architektur, dargestellt an 20 Beispielen / The New Architecture, Examinated on 20 examples* [sic]. Zurich: Girsberger, 1940.

Roth, Curtis. "Software Epigenetics and Architectures of Life," *e-flux*, February 2019. Available at: https://www.e-flux.com/architecture/becoming-digital/248079/software-epigenetics-and-architectures-of-life/ (accessed May 7, 2022).

Rottner, Nadja. "Object Lessons." In *Claes Oldenburg*, edited by Nadja Rottner, 173–206. Cambridge, MA: MIT Press, 2012.

Rowe, Colin. "Robert Venturi and the Yale Mathematics Building." *Oppositions* (1976): 11–19.

Rowe, Colin. "Mannerism and Modern Architecture." *Architectural Review* 107 (May 1950): 289–299.

Rublowsky, John. *Pop Art*. New York: Basic Books, 1965.

Salmon, Frank, ed. *Summerson and Hitchcock: Centenary Essays on Architectural Historiography.* London: Yale University Press, 2006.

Scheppe, Wolfgang, and the IUAV Class on Politics and Representation. *Migropolis: Venice: Atlas of a Global Situation.* Ostfildern: Hatje Cantz; Venice: Fondazione Bevilacqua La Masa, 2009.

Schuman, Tony. "Labor and Housing in New York City: Architect Herman Jessor and the Cooperative Housing Movement." In *Architecture as a Political Act: Proceedings of the ACSA International Conference,* edited by Beth Young and Thomas C. Gelsanliter, 383–394. Berlin: Association of Collegiate Schools of Architecture, 1997. Available at: https://www.acsa-arch.org/chapter/labor-and-housing-in-new-york-city-architect-hemrna-jessor-and-the-cooperative-housing-movement/ (accessed May 7, 2022).

Scimemi, Maddalena. "Venezia Internazionale. La CIAM Summer School 1952–1957." *IUAV 83* (1983): 5–6.

Scimemi, Gabriele. "La quarta scuola estiva del CIAM a Venezia." *Casabella* 231 (November–December 1956): 69–73.

Scott Brown, Denise. "Activities as Patterns." In Robert Venturi and Denise Scott Brown, *Architecture as Signs and Systems for a Mannerist Time,* 120–141. Cambridge, MA: Belknap Press of Harvard University Press, 2004.

Scott Brown, Denise. "An Alternate Proposal That Builds on the Character of South Street." *Architectural Forum* 135, no. 3 (October 1971): 42–44.

Scott Brown, Denise. "Architecture as Patterns and Systems: Learning from Planning." In Robert Venturi and Denise Scott Brown, *Architecture as Signs and Systems for a Mannerist Time,* 103–224. Cambridge, MA: Belknap Press of Harvard University Press, 2004.

Scott Brown, Denise. "Architecture, Signs, and Social Values: Marta Nowak in conversation with Denise Scott Brown." *AN.ONYMOUS* (July 2013). Available at: https://www.an-onymous.com/denis-scott-brown (accessed May 9, 2022).

Scott Brown, Denise. "Between Three Stools: A Personal View of Urban Design Pedagogy." In Denise Scott Brown, *Urban Concepts,* edited by Andreas C. Papadakis, 8–20. London: Academy Editions, 1990 (Architectural Design Profile 83, published as part of *Architectural Design* 60, nos. 1/2).

Scott Brown, Denise. "Changing Family Forms." *Journal of the American Planning Association,* Spring 1983, 133–137; reprinted in Robert Venturi and Denise Scott Brown, *Venturi Scott Brown & Associates: On Houses and Housing,* 108–110. London: Academy Editions; New York: St Martin's Press, 1992.

Scott Brown, Denise. Commencement Address, University of Witwatersrand, July 21, 2011.

Scott Brown, Denise. "Co-op City: Learning to Like it." *Progressive Architecture* (February 1970): 64–73.

Scott Brown, Denise. "Denise Scott-Brown: An African Perspective. Interviewed by Jochen Becker (metroZones)" [video]. 1:16:35. Vienna: Dérive Verein für Stadtforschung, 2013. Available at: https://vimeo.com/312749292 (accessed May 7, 2022).

Scott Brown, Denise. "Denise Scott Brown in Conversation with Enrique Walker." In *The Ordinary: Recordings,* edited by Enrique Walker, 30–63. New York: Columbia Books on Architecture and the City, 2018.

Scott Brown, Denise. "Die Stadt als 'Zeichensystem.'" *Werk-Archithese* 66, nos. 33/34 (1979): 33–39, 67–68.

Scott Brown, Denise. "Drawing for the Deco District." *Archithese,* no. 2 (1982): 17–21.

Scott Brown, Denise. "Form, Design and the City—Reviews." *Journal of the American Institute of Planners* 28, no. 4 (1962): 293–299.

Scott Brown, Denise. "Functionalism, Yes Yes." *Space* 487 (August 2008): 22–23.

Scott Brown, Denise. "The Function of a Table." *Architectural Design* 37 (April 1967): 154.

Scott Brown, Denise. *Having Words.* London: AA Publications, 2009.

Scott Brown, Denise. "Invention and Tradition in the Making of American Place." *Harvard Architecture Review,* 5, 1986, 163–171; reprinted in *American Architecture* (1986), 158–170; *Transition,* Winter 1989, 67–75; in Denise Scott Brown, *Having Words,* 97–118, London: AA Publications, 2009; and in *MAS Context,* 13, Spring 2012, 6–31.

Scott Brown, Denise. "Las Vegas Learning, Las Vegas Teaching." In *Eyes That Saw: Architecture After Las Vegas,* edited by Stanislaus von Moos and Martino Stierli, 381–407. Zurich: Scheidegger & Spiess; New Haven, CT: Yale School of Architecture, 2020.

Scott Brown, Denise. "Learning from Brutalism." In *The Independent Group: Postwar Britain and the Aesthetic of Plenty,* edited by David Robbins, 203–206. Cambridge, MA: MIT Press, 1990.

Scott Brown, Denise. "Learning from Pop." *Casabella*, no. 359–60 (May/June 1971): 15–23; reprinted in Robert Venturi and Denise Scott Brown, *A View from the Campidoglio: Selected Essays 1953–1984*, edited by Peter Arnell, Ted Bickford, and Catherine Bergart, 26–34 (New York: Harper & Row, 1984).

Scott Brown, Denise. "Letter to Friends, Fine Arts, January 31, 1965." In *Everything Loose Will Land: 1970s Art and Architecture in Los Angeles*, edited by Sylvia Lavin, 83–86. West Hollywood, CA: MAK Center for Art and Architecture, Los Angeles, at the Schindler House; Nuremberg: Verlag für moderne Kunst Nürnberg; New York, NY: Distributed Art Publishers, 2013.

Scott Brown, Denise. "Little Magazines in Architecture and Urbanism." *Journal of the American Institute of Planners* 34, no. 4 (1968): 223–233.

Scott Brown, Denise. "Manierismuseum." In Jeremy Eric Tenenbaum, *Your Guide to Downtown Denise Scott Brown*, 96–99. Zurich: Park Book, 2018.

Scott Brown, Denise. "The Meaningful City." *AIA Journal* 43, no. 1 (January 1965): 27–32.

Scott Brown, Denise. "Natal Plans." *Journal of the American Institute of Planners* 30, no. 2 (1964): 161–166.

Scott Brown, Denise. "On Analysis and Design," In Denise Scott Brown, *Having Words*, 136–144. London: AA Publications, 2009.

Scott Brown, Denise. "On Architectural Formalism and Social Concern: A Discourse for Social Planners and Radical Chic Architects." *Oppositions* 5 (summer 1976): 99–112.

Scott Brown, Denise. "On Ducks and Decoration." *Architecture Canada* (October 1968): 48–49. Reprinted in *Architecture Culture 1943–1968: A Documentary Anthology*, edited by Joan Ockman, 446–448. New York: Rizzoli, 1993.

Scott Brown, Denise. "On Houses and Housing." In Robert Venturi and Denise Scott Brown, *Venturi Scott Brown & Associates: On Houses and Housing*, 10–13. London: Academy Editions, 1992; New York: St Martin's Press, 1992.

Scott Brown, Denise. "On Pop Art, Permissiveness and Planning." *American Institute of Architects Planning Journal* 35, no. 3 (1969): 184–186; reprinted in Denise Scott Brown, *Having Words*, 55–59. London: AA Publications, 2009.

Scott Brown, Denise. Oral History Interview with Peter Reed. Smithsonian Archives of American Art. October 25, 1990–November 9, 1991. Available at: https://www.aaa.si.edu/collections/interviews/oral-history-interview-denise-scott-brown-13059 (accessed May 7, 2022).

Scott Brown, Denise. "The Petition is My Prize—and it's Better than the Pritzker." *Architecture Review*, March 8, 2017. Available at: https://www.architectural-review.com/films/denise-scott-brown-the-petition-is-my-prize-and-its-better-than-the-pritzker (accessed May 7, 2022).

Scott Brown, Denise. "Planning the Powder Room." *A.I.A. Journal* XLVII, 4 (April 1967): 81; reprinted in Denise Scott Brown, *Having Words*, 128–135. London: AA Publications, 2009.

Scott Brown, Denise. "Questions of Style." *Art Forum*, October 2010, 264–65, 352. Available at: https://www.artforum.com/print/201007/denise-scott-brown-26154 (accessed May 7, 2022).

Scott Brown, Denise. "Reclaiming Frank's Seat at the Table." In Josef Frank, *Schriften / Writings, Band 1. Veröffentlichte Schriften von 1910 bis 1930*, edited by Tano Bojankin, Christopher Long, and Iris Meder, 21–45. Vienna: Metroverlag, 2012.

Scott Brown, Denise. "The Redefinition of Functionalism." In Robert Venturi and Denise Scott Brown, *Architecture as Signs and Systems: For a Mannerist Time*, edited by Robert Venturi and Denise Scott Brown, 142–174. Cambridge, MA: Belknap Press of Harvard University Press, 2004.

Scott Brown, Denise. "Remedial Housing for Architects Studio." In Robert Venturi and Denise Scott Brown, *Venturi Scott Brown & Associates: On Houses and Housing*, 51–57. London: Academy Editions; New York: St. Martin's Press, 1992.

Scott Brown, Denise. "The Rise and Fall of Community Architecture." In Denise Scott Brown, *Urban Concepts*, edited by Andreas C. Papadakis, 30–39, London: Academy Editions, 1990 (Architectural Design Profile 83, published as part of *Architectural Design* 60, nos. 1/2).

Scott Brown, Denise. "Room at the Top? Sexism and the Star System in Architecture." In Ellen Perry Berkeley and Matilda McQuaid, eds. *Architecture: A Place for Women*, 237–246. Washington, DC: Smithsonian Institute Press, 1989; reprinted in Denise Scott Brown, *Having Words*, 79–89. London: AA Publications, 2009.

Scott Brown, Denise. "Some Ideas and Their History." In Robert Venturi and Denise Scott Brown,

Architecture as Signs and Systems for a Mannerist Time, 105–119. Cambridge, MA: Belknap Press of Harvard University Press, 2004.

Scott Brown, Denise. "Studio: Architecture's Offering to Academe." ARPA Journal, no. 4 (2016). Available at: https://arpajournal.net/wp-content/uploads/2016/05/Denise-Scott-Brown-Studio-ARPA-Journal.pdf (accessed May 7, 2022).

Scott Brown, Denise. "Towards an Active Socioplastics." In Denise Scott Brown, Having Words, 22–54. London: AA Publications, 2009.

Scott Brown, Denise. Wayward Eye, [catalogue of the exhibition of the same title, July 11–28, 2018. London: Betts Project, 2018]. Available at: https://static1.squarespace.com/static/5336b2fee4b057e-83f9e14e3/t/5b4794ec-03ce6454bd30b6da/1531417923365/DENISE+SCOTT+BROWN-WAYWARD+EYE-BETTS+PROJECT-CATALOGUE-LR.pdf (accessed May 25, 2022).

Scott Brown, Denise. "Working for Giuseppe Vaccaro." Edilizia Popolare, no. 243 (1996): 5–13.

Scott Brown, Denise. "A Worm's Eye View of Recent Architectural History." Architectural Record 172, no. 2 (1984): 69–81.

Scott Brown, Denise. "Zeichen des Lebens. Symbole in der amerikanischen Stadt." Archithese, no. 19 (1976): 29–34.

Scott Brown, Denise, and Frances Hundt. "Erhaltung historischer Bauten und wirtschaftliche Neubelebung." Archithese, no. 3 (1980): 20–24.

Scott Brown, Denise, [and Andreas C. Papadakis, ed]. Urban Concepts. London: Academy Editions, 1990 (Architectural Design Profile 83, published as part of Architectural Design 60, nos. 1/2).

Scott Brown, Denise, and Robert Venturi. Architecture as Signs and Systems: For a Mannerist Time. Cambridge, MA: Belknap Press of Harvard University Press, 2004.

Scott Brown, Denise, [and Thomas Weaver]. From Soane to the Strip: Soane Medal Lecture 2018. London: Sir John Soane's Museum, 2019.

Scott, Joanne Patricia. "Origins in Excellence: The Practical Ethos of G. Holmes Perkins and the Philadelphia School." PhD diss., University of Pennsylvania, 2004.

Sessa, Rosa. "By Means of Rome: Robert Venturi prima del Post-Modern." PhD diss., Università degli studi di Napoli Federico II, 2017.

Shear, Mervyn. WITS: A University in the Apartheid Era. Johannesburg: Witwatersrand University Press, 1996.

Shearman, John. Mannerism. Harmondsworth: Penguin, 1967.

Shimoni, Gideon. "South African Jews and the Apartheid Crisis." American Jewish Year Book 88 (1988): 3–58.

Smith, C. Ray. Supermannerism: New Attitudes in Post-Modern Architecture. New York: Dutton, 1977.

Smith, Katherine. The Accidental Possibilities of the City: Claes Oldenburg's Urbanism in Postwar America. Oakland, CA: University of California Press, 2021.

Smith, Katherine. "Mobilizing Visions: Representing the American Landscape." In Instruction and Provocation, or Relearning from Las Vegas, edited by Michael J. Golec and Aron Vinegar, 97–128. Minneapolis: University of Minnesota Press, 2008.

Smithson, Alison, ed. "Team 10 Primer," Architectural Design 32 (December 1962): 559–602.

Smithson, Alison, and Peter Smithson. "Louis Kahn." Architects' Yearbook 9 (1960): 102–118.

Smithson, Alison, and Peter Smithson. Changing the Art of Inhabitation: Mies' Pieces. Eames' Dreams. The Smithsons. London: Artemis Press, 1994.

Sontag, Susan. "Notes on 'Camp.'" Partisan Review 31, no. 4 (1964): 515–530; reprinted in Susan Sontag, Against Interpretation, and Other Essays, 277–293 (New York: Farrar, Straus and Giroux, 1966), and separately as Notes on "Camp" (London: Penguin, 2018).

Sotomayor, Sonia. My Beloved World. New York: Random House, 2014.

Spence, Betty, and Barrie Bierman. "M'Pogga." Architectural Forum 116, no. 691 (October 1954): 35–40.

Stadler, Hilar, and Martino Stierli, eds., in collaboration with Peter Fischli. Las Vegas Studio: Images From the Archive of Robert Venturi and Denise Scott Brown. Zurich: Scheidegger & Spiess, 2008.

Steinmann, Martin. CIAM: Internationale Kongresse für Neues Bauen: Congrès internationaux d'architecture moderne: Dokumente 1928–1939. Basel: Birkhäuser, 1979.

Stierli, Martino. "In the Academy's Garden: Robert Venturi, the Grand Tour, and the Revision of Modernism." AA Files 56 (2007): 42–63.

Stierli, Martino. "Las Vegas and the Mobilized Gaze." In Eyes That Saw: Architecture After Las Vegas, edited by Stanislaus von Moos and Martino Stierli, 129–173.

Zurich: Scheidegger & Spiess; New Haven, CT: Yale School of Architecture," 2020.

Stierli, Martino. *Las Vegas in the Rearview Mirror: The City in Theory, Photography, and Film,* translated by Elizabeth Tucker. Los Angeles: Getty Research Institute, 2013.

Stierli, Martino. *Venturi's Grand Tour: Zur Genealogie der Postmoderne.* Basel: Standpunkte Basel, 2011.

Summerson, John. *The Classical Language of Architecture.* Cambridge, MA: MIT Press, 1966.

Summerson, John. *Heavenly Mansions and Other Essays on Architecture.* London: Cresset Press, 1949.

Taylor, Jennifer. "Strategy for 'Bigness': Maki and 'Group Form'." In *La Città Nuova. Proceedings of the 1999 ACSA International Conference,* edited by Katrina Deines and Kay Bea Jones, editors, 316–320. Rome: Association of Collegiate Schools of Architecture, 1999. Available at: https://www.acsa-arch.org/chapter/strategy-of-bigness-maki-and-group-form/ .

Tenenbaum, Jeremy. *Your Guide to Downtown Denise Scott Brown.* Zurich: Park Books, 2018.

Thiel, Philip. "A Sequence-Experience Notation for Architectural and Urban Spaces." *Town Planning Review* 32, no. 1 (April 1961): 33–52.

Thiel, Philip. "An Experiment in Space Notation." *Architectural Review* 131, no. 783 (May 1962): 326–329.

Thiel, Philip. *People, Paths, and Purposes: Notations for a Participatory Envirotecture.* Seattle: University of Washington Press, 1997.

Thiel, Philip. *Visual Awareness and Design: an Introductory Program in Conceptual Awareness, Perceptual Sensitivity, and Basic Design Skills.* Seattle: University of Washington Press, 1981.

Tschumi, Bernard. "Sanctuaries." *Architectural Design* 43, no. 9 (1973): 575–590.

Vaccaro, Carolina, and Frederic Schwartz. *Venturi, Scott Brown e Associati.* Bologna: Zanichelli, 1991.

Vaccaro, Giuseppe. "Roma: quartiere Ponte Mammolo nucleo sud." *Architettura Cantiere,* no. 15 (1957): 12–23.

van Bergeijk, Herman. "CIAM Summer School 1956." *OverHolland* 9 (2010): 113–124.

van der Waal, Gerhard-Mark. *From Mining Camp to Metropolis: The Buildings of Johannesburg 1886–1940.* Pretoria: C. van Rensburg Publications for the Human Sciences Research Council, 1987.

Van Eck, Caroline. "Sir John Summerson on Artisan Mannerism." In *Summerson and Hitchcock: Centenary Essays on Architectural Historiography,* edited by Frank Salmon, 85–104. London: Yale University Press, 2006.

Venturi, Robert. Acceptance Speech, Pritzker Prize [Mexico City, May 16, 1991]. Chicago: Pritzker Architecture Prize, 1991. Available at: https://www.pritzkerprize.com/sites/default/files/inline-files/1991_Acceptance_Speech.pdf (accessed May 8, 2022).

Venturi, Robert. *Complexity and Contradiction in Architecture.* New York: Museum of Modern Art, 1966.
— French translation: *De l'ambiguïté en architecture,* translated by Maurin Schlumberger and Jean-Louis Vénard. Paris: Dunod, 1971.
— German translation: *Komplexität und Widerspruch in der Architektur,* edited by Heinrich Klotz, translated by Heinz Schollwöck. Braunschweig: Vieweg, 1978.

Venturi, Robert. *Iconography and Electronics upon a Generic Architecture: a View from the Drafting Room.* Cambridge, MA: MIT Press, 1996.

Venturi, Robert, and Denise Scott Brown. *Architecture as Signs and Systems: For a Mannerist Time.* Cambridge, MA: Belknap Press of Harvard University Press, 2004.

Venturi, Robert, and Denise Scott Brown. "Functionalism Yes, But ..." In *Venturi and Rauch 1970–74, A+U: Architecture and Urbanism* 4, 37 (November 1974): 33–34.
— German translation: "Funktionalismus ja, aber ..." *Werk-Archithese* 64, no. 3 (1977): 33–35.

Venturi, Robert, and Denise Scott Brown. "A Significance for A&P Parking Lots, or Learning from Las Vegas." *Architectural Forum,* March 1968, 37–43.
— German translation: "Der Parkplatz von Atlantic & Pacific oder: Was lehrt uns Las Vegas?" *Werk,* no. 4 (1969): 257–266.

Venturi, Robert, and Denise Scott Brown. *A View from the Campidoglio: Selected Essays, 1953–1984,* edited by Peter Arnell, Ted Bickford, and Catherine Bergart. New York: Harper & Row, 1984.

Venturi, Robert, and Denise Scott Brown. *Venturi Scott Brown & Associates: On Houses and Housing.* London: Academy Editions; New York: St. Martin's Press, 1992.

Venturi, Robert, Denise Scott Brown, and Steven Izenour. *Learning from Las Vegas.* Cambridge, MA: MIT Press, 1972.
— Revised edition: *Learning from Las Vegas: the*

Forgotten Symbolism of Architectural Form. Cambridge, MA: MIT Press, 1977.

— Facsimile of 1972 edition: *Learning from Las Vegas.* Cambridge, MA: MIT Press, 2017. German translation: *Lernen von Las Vegas. Zur Ikonographie und Architektursymbolik der Geschäftsstadt.* Braunschweig: Vieweg, 1979.

Venturi, Scott Brown and Associates May 21–31, 1992. Seoul Arts Center, Art Museum, Seoul: Plus Publishing, 1992. [exhibition catalogue]

Vinegar, Aron. "Ed Ruscha, Heidegger, and Deadpan Photography." In *Photography After Conceptual Art*, edited by Diarmuid Costello and Margaret Iversen, 28–49. London: Wiley-Blackwell, 2010.

Vinegar, Aron. *I am a monument: on Learning from Las Vegas.* Cambridge: MIT Press, 2008.

Vinegar, Aron. and Michael J. Golec, eds. *Relearning from Las Vegas.* Minneapolis: University of Minnesota Press, 2009.

von Moos, Stanislaus: *see* Moos, Stanislaus von

Waite, Richard. "Call for Denise Scott Brown to be given Pritzker recognition." *Architects' Journal*, March 21, 2013. Available at: https://www.architectsjournal.co.uk/archive/call-for-denise-scott-brown-to-be-given-pritzker-recognition.

Weisbach, Werner. "Gegenreformation—Manierismus—Barock." *Repertorium für Kunstwissenschaft* 49 (1928): 16–28.

Wheeler, Elizabeth. "More Than the Western Sky: Watts on Television, August 1965." *Journal of Film and Video* 54, no. 2/3 (2002): 11–26.

Williams, Tom. "Lipstick Ascending: Claes Oldenburg: Claes Oldenburg in New Haven in 1969." *Grey Room*, no. 31 (Spring 2008): 116–144.

Wigley, Mark. "Network Fever." *Grey Room*, no. 4 (2001): 82–122. Available at: https://doi.org/10.1162/152638101750420825 (accessed May 21, 2022).

Wittkower, Rudolf. *Architectural Principles in the Age of Humanism.* London: Warburg Institute, 1949.

Wittkower, Rudolf. "Michelangelo's Biblioteca Laurenziana." *Art Bulletin* 16, no. 2 (1934): 123–218.

Wolpe, AnnMarie. *The Long Way Home.* London: Virago, 1994.

Wrede, Stuart. "*Complexity and Contradiction* Twenty-Five Years Later: An Interview with Robert Venturi." In *Studies in Modern Art: American Art of the 1960s*, edited by John Elderfield, 142–163. New York: Museum of Modern Art, 1991.

Wrede, Stuart. "Revisiting 1968–69: On *Novum Organum* and *Lipstick (Ascending) on Caterpillar Tracks.*" *Perspecta* 44 (2011): 128–134, 201.

Young, Michael, and Peter Willmott. *Family and Kinship in East London.* London: Routledge & Kegan Paul, 1957.

Zamarian, Patrick. *The Architectural Association in the Postwar Years.* London: Lund Humphries, 2020.

Contributors

Françoise Blanc is an architect and Professor Emeritus at Toulouse School of Architecture, France. Blanc holds a Ph.D. in the history of architecture from the University of Toulouse–Jean Jaurès. She collaborated with Denise Scott Brown and Robert Venturi (VSBA) on the project for and construction of the Provincial Capitol Building in Toulouse (1999).

Dr. ir. Marianna Charitonidou is an architect-engineer and urban planner, historian and theorist of architecture and urbanism, expert in sustainable environmental design, and a curator. She is currently conducting a postdoctoral research project entitled "Constantinos A. Doxiadis and Adriano Olivetti's Postwar Reconstruction Agendas in Greece and in Italy: Centralising and Decentralising Political Apparatus" at the Department of Art Theory and History of Athens School of Fine Arts.

Denise Costanzo is Associate Professor of Architecture at Pennsylvania State University, author of *What Architecture Means: Connecting Ideas and Design* (Routledge, 2016), and coeditor (with Andrew Leach) of *Italian Imprints on Twentieth Century Architecture* (Bloomsbury, 2022). Her current book project is *Modern Architects and the Problem of the Postwar Rome Prize: France, Spain, America, and Britain, 1946-1960* (forthcoming with University of Virginia Press).

Lee Ann Custer is a historian of the art, architecture, and urbanism of the United States. Her intellectual interests center on the limits of the urban built environment in both physical form and representation. In 2016, she cocurated the exhibition "Back Matter: The Making of Robert Venturi's Complexity and Contradiction" at the Architectural Archives of the University of Pennsylvania. Custer holds a Ph.D. from the University of Pennsylvania and a B.A. from Harvard University.

Valéry Didelon is an architecture critic and historian. He is professor of Theory and Design at the École nationale supérieure d'architecture de Normandie. He is co-founder and editor of the magazine *Criticat* and is a contributor to many architecture journals. Didelon is the author of several books, including *La déconstruction de la ville*

européenne: Euralille 1988–1995 (Éditions de la Villette, 2021) and *La controverse Learning from Las Vegas* (Éditions Mardaga, 2011).

Frida Grahn is an architect and historian of architecture based in Zurich. She holds a Master of Science in Architecture and a Master of Advanced Studies in History and Theory of Architecture from the Swiss Federal Institute of Technology (ETH) in Zurich. She is currently a Ph.D. candidate in the history of architecture at the Accademia di architettura Mendrisio, Università della Svizzera italiana (USI).

Jacques Herzog studied architecture at the Swiss Federal Institute of Technology (ETH) in Zurich from 1970 to 1975. Together with Pierre de Meuron, he established Herzog & de Meuron in Basel in 1978. He has been Visiting Professor at the Graduate School of Design, Harvard University, since 1989, and was professor at ETH Zurich and co-founder of ETH Studio Basel – Contemporary City Institute, from 1999 until 2018.

Inès Lamunière is a Professor Emerita at the Swiss Federal Institute of Technology (EPF) in Lausanne and Architect EPFL SIA FAS. She has been Visiting Professor at the Graduate School of Design, Harvard University. She was Chair of the Department of Architecture, EPF Lausanne, from 2008 to 2011 and a member of the Board of Archizoom from 2008 to 2012.

Sylvia Lavin is a Professor of History and Theory of Architecture at Princeton University, School of Architecture, previously Professor of Architectural History and Theory at UCLA. She is a member of the Board of Trustees of the Canadian Centre for Architecture (CCA) in Montreal. Lavin curated the exhibition "Architecture Itself and Other Postmodernist Myths" at the CCA in 2018, which explores the impact of the postmodernization of architectural procedures.

Andrew Leach teaches history of architecture at the University of Sydney. Among his books are *Manfredo Tafuri* (A&S Books, 2007), *What is Architectural History?* (Polity Press, 2010), *The Baroque in Architectural Culture 1880–1980* (edited with Maarten Delbeke and John Macarthur; Ashgate, 2015), *Crisis on Crisis, Rome* (Standpunkte, 2017), *Sydney School* (edited with Lee Stickells; Uro Publications, 2018), and *Gold Coast: City and Architecture* (Lund Humphries, 2018).

Craig Lee is Daniel F. and Ada L. Rice Postdoctoral Curatorial Fellow in Architecture and Design at the Art Institute of Chicago. He is a Ph.D. candidate in art history at the University of Delaware and earned a master's degree at the Bard Graduate Center and a bachelor's degree at Dartmouth College.

Christopher Long is Martin S. Kermacy Centennial Professor of Architectural and Design History at the University of Texas at Austin. He has published widely on various aspects of Central European and American modernism.

Mary McLeod is a Professor of Architecture at Columbia University's *Graduate School of Architecture, Planning and Preservation (*GSAPP), where she teaches architecture history and theory. Her research and publications have focused on the history of the modern movement and on contemporary architecture theory, examining issues concerning the connections between architecture and ideology.

Robin Middleton studied architecture at the University of Witwatersrand and wrote a Ph.D. dissertation on "Viollet-le-Duc and the Rational Gothic Tradition" at Cambridge University (1958). He was technical editor of *Architectural Design* from 1964 to 1972, head of general studies at the Architectural Association, London, and librarian and lecturer in the Faculty of Architecture and Art History at Cambridge University from 1972 to 1987. He joined the Columbia faculty in 1987 and retired in 2003.

Stanislaus von Moos is a Swiss art historian, founder and editor-in-chief of *Archithese,* Professor Emeritus, curator, and author of numerous publications. His interest in and concern with Venturi and Scott Brown has been highly influential, as seen in his often-cited articles, in two monographs on the office (1987 and 1999), and in the anthology *Eyes That Saw: Architecture after Las Vegas* (Scheidegger & Spiess, 2020).

Sarah Moses is an architectural historian with a particular interest in sites with "difficult" or contentious histories. Her work examines the conflict between a collective desire to memorialize and a protective impulse to stigmatize, sanitize, or obliterate sites with traumatic or violent associations.

Joan Ockman is Vincent Scully Visiting Professor of Architectural History and Director of Doctoral Studies at Yale School of Architecture. She also holds senior appointments at the University of Pennsylvania's Weitzman School of Design and at Cooper Union in New York.

Hilary Sample is the IDC Professor of Housing Design at Columbia University's *Graduate School of Architecture, Planning and Preservation (*GSAPP), and is a co-founder of the New York–based architecture and design studio MOS. Since its establishment in 2007, MOS has won major national and international awards and has been recognized in significant publications.

Katherine Smith is Professor of Art History at Agnes Scott College (Decatur, Georgia). Her research focuses on intersections in American art and architecture from the 1960s to the present, with emphases on sculpture and urbanism.

Jeremy Eric Tenenbaum has worked with Denise Scott Brown and Robert Venturi, as well as their successor firm, VSBA Architects & Planners. He designed the major retrospective "Downtown Denise Scott Brown" at the Architekturzentrum Wien in Vienna, and wrote and designed its accompanying monograph, *Your Guide to Downtown Denise Scott Brown* (Park Books, 2018).

Carolina Vaccaro is an architect based in Rome. She holds an architecture Ph.D. from Sapienza University of Rome. She is a design professor at Sapienza University of Rome and currently at Temple University Rome. She was curator of the exhibition *DSB: Learning to See* at the Tyler School of Art and Architecture Gallery in Philadelphia (2021).

Aron Vinegar is a Professor in the Department of Philosophy, Classics, History of Art and Ideas at the University of Oslo. He is the author of *I am a monument: on Learning from Las Vegas* (MIT Press, 2008).

James Yellin is a former United States career diplomat. His assignments included serving from 2002 to 2005 as the United States Ambassador to Burundi and as the principal United States representative at the Burundi peace talks in Arusha, Tanzania.

Image Credits

Front cover © Lynn Gilbert.
Back cover Courtesy of VSBA.

Frontispiece Courtesy of Denise Scott Brown.

Preface
Mary McLeod
gta Archives / ETH Zurich, Stanislaus von Moos.

Introduction: Portraits of an Architect
Frida Grahn
Courtesy of Denise Scott Brown.

On the Outside Looking Around: "Mine is an African View of Las Vegas"
Craig Lee
Figure 1 Reproduced by permission of MIT Press; ©1972 Massachusetts Institute of Technology.
Figure 2 Reproduced by permission of MIT Press; ©1977 Massachusetts Institute of Technology.
Figure 3 From Phyllis Lakofski's photo album, given to Ruth Lakofski. Courtesy of Robin Middleton.
Figure 4 Courtesy of Denise Scott Brown.
Figure 5 Courtesy of Denise Scott Brown; Venturi, Scott Brown and Associates, Inc.
Figure 6 Photograph by Elizabeth MacCrone. Courtesy of Denise Scott Brown.
Figure 7 Photograph by Denise Scott Brown. Courtesy of Denise Scott Brown.
Figure 8 From Ruth Lakofski's photo album, courtesy of Robin Middleton.
Figure 9 Photograph by Steven Izenour. Courtesy of Venturi, Scott Brown and Associates, Inc.
Figure 10 Crystal Bridges Museum of American Art, Bentonville, Arkansas, Gift of The Andy Warhol Foundation for the Visual Arts, 2013.32.7. © 2022 The Andy Warhol Foundation for the Visual Arts, Inc. / Licensed by Artists Rights Society (ARS), New York.

Recollections I: Man Made Johannesburg
Robin Middleton with an introduction by Mary McLeod
Figure 1 Photograph by Diana Murphy.

Figure 2–6 *South African Architectural Record,* January 1952.

Encountering Architectural History in 1950s London
Andrew Leach
Figure 1 Photograph by Bill Toomey (1952), RIBA Collections.
Figure 2 Drawn by Jacque Gentilhatre (1571), RIBA Collections.
Figure 3 Photograph by Crispin Boyle (1978), RIBA Collections.
Figure 4 Drawn by R. William Backhouse (1786), RIBA Collections.

The Function of Functionalism for Denise Scott Brown
Denise Costanzo
Figure 1 Photograph by IDZ Berlin/Christian Ahlers; Courtesy of Venturi Scott Brown Collection, The Architectural Archives, University of Pennsylvania.
Figure 2 Photographs by Dan Brewer, 1965; Courtesy of Venturi Scott Brown Collection, The Architectural Archives, University of Pennsylvania.
Figure 3 Gabriele Scimemi. "La quarta scuola estiva del CIAM a Venezia." *Casabella* 213 (November–December 1956): 71.
Figure 4 Courtesy of Venturi Scott Brown Collection, The Architectural Archives, University of Pennsylvania.
Figure 5 Courtesy of Venturi Scott Brown Collection, The Architectural Archives, University of Pennsylvania.

Recollections II: The Mutual Experience—in Giuseppe Vaccaro's Office in Rome
Carolina Vaccaro
Figure 1 Courtesy of Denise Scott Brown.
Figure 2–7 Courtesy of Archivio Vaccaro, Rome.

Denise Scott Brown's Nonjudgmental Perspective: Cross-Fertilization between Urban Sociology and Architecture
Marianna Charitonidou
Figure 1–3 Courtesy of Venturi Scott Brown Collection, The Architectural Archives, University of Pennsylvania.

Teaching "Determinants of Urban Form" at the University of Pennsylvania, 1960–1964
Lee Ann Custer
Figure 1   George Pohl Collection, negative set #43, The Architectural Archives, University of Pennsylvania.
Figure 2–5 George Pohl Collection, The Architectural Archives, University of Pennsylvania.

Recollections III: Learning from Denise Scott Brown and Paul Davidoff
James Yellin
Figure 1–2 Reproduced by permission of MIT Press; ©1977 Massachusetts Institute of Technology.

Positioning Denise Scott Brown: Los Angeles, 1965–1966
Sylvia Lavin
Figure 1–4 Courtesy of Denise Scott Brown.
Figure 5   From: "A Sequence-Experience Notation for Architectural and Urban Spaces," *Town Planning Review* 32, 1 (April 1961): 33–52. Originally published by Liverpool University Press. Reproduced with permission of the licensor through PLSclear.
Figure 6   Courtesy of UCLA Library, Arts Library.
Figure 7   Courtesy of Denise Scott Brown.
Figure 8   Courtesy of Samueli School of Engineering, UCLA.
Figure 9   Courtesy of The Architectural Archives, University of Pennsylvania.

With Lots of Love: South Street, 1968–1972
Sarah Moses
Figure 1–3 Courtesy of Denise Scott Brown.
Figure 4   Philadelphia City Planning Commission.
Figure 5   Courtesy of Denise Scott Brown.

"Strange" Appearances: On Pop Art, Hamburgers, and Urbanists
Katherine Smith
Figure 1   Courtesy of Venturi Scott Brown Collection, The Architectural Archives, University of Pennsylvania.
Figure 2   Courtesy of Ken Heyman.
Figure 3   Courtesy of Venturi Scott Brown Collection, The Architectural Archives, University of Pennsylvania.

Figure 4   Art Gallery of Ontario, Toronto [purchased 1967]. Photograph by Rudy Burckhardt © 2022 Estate of Rudy Burckhardt/Artists Rights Society (ARS), New York. Digital image © The Museum of Modern Art / Licensed by SCALA / Art Resource, New York.
Figure 5   Courtesy of Venturi Scott Brown Collection, The Architectural Archives, University of Pennsylvania. Photograph by Spencer Parsons.

Recollections IV: Denise and Bob on My Mind
Inès Lamunière
Figure 1   Inès Lamunière.
Figure 2   Photograph: Alain Grandchamp.
Figure 3–4 dl-a, designlab-architecture.

"Make Little Plans": Scott Brown at the Fiftieth Anniversary of CIAM
Frida Grahn
Figure 1   ETH-Bibliothek Zürich, Bildarchiv; photographer: Comet Photo AG (Zürich) / Com_F69-15275 / CC BY-SA 4.0.
Figure 2   Courtesy of Venturi Scott Brown Collection, The Architectural Archives, University of Pennsylvania.
Figure 3   Archives de la construction moderne – EPFL, Henri-Robert Von der Mühll. © Emile Gos, Lausanne.
Figure 4–5 Courtesy of Venturi Scott Brown Collection, The Architectural Archives, University of Pennsylvania.

The Rule of Flux: Notes on Denise Scott Brown and Venice
Stanislaus von Moos
Figure 1   © Jacques Herzog und Pierre de Meuron Kabinett, Basel.
Figure 2   © ETH Studio Basel, Basel 2005.
Figure 3   From Giorgio Bellavitis and Giandomenico Romanelli, *Venezia* (1985).
Figure 4   Courtesy of Denise Scott Brown.
Figure 5   From Pippo Ciorra, *Ludovico Quaroni 1911–1987. Opere e Progetti* (1989).
Figure 6   Courtesy of VSBA.
Figure 7   Courtesy of VSBA.
Figure 8   © 2022, ProLitteris, Zurich.
Figure 10   Courtesy of VSBA.

Recollections V: Exploring Denise Scott Brown's
Methods
Françoise Blanc
Figure 1-5 Courtesy of VSBA.

1+1>2: Letter to Biljana, Notes to Frida
Denise Scott Brown
Figure 1   Photograph by George Pohl. Courtesy of
             VSBA.
Figure 2   gta Archives / ETH Zurich, Stanislaus von
             Moos.
Figure 3   Photograph by George Pohl. Courtesy of
             VSBA.
Figure 4–6 Photograph by Matt Wargo. Courtesy of
             VSBA.
Figure 7   Photograph by Ke Feng. Courtesy of VSBA.
Figure 8   Photograph by Carl C. Paatz.

"So You'd Like To See The World?"
Jeremy Eric Tenenbaum and Denise Scott Brown
Figure 1–9   Courtesy of Denise Scott Brown.